HOME EC *FOR* EVERYONE

HOME EC FOR EVERYONE

PRACTICAL LIFE SKILLS IN 118 PROJECTS

SHARON & DAVID BOWERS

ILLUSTRATIONS BY SOPHIA NICOLAY

WORKMAN PUBLISHING | NEW YORK

FOR HUGH AND PEARSE

Library of Congress Cataloging-in-Publication Data is available.

ISBN 978-1-5235-1237-9

This book has been adapted from *The Useful Book*, © 2016.

Design by Janet Vicario

Workman books are available at special discounts when purchased in bulk for premiums and sales promotions as well as for fund-raising or educational use. Special editions or book excerpts can also be created to specification. For details, contact the special sales director at specialmarkets@workman.com.

Workman Publishing Co., Inc.
225 Varick Street
New York, NY 10014-4381
workman.com

WORKMAN is a registered trademark of Workman Publishing Co., Inc.

Printed in China

First printing March 2021

10 9 8 7 6 5 4 3 2 1

ACKNOWLEDGMENTS

So many people have helped make this book happen and we are so grateful to them all.

Our sincere thanks again to Lynn Cohen, Garth Sundem, Jennifer Griffin, and Angela Miller.

In this latest edition we were thankful to have the watchful eye and steady hand of Sun Robinson-Smith. Thanks also to Megan Nicolay, who has been with this book since it originally stemmed from an idea by Raquel Jaramillo. Sophia Nicolay's lovely and clear illustrations continue to brighten the pages, and we are lucky to have her on board.

Warmest thanks to the talented team at Workman, many of whom also worked on the original edition: Samantha Gil, Janet Vicario, Orlando Adiao, Eric Brown, Annie O'Donnell, Barbara Peragine, Kate Karol, Julie Primavera, Claire Gross, Abigail Sokolsky, Claire McKean, Page Edmunds, and Suzie Bolotin.

CONTENTS

COOKING 1

Learning how to feed yourself (and others) starts here

SEWING 119

Simple sewing tasks can be impressive when done the right way

LAUNDRY & CLOTHING 155

From laundry labels to shrunken sweater care

DOMESTIC ARTS

The life-changing magic of keeping a clean home

LIFE SKILLS

Grace notes to put the finishing touches on a settled and pleasant life

INTRODUCTION

As technology keeps advancing, it feels like we can do anything if we've got the right device. We can order things online and have them delivered within a couple of hours. We can use our voices to control the lights in our homes. For decades experts have declared that computers were going to make offices "paperless," and the powers that be decided America would henceforth specialize in producing "information workers." What's more, fast food became more convenient than ever, so presumably we'd all just order takeout while sitting in our cubicles, working diligently at our computers. With an eye on this promised future, many school systems, faced with budget cuts and waning interest, have discontinued their Home Ec and domestic arts courses. (But shouldn't someone have checked first to see if our offices actually became paperless? Mine sure didn't!)

Of course, modern life doesn't quite look like a sci-fi movie. And even in space, someone's got to clean the common areas and feed hungry astronauts! Unfortunately, the eradication of classes that taught essential how-tos and shared practical knowledge has had serious consequences: a whole population of people who never learned to cook, do basic mending, or follow a monthly budget. The challenges and global crises of 2020 made it clear that we need more than our screens to stay healthy and keep a household together. We need basic skills that we can build on to adapt to life's unexpected difficulties.

Becoming more self-sufficient is not only easier than many people imagine, it's also extremely satisfying. Work that you do with your own hands is work held to a single standard: Did I fix it? And if the answer is yes, you're finished. It's a feeling of accomplishment that a day spent scrolling through social media, ordering on apps, or poring over spreadsheets can't approach. By the same token, a delicious homemade meal—made with attention and care and not ordered from a drive-through or reheated from a box—is well within the reach of anyone who takes a few minutes to learn the kitchen basics. Whether you aspire to brew the perfect cup of coffee, make fluffy scrambled eggs, hem your own pants, or fold a fitted sheet (don't we all!), those skills are now literally within your grasp. Read on, then get busy.

COOKING

Are you going to spend the rest of your life calling for takeout when you're hungry? The fascinating little secret about being able to cook is being able to make what you want, and make it taste the way you want it to, at any time you like. The other interesting thing to know is that it's not that hard. Learn some basics and pretty soon you can improvise like a pro.

A FULL PANTRY
DRY, CANNED, FRESH, FROZEN . . .

IN THE PANTRY

Baking powder

Baking soda

Bouillon cubes (beef, chicken, vegetable)

Bread

Canned beans (black, cannellini, kidney, pinto)

Canned soups

Canned tomatoes

Chocolate chips

Cocoa

Coffee

Cooking oil

Cornmeal

Cornstarch

Flour

Honey

Hot sauce

Nuts

Olive oil

Pasta

Peanut butter

Raisins

Rice

Rolled oats

Soy sauce

Spices and dried herbs

Sugar (brown and white)

Tea

Tomato paste

Tuna

Vanilla extract

Vinegar

Worcestershire sauce

IN THE REFRIGERATOR

Butter or dairy-free spread

Cheeses

Cottage or ricotta cheese

Cucumber

Eggs

Fresh herbs (basil, parsley, rosemary)

Jam or jelly

Ketchup

Lettuce

Mayonnaise

Mustard

Orange (or other fruit) juice

Plain yogurt

Sour cream

IN THE FREEZER

Bread

Chicken breasts
and fillets

Fish fillets

Frozen vegetables
(corn, peas, spinach)

Hamburger
(in 1 or ½ pound packs)

Ice

Steak or pork chops

IN THE VEGETABLE BASKET & IN THE FRUIT BOWL

Apples

Bananas

Cabbage

Carrots

Celery

Garlic

Ginger

Grapefruit

Lemons

Onions

Oranges

Potatoes

Sweet Potatoes

COOKING TOOL KIT

POTS & PANS

Stoneware or glass casseroles and baking dishes

Wok

Large cast-iron skillet

Stock pot

Nonstick sauté or omelet pan

Steamer basket

Dutch oven

Baking sheets, with and without rims

Muffin tin

Stainless steel saucepans

Loaf pan

Insulated baking sheet

POWER APPLIANCES

Stand or handheld electric mixer

Toaster oven

Microwave

Food processor

Hand or stick blender

Blender

Slow cooker

KNIVES & UTENSILS

Pastry brush

Corkscrew

Garlic press

Can opener

Small grater/ zester for citrus, nutmeg, or Parmesan (Microplane)

Kitchen shears

Whisk

Potato masher

Standard spatula

Frosting spatula

Grater

Vegetable peeler

Rubber or silicone spatula

Tongs

Extra-large serving spoons

Wooden spoons

Slotted spoon

Ladle

Large chef's knife

 Midsize utility knife

Paring knife

Serrated bread knife

 Meat cleaver

Magnetic knife rack

MISC. EQUIPMENT

Colander

Salad spinner

Wooden cutting board

Plastic cutting board

Measuring cup

Salt and pepper mills

Cup and spoon measures

Mixing bowls

Juicer

#1 How to Boil Water
(The First Step to Cooking at Home)

There are fancier culinary techniques, but I can't think of many foods that can't be cooked in (or over) a pot of boiling water. Simple, straightforward, accessible. If you're ever stumped about what to make for a meal, put a pot of water on the stove, open your refrigerator and pantry, and start grabbing what looks good. Within minutes, you could be heading down the road toward chicken salad, spaghetti and meatballs, vegetable soup, or deviled eggs.

1 Pick your pot. Always use one bigger than you think you'll need in order to accommodate the displacement of the water by the food you'll be adding. (If you bring your water to a boil and then add, say, a bunch of potatoes, once the water reaches the boiling point again, it may spill over onto your stovetop.)

2 Fill your pot with cold water. (But don't fill it all the way to the top!) It feels counterintuitive to use cold water, but hot water has been sitting in your taps longer, possibly pulling unwanted residue from your pipes.

3 Put the pot on a burner set to high heat. You can always reduce the heat later if you are after a simmer or a gentle poach.

4 Cover your pot with a close-fitting lid. This prevents steam from escaping and speeds up the process.

What's the Point?

The boiling point is the temperature at which a liquid becomes a gas. Water's boiling point is 212 degrees Fahrenheit (100 degrees Celsius) at sea level. A higher elevation will change the equation: The lower the air pressure (that is, at higher altitudes), the easier it is for water molecules to push out of their liquid prison. In a nutshell, water will boil at the top of a mountain at 185 degrees Fahrenheit. That means, if you're trying to boil an egg, you'll have to leave it in the pot longer. So cooking times will vary from Albuquerque to Aspen, and if your dish must reach a specific temperature to be safe to eat, it's smart to have an instant-read thermometer at the ready.

Try an Electric Kettle

The fastest and most efficient way to boil water is in an electric kettle, which can bring two quarts to 212 degrees Fahrenheit in less than two minutes. It's an inexpensive gadget that can make your life a lot easier. Boil the kettle, pour it in the pot, and speed up dinner.

✕ ✕ ✕ ✕ ✕ ✕ ✕ ✕ ✕ ✕ ✕ ✕ ✕ ✕ ✕ ✕ ✕ ✕ ✕ ✕

Worth Your Salt?

Adding anything to water—salt included—elevates its boiling point, increasing the time it takes the water to bubble. The difference in temperature between unsalted and salted water—based on a ratio of 1 teaspoon of salt per quart of water—is 1 or 2 degrees Fahrenheit, a difference that can matter for foods that cook quickly and in recipes that require precision. (The same principle applies to so-called hard water, which has a high mineral content.)

Some recipes call for salt in the water because it makes for a hotter boil, which cooks foods faster and more thoroughly. Mostly, though, salting simply adds flavor. For pasta, you'll want to salt the water in the cooking pot just as it comes to a boil. The salt dissolves in the water, and the pasta absorbs some of it as it cooks, so it gets salted from the inside out. If you salt already cooked pasta, it can't permeate the toothsome noodles. For a 4-quart pot, add about 1 tablespoon of salt to the water. ✕

Top Ten Reasons to Cook

To nourish your body, mind, and soul, nothing beats the fruits of your own labor, in your own kitchen. Here are ten reasons why:

1. It's cheaper. Dining out means paying a mark-up on your meals to cover the restaurant's operating costs, plus tipping the staff (not to mention the cost of getting there and back). If you outline your menus in advance, stock your pantry, use coupons, buy in bulk, and prepare batches to freeze, you can really stretch your food dollar.

2. It's healthier. American restaurants often plate portions that are 30 to 50 percent larger than the recommended size. And diners often view meals out as a splurge or treat, which can translate to fried food, dishes drenched in melted cheese, or big hunks of red meat, as well as sugary drinks and desserts. In short, lots of what's bad for you. At home, you control the freshness (therefore peak nutritional content) of foods, as well as choose the fat, salt, and sugar content of sauces and condiments. Plating your own food gives you control over portion sizes and helps prevent unwanted weight gain.

3. You get what you want. Hate mushrooms? Don't put them in the sauce. Love black pepper? Grind away without the embarrassment of having to signal for more . . . more . . . just a little more. If you're gluten free, you don't have to wonder if the chef *really* used rice flour in that batter—because *you're* the chef.

4. It saves you time. By the time you decide on a restaurant, walk or drive yourself there, wait for your food, and eat it or bring it home and serve it, you could have easily made a salad, omelet, pasta dish, burger, or stir-fry from scratch. If you've cooked ahead and stored individual portions, it takes just a quick reheat and some garnishing before you are ready to sit down to a wholesome meal in a matter of minutes.

5. You're less likely to get food poisoning. The Centers for Disease Control and Prevention estimate that about 75 million people per year in the United States experience food poisoning. Food-borne pathogens such as bacteria, viruses, and parasites can sicken or even kill. Improper cooking temperatures, cross-contamination between raw and cooked

(continued)

Recommended portion

Restaurant portion

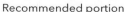

foods, and poor sanitation are risk factors. At home, you can control cooking temperatures, sanitize surfaces and hands, and properly wash raw produce—steps often overlooked or skipped by inexperienced or rushed employees in fast-food kitchens.

6. You can balance your diet. At home, you're not limited to "one from column A and one from column B." By serving yourself appropriate combinations of foods from the Food and Drug Administration's recommended guidelines—once a pyramid, now a plate—you can ensure you are getting the proper daily balance of fat, protein, carbohydrates, and fiber.

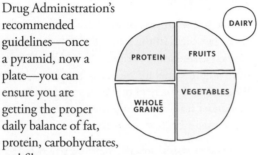

7. It promotes friendship and family. Planning meals, cooking side by side, laying the table with special touches, and relaxing over good food and conversation bond people together. For humans, eating means survival. Sharing food is like a primal signal for "I've got your back."

8. Practice makes perfect. Or at the very least, practice assures progress. If you think you can't cook, there's no better cure for that than getting in the kitchen. If you start by following step-by-step recipes, with repetition, you'll begin to identify basic techniques such as searing, thickening sauces, and caramelizing vegetables, and they'll become muscle memory. Soon, you'll be able to grab ingredients from the fridge and cook a meal without cracking a book.

9. It's good for the planet. Restaurant dining leaves a pretty huge carbon footprint: Driving there requires fuel, sit-down restaurants generate lots of food waste (think of the uneaten breadbaskets that must be dumped),

and takeout restaurants require a veritable mountain of wrappers, containers, and disposable cutlery.

10. It gives you a sense of pride. Whether it's building bookshelves, knitting a scarf, or preparing a nourishing and delicious dinner, we feel a sense of accomplishment when we create something from nothing and embellish it with unique personal touches.

A Boil by Any Other Name

Scald. A moist-heat cooking technique using liquid or steam to help dissolve solids such as salt, sugar, chocolate, or flour. Think hot cocoa: scalded milk with sugar and cocoa powder dissolved into it.

Poach. The gentlest boil. Use this technique for foods that can fall apart, dry out, or overcook easily. Poaching preserves the flavor of delicate

✕ ✕ ✕ ✕ ✕ ✕ ✕ ✕ ✕ ✕ ✕ ✕ ✕ ✕ ✕ ✕ ✕ ✕ ✕

Nuke It! Boiling Liquids in the Microwave

You can use your microwave to boil, but be extremely cautious of "superheating." This occurs when water heats past the boiling point without forming bubbles to release air, then erupts in a dangerous, scalding volcano. Here are some tips for safer microwaving:

• Before heating, stir the liquid thoroughly to add air.

• Before heating, place a nonmetal object in your bowl or cup to encourage the formation of bubbles. A wooden chopstick works well.

• Heat in short stints, carefully stirring at intervals.

• Heat in a vessel with an irregular interior. Ridges and bumps offer what scientists call a "nucleation site," serving as a starting point for bubbling. ✕

foods. Think fish, eggs (out of the shell), pears, and chicken breasts.

Blanch. A French cooking technique whereby you plunge food briefly into rapidly boiling water to cook it but maintain its color and crispness. Think haricots verts (green beans) and asparagus. Also used to loosen the skins on soft fruits such as tomatoes and peaches, so they can be easily slid off.

Simmer. Stopping just short of a boil, with liquid cooking at 180 to 205 degrees

Fahrenheit so that the flavor isn't cooked away and the amount of liquid isn't reduced. Think stocks and soups.

Rolling boil. The most vigorous boil, often called for when a food isn't introduced until the liquid is as hot as possible. Think pasta.

Reduce, aka "making a reduction." Used to thicken and intensify the flavor of a liquid by boiling off the water. Often done in a wide, shallow pan with no lid in order to enable evaporation. Think glazes and sauces.

#2 How to Boil an Egg

Just drop an egg in boiling water, right? Sure, you'll wind up with something technically edible that way, but to avoid pitfalls like funky green yolks and rubbery whites, read on. Just a little care is all that's needed for boiled eggs that are tender, creamy, and fresh tasting.

1 Start with cold eggs from the refrigerator, and place them in a single layer in a heavy-bottomed saucepan or pot with a tightly fitting lid.

2 Cover with cold water, to at least 1 inch above the top of the eggs.

3 Place the pot over medium heat, uncovered, and bring to a rolling boil.

4 Remove the pot from the heat, cover it, and let it stand for 12 minutes to hard-boil and 6 minutes to soft-boil.

5 Using a heatproof slotted spoon, scoop out the eggs and place them in a bowl of ice water. Let stand for 10 minutes.

6 Peel and serve right away (see How to Peel a Boiled Egg, page 12) or refrigerate the unpeeled eggs for up to a week.

TIP: If you notice the white seeping out of a cracked egg during boiling, add a little vinegar to the water. This helps the proteins in the egg white coagulate faster, sealing the crack.

#3 How to Peel a Boiled Egg

Nothing dampens enthusiasm for this tasty, high-protein snack like the struggle to free it from its natural wrapper. Here's how to peel eggs with ease and keep the whites smooth and even.

1 Start with older eggs. The higher pH of older eggs strengthens the membrane, making it easier to separate from the white. Eggs less than 3 days old are harder to peel. I like to keep eggs in the fridge for up to 2 weeks before boiling them, for easier peeling. Don't know how old your eggs are? Put them in a bowl of water. If they stand on their ends, they're old enough. (Older eggs have bigger air cells, the concave part at the flat end of a hard-boiled egg.)

2 Before boiling your eggs, try doing one of the following: Make a crack or pinhole in the large end of the uncooked eggs. (This allows carbon dioxide to escape.) Add a teaspoon of salt to each quart of egg-boiling water. (When salt permeates the egg, its proteins coagulate and firm up, making the white easier to pull from the shell.)

3 After removing the cooked eggs from the hot water, gently crack the shells before plunging them into ice water.

TIP: You can avoid the peeling issue completely by slicing the whole, boiled egg, shell on, in half with a very sharp knife, then scooping out the good stuff with a fine-edged spoon.

✕✕

What to Do with Hard-boiled Eggs

If a carton of eggs has been sitting in your fridge for two to three weeks, hard-boil them all. Not only will they last another week or so, but you can make...

- **Egg Salad:** Dice or mash the whole peeled eggs with a fork and add mayonnaise, salt, pepper, diced celery, chopped scallions, chives, parsley, or any other aromatic ingredient that catches your fancy.

- **Deviled Eggs:** Split lengthwise and spoon the yolks into a bowl. Stir in mayo (or a little softened butter) and a bit of mustard or cider vinegar. Add salt and pepper to taste, along with a little hot sauce if desired. Spoon back into the halved whites and top with a dash of paprika or some crumbled bacon or finely sliced scallions.

- **Toppings:** Crumble them over a green salad, dice and toss into tuna, cube them up and add to your favorite potato salad, or lay slices over a dish of hummus drizzled with olive oil. ✕

Boiled Eggs: Troubleshooting

Ick! My yolk is green. Can I still eat it?

Green yolk is simply a formation of ferrous sulfide where the yolk meets the white. This normal, harmless chemical reaction occurs when the yolk's iron touches the white's hydrogen sulfide. Yolks and whites cook at different temperatures, and overcooking contributes to this unsightly coloration. To prevent it, start with cold eggs in cold water, and once the eggs are cooked, plunge them into an ice-water bath to stop the cooking process.

Why are my egg whites rubbery?

Simply put: overcooking. Egg whites are largely protein, and like meat, when overcooked, they become tough. Start with cold water and cold eggs in order to gently raise the temperature of the whites while ensuring that heat permeates to the center in order to fully cook the yolk.

All of my boiled eggs are cracked. Help!

Never stack eggs—cook them in a single layer. This will reduce jostling. Also, as eggs cook, the gases inside them expand, forming hairline cracks and holes in the shell. Bringing an egg to high heat rapidly causes an internal explosion. Start cold and heat gradually.

#4 How to Crack an Egg

Eggs are a basic building block for cooks, with properties that can seem almost magical. They add lift, fluffiness, and silkiness; they serve as a binder (the "glue" in a meatloaf or veggie burger!); and they make for a quick snack or meal at any time of day.

1 Holding the egg in one hand, rap it sharply on the side of the bowl you're breaking it into. Always crack with conviction! If you rap hesitantly, you're more likely to get a messy break and egg all over your fingers.

2 Holding the egg with both hands, with the cracked side facing down into the bowl, put the tips of your thumbs into the broken spot and pull.

3 Wash your hands with soap when you're done; don't just wipe them on a towel!

4 If a bit of shell has dropped into the bowl, use the tip of a spoon or your washed fingertips to pull out any broken bits. (Resist the urge to use one half of the shell to scoop it out—there are bacteria on the outside of the shell.)

Skillet Savvy

Use a cast-iron skillet for cooking nearly everything—except scrambled eggs. It can leave tiny bits of black from the iron pan visible on the eggs' surface; scrambled eggs also adhere so strongly to the pan that they can ruin its finish. An enamel-coated or nonstick skillet will make eggs fluffier and cleanup easier.

Recipe:
PERFECT SCRAMBLED EGGS

One of the most trusted recipes in your arsenal should be the perfect scramble. The trick is not to touch them too much.

Serves 2 to 4

4 large eggs

2 tablespoons unsalted butter

1 tablespoon milk

Salt and freshly ground pepper

1. Crack the eggs into a medium-size bowl and discard the shells.

2. Put a medium-size (8- or 10-inch) skillet on a burner over medium heat. Place the butter in the pan to melt.

3. While the butter melts, use a fork or a whisk to beat the eggs vigorously. If using a fork, hold the tines of the fork parallel to the bottom of the bowl and whip the eggs over and over in a circular motion to break the yolks and incorporate them into the whites.

4. Beat in the milk (it helps make the eggs creamier) and a pinch of salt and pepper. As the butter starts to sizzle, tip the eggs into the pan.

5. Use a wooden spoon or a heatproof silicone spatula to turn the eggs over gently as they cook (infrequently, so you're not touching them too much), pulling a track through the eggs as they set so that more uncooked egg touches the pan.

6. After a minute or two, when there is still a little runny egg visible, turn the scrambled eggs into a serving bowl or onto plates. The residual heat will continue cooking the eggs so that they're perfect by the time they reach the table.

The Freshness Test

Eggs can be stored in the fridge for several weeks without much quality loss, but the shells are permeable to air. As an egg ages, the white shrinks and an air pocket grows until, eventually, it turns. To tell if an egg is fresh, fill a cup with cold water and set the egg into it. A fresh egg will lie on the bottom of the cup. An older egg, with a larger air pocket, will stand on its end or float.

A super-fresh egg is perfect for scrambling. But for poaching or boiling, a slightly older egg is best. When you boil a fresh egg, the white is still closely bound to the shell, so it will also peel off in raggedy chunks; the shell will peel smoothly from an egg that's a week or so old. Similarly, an older egg forms a neater oval shape when poached, without lots of trailing threads of white.

Size It Up

Eggs at the grocery store are available in a dizzying range of sizes and "grades": small, medium, large, extra-large, jumbo, and AA. The letter grades identify quality, as determined by the USDA; the highest grade is AA. Size is determined by weight per dozen, and most recipes assume you are using large eggs, unless a different size is specifically called for. Any size egg that you have in your refrigerator will work just fine. In small amounts, the volume difference is not so great that it will have a massive impact.

Organic—Worth the Price?

A certified organic egg comes from a hen that eats organic feed, is grown without pesticides, and is not fed antibiotics. That chicken, however, might live in a "battery" farm, where chickens are subjected to inhumane treatment and exceedingly crowded conditions. The best eggs—in terms of flavor as well as animal welfare—are organic and "free range," meaning the chickens have constant or daily access to the outdoors, to roam freely and peck at insects and plants.

The best eggs are from a farmers' market, where the vendor can probably tell you personally about the chickens' living conditions. In summertime, a farm egg has a deep orange yolk that's particularly thick and rich, and this is the benchmark for the best eggs. In a supermarket, you can't always be sure from the box.

Are Brown Eggs Better?

Only if you prefer the color. Otherwise, brown eggs and white eggs are eggs-actly the same. They are no more natural or farm-fresh than white eggs; they're just from a breed of chicken that lays brown eggs, just as some birds lay pale green or blue eggs. If you want an egg to taste different, you have to switch birds: Try duck, goose, or quail eggs for a different flavor.

Red Alert

That red dot on the yolk does not mean that the egg was fertilized. It is simply a tiny bit of blood that got into the egg as it formed in the hen. It won't hurt you at all, but it's a little unappetizing. Use the tip of a spoon to dip it out and discard it.

#5 How to Whip Cream

Walk right past those containers of "whipped topping" in the freezer section of the supermarket—they are an unappetizing concoction of sugar, vegetable oils, thickeners, and emulsifiers, often containing no dairy at all—and skip those cans of prewhipped cream, which also contain stabilizers and emulsifiers. All you need is heavy cream (not "whipping cream"), usually sold in ½ pint (8-ounce) containers. One container will yield 1 cup of cream that will whip into 2 cups. For peaky, airy whipped cream, I have just two words for you: cold and fast.

1 Put a large metal mixing bowl and a whisk in the freezer for at least 1 hour before you make your whipped cream.

2 Pour 1 cup of very cold heavy cream into the bowl. To keep the bowl steady on the counter, dampen a kitchen towel and coil it around the base of the bowl.

3 Tip the bowl slightly toward you with one hand and use the whisk in the other hand to beat the cream with broad oval strokes. Don't beat in a small circle, or it will take longer. If you beat in a large circle, you're more likely to splash the cream everywhere.

4 Beat the cream until soft peaks form, 3 to 5 minutes, depending on room temperature. If you beat past the soft peak stage, the cream will stiffen perceptibly and may turn into butter.

5 Use the whipped cream immediately. Store any leftover cream tightly covered in the refrigerator and use within a few days, beating it with a whisk again to reincorporate some air, if needed.

Soft Peak   Stiff Peak

Sweetened Whipped Cream

Plain whipped cream is ideal for topping sweet and rich desserts. If you prefer sweetened whipped cream, add 2 tablespoons granulated sugar (or more or less to taste) and ½ teaspoon vanilla extract before beating. ⅹ

The Lowdown on Dairy

Discover after a day or two that your milk product has gone off? It may have been because low-fat and nonfat dairy products don't stay fresh nearly as long as their creamier counterparts. Fat retains not only flavor, but also freshness. Understanding the various products offered in the dairy case can help you wisely choose—and use— your milk products.

WHOLE, SKIM, OR IN BETWEEN?

Depends on what you need it for. Nutritionists usually recommend whole milk for children to drink until the age of two, then low-fat versions for all ages after that, but lower-fat milks typically have more sugar. In the end, you might as well go with your personal preference.

WHAT ABOUT THE CREAMY STUFF?

Half-and-half is a mixture of equal parts heavy cream and whole milk, with a butterfat content of about 15 percent.

Light cream ranges from 15 to 30 percent butterfat. Heavy cream can be 36 to 40 percent butterfat. Half-and-half and light cream will not whip, but they're ideal for coffee or cooking, allowing you to add some richness with less fat.

HOW MUCH FAT IS IN YOGURT? AND WHAT MAKES YOGURT "GREEK"?

It depends on what you start with. All yogurt can be made with whole or skim milk, or any of the percentages in between. Greek-style yogurt can be nonfat if it's made with skim milk, or it can taste as rich as heavy cream if made with whole milk. That's because the milk is treated with a yogurt culture to slightly sour and thicken it. Greek-style yogurt is strained to remove excess liquid, resulting in a much thicker product. Whatever you prefer, consider buying yogurt without added sweeteners and then add fruit or sweeten it yourself. Flavored yogurts are far more likely to contain chemical flavors, colors, and

stabilizers than plain yogurt, and typically cost more, too.

IS THERE BUTTER IN BUTTERMILK?

Real buttermilk is the by-product of the butter-making process. When fresh cow's milk, with the cream still in it, is churned, the butterfat separates into a lump of butter, and the remaining liquid is buttermilk. Most of what you find in the supermarket, however, is cultured buttermilk—a low-fat milk that has been treated with a culture to give it the tangy flavor and acidity of real buttermilk.

HOW LONG WILL IT KEEP?

Stored in the refrigerator at 38 degrees Fahrenheit, whole milk will easily stay fresh for a week or more, a bit longer than low-fat. Half-and-half or light cream will last longer than whole milk, and heavy cream can sit in your refrigerator for nearly a month with no loss in quality.

The date on the label is the date after which the store must not *sell* the product, in

ⅹ ⅹ

Sweet or Salty?

Most cooks prefer unsalted butter, also called "sweet cream" butter, in part because it's believed to be fresher (salt acts as a preservative) but mostly because it won't add unwanted extra salt to a recipe. Salted butter, though best for buttering toast or baked potatoes, can be tricky to work with, especially in baking, because different butter-makers use different amounts of salt in their product. If you add salted butter to a recipe that calls for unsalted butter, always decrease the amount of table salt called for by ¼ teaspoon (per stick). ⅹ the interest of public health. But if your milk, cream, buttermilk, or yogurt is only a day or two past its date, has been kept at 38 degrees or colder, and, most important, has not been opened, it may still be fresh enough to drink. Opening a container allows oxygen to contact the product, making it degrade more quickly. An unopened carton of milk (particularly whole milk) may still be good a few days past the sell-by date, and yogurt almost always is. Just give it the sniff test: If it smells fine, it's probably fine to drink. But if there's any question, throw it out.

#6 How to Stock Up
(Weekly Shopping and Long-Term Planning)

Planning grocery purchases in advance helps save you money, minimizes trips to the store, and guarantees that you will always have staples on hand. Shop with menus in mind, and you'll never find yourself desperate for fresh cilantro in the middle of chopping tomatoes for your famous salsa.

1 Set the standard. Taking the time for this step will pay off again and again. Head to your favorite supermarkets and big-box stores—wherever you like to shop—with a pen and paper. Starting at one end of the store (I suggest the dairy case), write down the prices for the items you usually buy or are likely to buy. Don't skip any aisles—this list is your shopping bible, and you want it to be comprehensive. At home, write a multipage checklist for each store, grouping the items by type (produce, meat, etc.) or by aisle number. If you do this in your regular stores, you'll quickly figure out that some places are ideal to stock up on, say, olive oil, flour, and sugar, whereas others are less expensive if you're just running in for a gallon of milk and some eggs.

2 Collect coupons. Keep an envelope or folder for clippings and/or use a couponing website or app. Before hitting the supermarket, go through your coupon stash and compare it with your list. Saving a few pennies on items you don't need or won't eat isn't smart, but reducing the bill on shelf-stable staples or needed weekly menu ingredients makes sense (and cents!).

Coca-Cola inventor John Pemberton is considered by many to be the godfather of coupons. In 1887, he offered certificates for a free drink to entice customers.

3 Hit the books. Before your weekly shopping trip, look through your cookbooks and recipes and plan what meals you'd like that week, along with big-batch freezables such as chili, soups, stews, and casseroles like lasagna. This curbs impulse buying and helps prevent overbuying and waste.

(continued)

4 Cross-reference. If you know you need fresh parsley for chicken soup, and bunches are twice as big as you'll need, plan to also make tabbouleh or chimichurri sauce. Then check those recipes and list their ingredients so you're not caught short.

5 Check your supply of perishables. With fresh staples such as milk, eggs, bread, and cheese and the addition of pantry items such as olive oil, dried pasta, canned tomatoes, canned fish, jarred olives, and jams on hand, you'll be able to make a quick, hearty meal, any time of day.

#7 How to Be a Thrifty Shopper

Remember: A penny saved is a penny earned. And coupons aren't the only way to save at the grocery store. Here's how to shop on a budget.

1 The bigger, the better. Buy nonperishable items in bulk and large sizes. Prices are better per unit, and you can repackage at home to make storage more convenient.

2 Extra! Extra! Read supermarket circulars in the Sunday papers, or check out advertised sales as you enter the store and adjust your list accordingly. Be flexible: Ground turkey can replace ground beef in your recipes if it's being offered at a better price.

3 Go generic. In many cases, the food inside the ho-hum packaging of generics and store brands is the same, produced by the same manufacturer, differing only in label and price. My family likes only a certain brand of mayonnaise, so I splurge or use coupons. With frozen peas, however, one brand (or nonbrand) is as good as another.

4 Keep it simple. Less processing usually means lower costs. A whole chicken (which you can cut up at home) is typically cheaper than a chicken cut into parts. Similarly, dried beans and peas are cheaper than canned, and cooking them isn't labor-intensive. Pop your own corn and save big compared to microwave style (bonus: no nasty chemical "flavorings").

5 Put it on ice. Buy meat or produce when it's cheap, then clean it (in the case of meat) or cook it (in the case of vegetables) and freeze it in individual portions.

#8 How to Freeze Hamburger Meat
(or Anything Else)

The invention of the freezer was a godsend for thrifty cooks. When our forebears slaughtered a cow or chicken, they had to eat it in short order to prevent spoilage and, therefore, illness. Freezing meat gives us access to safe, quality, high-protein meals on demand. In the United States, ground beef plays a starring role in most kitchens as a versatile and economical staple. Understanding how to buy, store, and freeze it is key to learning best practices in shopping, storing, and cooking all manner of meats and prepared dishes.

1 At the store, look for tears in the packaging and check the expiration date. The meat should look bright red—browning indicates age or unsafe storage—and have uniform fat marbling.

2 At home, remove the meat from its packaging and divide it into recipe-size portions (½ pound, 1 pound, 2 pounds, etc.) or form it into burger patties. Using freezer paper, with the shiny side in, tightly wrap each portion of meat, forcing out as much air as possible, and tape it tightly shut. Do this twice, for an additional protective layer. Patties must be wrapped individually, or they'll freeze in a single block. If you don't have freezer paper, wrap in plastic wrap or foil, then place them inside gallon-size freezer bags, forcing out the air before sealing. Label and date all frozen parcels. The USDA suggests freezing for no more than 4 months. If you will be using the meat within 2 days, no need to freeze it—stash it immediately in the coldest part of your refrigerator.

3 When you are ready to use the ground beef, you have a few options for thawing.

To thaw it in the refrigerator, simply place the package on a plate to catch any juices that might leak; allow 24 hours to fully thaw.

For a quicker thaw, unwrap the ground beef and seal it in a zip-top bag (if it's not already in one). Stopper the sink, fill it with cold water, and fully immerse the meat in the water. Change the water every half hour until the meat is thawed. Do not use hot water because bacteria can form under warm conditions.

To thaw it in the microwave, remove all wrapping and place the ground beef on a microwave-safe plate. Thaw it on the lowest defrost setting, checking frequently so that it doesn't begin to cook. Once the meat is thawed, cook it immediately and do not refreeze or re-refrigerate it.

How Much Should I Buy?

If ground beef (or any other freezer staple) is on deep sale, buy as much as you can reasonably store. Familiarize yourself with standard prices by reading store circulars, talking with butchers, and reading the cost-per-pound breakdowns at the meat counter. Bulk is usually cheaper than prepackaged. Four ounces (about ½ cup) of cooked ground beef is considered one serving, and 1 pound of raw beef will equal 2 cups of cooked ground beef.

A Cut Above

Types and grades of ground beef differ depending on which part of the cow they came from and the percentage of fat they contain. Use this basic guide when shopping.

Ground beef (aka hamburger meat). For this classification, there is no assurance about which part of the cow is used. Scraps from any butchered beef cuts can be included, but no innards are permitted. USDA standards allow up to 30 percent fat in ground beef, though some labels indicate the amount of fat and say "75 percent lean." It is good for stretching your food dollar by adding flavor to pasta sauces, chili, and soups, and it makes for juicy burgers.

Ground chuck. This comes from the "chuck," or shoulder, of the cow. Generally, these cuts are more expensive because of the popularity of chuck roasts and chuck steak. They feature a lot of connective tissue and benefit from long, slow cooking. When ground, chuck offers drier, leaner meat that is good for meatballs or meat loaves, goulashes that stand up to noodles and gravy, or any recipe that benefits from a firm texture.

Ground sirloin. Sirloin comes from the hip region of the cow. It's also more expensive than hamburger. The fat content of ground sirloin varies between 7 and 10 percent. Tender, with a pronounced beef flavor, it enjoys cult status among health-conscious cooks. Use it in heavily spiced chilis or for burgers piled high with add-ons such as mushrooms, peppers, and onions.

Ground round. The round comes from the rump area of a cow. Leaner than chuck, round's fat content hovers between 10 and 15 percent. The resulting burgers may be more steaklike, so they are tastiest when cooked medium or medium-rare and topped with juicy condiments. Ground round is a good choice for thick, meaty pasta sauces, lasagna, and tacos.

Recipe: PERFECT MEAT LOAF

Meat loaf is a favorite everywhere, loved for its economy, ease, and flexibility. Go basic with mashed potatoes and gravy, fancy with grilled vegetables and capellini (angel hair pasta), or enjoy it cold on a next-day sandwich! This is the way my mother made it, but once you master this recipe, improvise and customize to your heart's content. Wrap it in bacon, glaze it with sweet and sour sauce, top it with ketchup and hot sauce, or spice it with garam masala and serve it with basmati rice.

Serves 8

1 large yellow onion, diced

2 pounds ground beef (I prefer ground chuck)

½ cup ketchup

½ cup Dijon mustard

2 eggs, beaten

1¼ cups bread crumbs

Salt and freshly ground black pepper

1. Preheat the oven to 350°F. Line a baking sheet with foil.

2. In a large mixing bowl, combine all ingredients and mix with slightly wet hands until evenly combined.

3. Scoop the mixture onto the prepared baking sheet and form it into 1 large loaf or 2 small loaves. Bake a large loaf for 1 hour or smaller loaves for 45 minutes.

4. Let the meat loaf stand for 15 minutes before slicing so it doesn't fall apart.

TIP: Bread crumbs can be store-bought or you can whir chunks of bread in a blender or food processor. In a pinch, slice bread thinly with a bread knife and then chop.

Fruit   Nuts   Cheese   Bread

Make It Last   HERE'S A QUICK GUIDE TO STORING COMMON GROCERY ITEMS:

Meat. Ground meat and fresh poultry will store safely in the refrigerator for one to three days, and chops, roasts, and steaks for three to four days. If sealed properly and stored in the freezer, uncooked meat can last for four to twelve months. Buy meat in bulk for economy, and once home, divide it immediately among zip-top bags, forcing out as much air as possible when you seal the bag. If you're planning to freeze meat for several months, it's worth it to buy heavy-duty freezer bags.

Fruit. In general, fruit stays fresh longer left unpeeled and uncut. Seal whole fruit such as apples, peaches, and pears in plastic bags and keep them in the crisper drawer. Don't put any fruits on the top shelf because many refrigerators freeze food at this level. Berries and grapes are better left in the vented plastic store packaging; before refrigerating, slide the whole package into a brown paper bag to protect them from light and humidity. Bananas keep longer in the fridge,

but the peel will brown. Pineapples and mangoes should be peeled, sliced, and stored in an airtight, lidded bowl. To discourage browning, toss cut fruit with a few teaspoons of lemon juice.

Nuts. Shelled nuts, if not used quickly, get rancid and soggy faster than you'd think. Store them in a zip-top bag with the air pushed out, inside of a sealed container in the refrigerator for up to three months, or stashed in the freezer for up to a year. Always do a taste test with older nuts before using them in baked goods or salads.

✕ ✕ ✕ ✕ ✕ ✕ ✕ ✕ ✕ ✕ ✕ ✕

What Is Freezer Burn?

Those leathery, brownish patches and wrinkled, crystallized spots on frozen foods are caused by a combination of dehydration and oxidization. Freezer burn isn't harmful; it just doesn't taste good. Airtight packaging helps stave it off, and some experts recommend freezing water in open, plastic containers in your freezer to maintain humidity. ✕

Cheese. The first thing to know is that cheese is a living, breathing thing. The most common mistake is wrapping it in plastic, suffocating the flavor. For cheese that comes in plastic, unwrap it immediately at home, and then repackage it by wrapping it tightly in parchment, waxed paper, or paper towels. Then put it in a partially sealed zip-top bag. Rub the outer layer of firm cheeses (not blue or Stilton!) with olive oil. If mold begins to form, you can then wipe and rinse it away, or cut off the outermost layer, preserving the bulk of it.

Bread. Moist breads last longer in the fridge or freezer (where they will keep for three to six months), but I abhor cold bread. When I'm forced to prolong the shelf life of bread by chilling it, I designate those loaves for toast, bread pudding, or stuffing. Storing home-baked or artisanal breads made without preservatives can be tricky; don't use plastic wrap

(continued)

or plastic bags. The bread will turn gummy and quickly grow mold. My grandmother had the right idea with her ceramic bread box—it kept out air (and critters!) but allowed for breathing. No room for a bread box? Wrap your bread in a clean dishtowel and put it in a paper bag.

Vegetables. Onions and potatoes can be stored at room temperature, preferably in a cool, dry place. But most veggies—including carrots, cabbage, and cauliflower—do better in the fridge. In fact, you can also store onions in the refrigerator to reduce tears when chopping. If you have a "vegetable" setting on your fridge drawers, use it—the purpose is to reduce humidity, which most veggies prefer.

#9 How to Buy an Apple
(or, How to Shop for Produce)

Fresh, ripe natural foods nourish the body and delight the senses. If you shop smart, they also offer excellent mileage for your food dollar. Choosing the best the market has to offer isn't rocket science, but it takes some know-how and a little common sense.

1 There are no stupid questions. Don't know the difference between a Mutsu and a Winesap? Ask the seller. Whether it's the produce manager at your grocery store or the stall-keeper at the farmers' market, they should know the answer or can find out for you.

2 Inspect for "yuck" factors. You know what you don't like to eat: bugs, rotten spots, bruised flesh, weird bumps. If it's not appetizing, pick another one off the pile.

3 Use your five senses. If a peach doesn't smell like a peach, don't buy it. If it's green when it's supposed to be red, keep searching. If there are samples, taste them. If you shake a melon or squash and it sounds like a baby's rattle, it's dried out—and shouldn't go in your cart.

4 Look for average sizes and shapes. Comically large produce (like strawberries) often means it's either old or has been bred for something other than flavor.

5 Buy local, when possible. Generally, the less it has traveled, the fresher, riper, and less chemically treated it is.

6 Buy what you'll realistically eat. Don't buy spinach if you hate it, and buy only as much produce as you will eat in a few days, or up to a week. More than that, and it loses precious nutrients or, worse, goes bad.

7 Try to buy what's in season. If you don't know, ask. Usually, in-season produce is at its peak of flavor and (bonus!) at its cheapest because it's abundant.

Is Organic Really Better?

Ideally, *organic produce* would be defined as produce grown without pesticides or chemicals, from seeds that weren't genetically engineered, in a way that doesn't harm the soil or the water table. In truth, the standards vary. Even though the USDA has a certification for organic foods, the edges are fuzzy. For example, organic soup need contain only 95 percent organic ingredients, and the standards don't apply at all to growers who sell less than $5,000 worth of goods yearly.

The USDA and the government set allowable pesticide residue limits deemed safe for humans to eat, and groceries must meet those standards. Doctors, nutritionists, and pro-organic activist groups say that the benefits of eating fresh produce outweigh the known risks of pesticide residue. Your body and brain thrive on the vitamins, minerals, and fiber from fresh foods. Make the best choices you can, given your budget and options.

Note that conventional (nonorganic) produce such as bananas, grapefruits, onions, and avocados are fine choices because we don't eat the peels; other items are best bought organic because they are pesticide-heavy and we eat the outer layers. Go organic if you can for apples, bell peppers, blueberries, celery, grapes, leafy greens, peaches, and strawberries. Organic or not, all produce should be carefully washed before eating, especially foods with edible peels. Using warm water, either place your produce in a colander and rinse, or for extra-dirty vegetables like spinach or potatoes, soak in a stoppered sink. If using a brush, make sure the bristles aren't too stiff, or you'll tear delicate skins and peels. The FDA doesn't recommend soap; however, some stores sell food-grade sprays and washes to remove oil-based residues that are not entirely water-soluble, such as pesticides, waxy preservatives, and oils from human skin.

Rethink Salad

You shopped for a mountain of vegetables, determined to increase your intake. And then, guiltily, you found yourself tossing away soft cucumbers and limp lettuce, deflated radishes, and eggplant that's withered and brown. It's disheartening, when your intentions were so good! It's no use forcing yourself to eat produce plain, so think instead of *what* would make those vegetables be tempting to you?

Roasting is always good: You can toss practically anything with olive oil, salt, and pepper and roast it on a baking sheet at 375°F until it's brown and crisp-edged, tender and delicious: cauliflower florets, broccoli stems, onion half-moons, green beans, asparagus, eggplant, even wedges of cabbage or romaine. Don't be stingy with the oil, shake the pan now and then, and consider lining your baking sheet with foil, baking paper, or a nonstick mat.

You could also rethink your definition of "salad." It doesn't have to be just a pile of lettuce. Any cooked vegetable, dressed with vinegar and olive oil, becomes "salad," as does any raw vegetable cut thin or small enough to eat with ease. Think thinly sliced fennel with hazelnuts and vinaigrette. Shredded carrots with Greek yogurt, raisins, cumin, and a dash of honey. It doesn't even have to be a vegetable: Diced plums and apricots with almonds, red wine vinegar, olive oil, chopped parsley, and a sprinkle of smoked paprika is a fantastic side dish for roast chicken. Or, dice up melon and cucumbers, toss with soy sauce, sesame oil, cilantro, and mint, and top with roasted peanuts.

A new approach (along with a little help from the Internet) can help transform your vegetable drawer from a place where good intentions go to die into a place where a hearty, healthful dinner can be harvested any night of the week.

#10 How to Handle Lettuce
(or, How to Avoid Waste)

Americans throw out food so often that we barely stop to consider what a waste of money it is. In economics, "slippage" means the difference between the estimated cost of a transaction and what you actually pay. Restaurant managers and chefs have borrowed the term and applied it to food: Slippage is when you buy five tomatoes, eat three, and throw away two because they rotted. In any kitchen, waste not want not is the goal.

Is That Radioactive Waste in My Crisper Drawer?

It's happened to the best of us. After a week of eating out, vows to eat fresh, healthful food are renewed. With green salad in mind, you fling the fridge door open only to find a wilted green puddle where lettuce once was.

This may be a discouraging sight, but don't give up on salads made at home! If you're willing to invest twenty minutes once every two weeks, you'll have a ready supply of crisp lettuce (or spinach or parsley or collards . . . any leafy greens!).

Before we start: Get a salad spinner. In general, I don't tout specific gadgets, but in this case, the right tool for the job is essential. Wetness is the enemy of crisp lettuce. Centrifugal force removes water. Enough said.

1 Fill a clean sink with very cold water. Separate the leaves of lettuce, put them in the water, and swish them around. For limp leaves, break off the bottom to create a fresh edge, soak them for 30 minutes, and they will miraculously rejuvenate.

2 Drain the water. If the leaves were particularly sandy or dirty, fill the sink again, let soak for 15 minutes, then drain again. Next, rinse each individual leaf under cold running water, and then place the leaves in the basket of your salad spinner. (Give each leaf a quick once-over to check for clinging bugs!) For large leaves, as with romaine, you can tear them in halves or quarters before placing them in the basket.

3 When the spinner is full, but not too tightly packed, spin the lettuce until dry.

4 Roll out several paper towels on a countertop and stack the dry leaves in the center. Wrap the lettuce loosely with the paper towels.

5 Place the wrapped lettuce in a gallon-size zip-top bag, gently press out the air, and close the bag. Store in the refrigerator and use as needed. When the bag is empty, simply rinse, air-dry, and reuse it.

TYPES OF LETTUCE

Buttercrunch

Chicory

Mignonette

Oak leaf

Radicchio

Red coral

Arugula

Romaine

Watercress

More About Salad Spinners

Some salad spinners have holes in the bottom of the outer container so that the water can drain directly into the sink. Which is great if you don't mind leaning down into your sink to turn the handle or crank the knob or pull the cord.

However, what's great about the spinners with a solid exterior bowl is that they can serve first as a lettuce refresher. If your lettuce is not looking as crisp as you might wish, fill the spinner with cold water and let the lettuce soak in it for 10 or 15 minutes while you get dinner ready. Then lift the wet leaves into the inner sieve. If any dirt has soaked off, it will fall to the bottom, and you want to lift the greens off the grit, not pour it back over. Spin vigorously, then pour off any water and spin again.

(continued)

UP THE CREEK WITHOUT A SPINNER

If you find yourself without a salad spinner—such as in a vacation kitchen—you can use an old French trick for the most effective spinning ever. Wash the lettuce under running water, and tear up the leaves into serving pieces directly onto a clean dishtowel. Gather up the four edges of the towel, go outdoors, and swing your arm in a big circle, like a baseball pitcher winding up. Family and friends may want to line up in the doorway to watch but tell them to stay back. Water flies out in a massive arc around you! The lettuce will be perfectly dry and crisp, even if the bottom of the towel is soaked. It's a great way to dry a salad, and a terrific party trick.

#11 How to Care for Iceberg Lettuce

A fresh head of iceberg lettuce requires slightly different handling than other less densely packed varieties.

1 Remove the core by sharply knocking the head, stem down, against a countertop or cutting board until it's loose.

2 Twist the stem until it pulls out easily. Discard the core, along with the outer layer of leaves.

3 Rinse the whole head of lettuce well under very cold, running water and shake it dry over the sink.

4 Wipe off the excess water with a clean dish towel or paper towels.

5 Wrap the whole head in paper towels, place it in a zip-top bag, press out the air, seal it, and store it in the fridge.

6 Keep it up to a week, maybe even a few days longer, ready to pull off a few leaves for sandwiches, shred finely to top tacos or nachos, or cut off a wedge to eat with blue cheese dressing.

#12 How to Make Vinaigrette

The simplest salad dressing of them all is also perhaps the most delicious—classic vinaigrette is tangy and light, with just enough flavor to make any salad sing. I like a lot of mustard, which acts as an emulsifier, meaning it makes it possible for the vinegar and oil to mix. The salt counters the blandness of the oil, the vinegar adds tanginess, and the pepper offers bite. It's remarkably versatile; dress any pile of greens or veggies (or even pasta) with it. You can halve this recipe, but it stores well for at least a few days.

Makes 1 cup

3 tablespoons red wine vinegar

1 clove garlic, minced

Pinch of kosher salt

2 tablespoons Dijon mustard

¾ cup extra-virgin olive oil

Freshly ground black pepper

1. Put the vinegar, garlic, and salt in a small glass jar and let sit for 2 minutes. (This lessens the garlic's bite and dissolves the salt.)

2. Add the mustard, olive oil, and pepper to taste. Cap the jar tightly and shake vigorously.

Variations: Chopped fresh herbs are nice. Use grainy or mild mustard. Try balsamic vinegar for a robust fragrance; apple cider vinegar for a fruity finish; or lemon juice for extra tartness. Experiment with different oils, including nut oils and infused oils.

#13 How to Make Caesar Salad

(or, How to Construct a Salad and Make Dressing)

Tossed tableside at supper clubs by tuxedoed waiters, the Caesar salad is arguably the most sophisticated and romantic of all lettuce-based dishes. Once a mere starter, the Caesar salad has become a favorite entrée with the addition of extras such as grilled chicken, shrimp, or steak.

The original recipe, attributed to chef and restaurateur Caesar Cardini, was said to have included olive oil, coddled eggs, and whole romaine lettuce leaves, meant to be plucked from the plate by the stem and nibbled by hand. (The lore goes that Caesar Cardini invented the Caesar salad out of desperation one summer's night when his kitchen was running out of staple menu ingredients.) Chopping it makes for tidier eating, but eating salad with your hands is a fun change of pace.

(continued)

1 Select a salad bowl. I have a favorite, large wooden bowl that's functional and beautiful. For a classic Caesar, use romaine lettuce, torn into large chunks. As with all green salads, it's imperative to make sure the leaves are dry (see How to Handle Lettuce, page 24). Use a salad spinner and allow the lettuce to air dry. If needed, pat with a clean dish towel.

2 Make the Classic Caesar Dressing (shown at right).

3 Pour on the dressing, and then toss with your salad spoons or a pair of tongs. How much dressing to use is a matter of taste—some people like their salad really wet, some like it really dry—but a rough estimate is 1 tablespoon of dressing for every 2 cups of leaves. Start with that and add more as needed. First, be sure to toss well so each leaf is coated in a very thin layer of dressing. Once tossed, top with homemade croutons (see How to Make Croutons page 50), a final grind of pepper, and some big, flat shavings of Parmesan cheese.

Recipe: CLASSIC CAESAR DRESSING

Ideas about the salad vary, but the real marker of a good Caesar salad is the dressing. I often use my blender to make salad dressings. For vinaigrettes, I simply add all the ingredients to a tightly sealed jar and shake it. But a blender helps make this dressing creamy. If you don't want to use one, simply whisk everything but the olive oil in a medium-size bowl, then drizzle in the oil while whisking.

Makes ½ cup, to dress enough salad for 3 or 4 people

3 anchovy fillets (or 1 tablespoon anchovy paste)
1 clove garlic, chopped finely or pressed
1 large egg yolk
Juice of 1 lemon (see How to Juice a Lemon, page 30)
¼ cup freshly grated Parmesan cheese
¼ teaspoon kosher salt
¼ teaspoon freshly ground black pepper
½ cup extra-virgin olive oil

1. Put the anchovy, garlic, yolk, and lemon juice in a blender. Pulse to combine.

2. Add the Parmesan cheese, salt, pepper, and ¼ cup of the olive oil. Pulse to make a smooth paste.

3. With the blender on medium speed, slowly drizzle in the remaining ¼ cup olive oil to make a creamy dressing. If the dressing seems too thick, add a little more olive oil, taste it for balance, and add a little salt, if needed. Use it right away; this dressing does not store well.

Anchovies–small saltwater fish rich in Omega-3 fatty acids–are a secret key ingredient in dressings and pastas, adding "umami," the savory depth our tongues crave.

Raw Eggs: Are They Safe to Eat?

The dressing for a Classic Caesar salad is traditionally made with raw egg. According to the FDA, raw eggs can carry a risk of salmonella contamination. In 2009, they did a study that showed the risk to be lower than originally thought: About 1 in 30,000 eggs was found to be contaminated, and even then, the bacteria may not have penetrated the shell. Since 2010, all commercially produced eggs have been treated to kill the bacteria, but there is no 100 percent guarantee that salmonella won't be present.

My family and I eat raw eggs. My children are past the vulnerable infant and toddler stages; we're all healthy and we get our eggs from reputable sources. I also make sure that the shells are washed and that the eggs stay refrigerated. I hard-boil all eggs that stand on end (instead of lie flat) in water, which indicates advanced age.

If you want to use raw eggs but have concerns, consider using those that are pasteurized in-shell or coddle them by slipping whole eggs into boiling water for one minute, then immediately plunging them into an ice-water bath to halt cooking. Then you can separate the white from the yolk, if called for. ×

#14 How to Zest a Lemon

Most citrus-accented recipes (lemon bars, orange chocolate chip cookies, Meyer lemon vinagrette, chicken a l'orange) will call for "zest." This simply means the colored part of the rind, minus the white part (called pith), which is unpleasantly bitter. Here's how to properly remove the zest and leave the pith.

1 Wash the lemon in running water or soak the lemon in a bowl of water and then rinse.

2 Grip the lemon in your palm from end to end, so that the pointier end touches your little finger and the other end touches your thumb.

3 Prop a Microplane grater against a clean cutting board, angling it at 45 degrees. Twist your wrist while scraping the fruit against the grater in a long stroke, from one end of the lemon to the other. Don't press too hard, or you'll scrape the pith.

4 Rotate the lemon. Repeat the zesting motion one strip at a time, until the whole fruit—or as much as you need—is scraped clean of the yellow part.

5 If you don't have a Microplane, you can use a lemon zester—a specialized peeler that pulls off 3 or 4 tiny strips at a time—or a vegetable peeler to pull off super-thin strips. If you use a peeler, you'll likely need to scrape off the pith and chop the zest finely with a knife. You can also put wide strips of zest in a food processor and process it finely.

If Life Gives You Lemons...

If you need lemon zest for a recipe, but not the juice, you'll be left with a naked lemon. What to do? Waste not, want not! Why not?

• Stuff it into the cavity of a chicken before roasting, along with aromatics like rosemary and sage. This lends a tangy citrus flavor and keeps the meat moist.

• Chop it into chunks, put them in a bowl, and cover liberally with granulated

(continued)

sugar. Scoop ½ cup of the lemon-sugar mixture into the bottom of a tall glass, add ice, and top with cranberry juice for a bracing summer cocktail.

• Cut it into wedges and freeze for later use. Add the frozen wedges to a pot of homemade chicken soup or a pitcher of water to brighten the flavor.

• Make lemon syrup by combining equal amounts lemon juice and sugar, heating the lemon juice gently in the microwave or on the stovetop to help the sugar melt. Add ice and gin for a cocktail, seltzer or water for lemonade.

• Bleach a stain out of cotton by rubbing lemon juice and salt into it. Lemon juice is especially good for removing food stains.

Recipe: ZESTY LEMON SEASONING

Fragrant, oily lemon rind enhances the flavor of both sweet and savory foods. For a seasoning that packs a punch, lemon pepper is the way to go on fish, fowl, fresh salads, and more. I love it on cantaloupe chunks or corn on the cob. Sprinkle it liberally all over the skin before you roast a chicken.

Makes about ½ cup

6 lemons

⅓ cup crushed black peppercorns

¼ cup kosher salt

1. Preheat the oven to 200°F and line a baking sheet with parchment paper.

2. Zest the lemons and set the zest aside.

3. Grind the peppercorns coarsely, either in a pepper mill, a clean coffee grinder, or with a mortar and pestle.

4. Mix the lemon zest and peppercorns together in a bowl, and then spread the mixture out on the prepared baking sheet. Bake until the zest is completely dried, about 25 to 30 minutes.

5. Transfer the dried lemon-pepper mixture to a spice grinder, clean coffee grinder, or mortar and pestle, and grind until blended and finer in texture.

6. Transfer the mixture to a small bowl, add the salt, and stir until well combined. Store in an airtight container for up to a month.

#15 How to Juice a Lemon

The thickest, fattest, prettiest lemons often have the least juice, oddly enough. For the juiciest squeeze, look for thin-skinned lemons. You can tell because the exterior is actually smoother, almost a little translucent, not knobby and bumpy as it is with thick skins.

A lemon will yield, roughly, 3 to 4 tablespoons of juice, so if a recipe calls for "juice of 1 lemon," you can feel safe squeezing whatever size you have at hand. A tablespoon more or less in a recipe is mainly about your own taste and it won't do any harm.

1 Start with a lemon at room
temperature. If you're taking a lemon
straight from the fridge, soak it in hot tap
water for 2 minutes or microwave it for 20
seconds.

2 Wash the lemon in clear running water or
soak it in a bowl of water and rinse.

3 Using the palm of your hand, roll the
lemon on a clean countertop or cutting
board, pressing down as firmly as you can
without popping the fruit. This bursts the
individual cells, releasing the juices inside.

4 With a sharp chef's knife, cut the lemon in
half widthwise.

5 Using a citrus reamer, if you have one, or a
fork if you don't, hold the lemon half over
a bowl and twist the tool and the lemon half in
opposite directions while squeezing.

6 Once most of the juice is out, fold the
lemon like a sandwich and squeeze with
your hands. Insert the tool and scrape left to
right inside the peel to get the last remaining
juice.

7 Strain the juice to remove seeds and any
bits of fruit pulp that may have fallen into
the bowl.

#16 How to Cut a Lemon Wedge Garnish

For everything from cocktails to grilled fish, a lemon wedge is a must. Here's how to cut
presentation-ready lemon garnishes.

1 Holding the lemon broadside against a
cutting board, use a sharp chef's knife
to cut off the pointy ends, just enough to
leave a clean, flat edge.

2 Place one of the cut ends down on
the cutting board and slice the lemon
lengthwise, leaving two long halves.

3 Lay one of the halves cut side down, peel-
side up, on the cutting board, and cut it in
half again, lengthwise. Repeat with the other
half so that you have 4 long quarters.

4 Cut each of the quarters in half again,
lengthwise, slicing at a beveled angle.

5 Slice off the outer ⅛ inch of membrane on
each wedge. This will allow you to push
the seeds out easily with your finger.

6 To store, seal the wedges in an airtight
container or zip-top bag and put them in
the fridge. They can last up to 3 days.

Recipe: **REAL LEMONADE**

Fresh lemonade offers a lot of refreshing flavor in return for very little effort. The secret is simple syrup—a solution of sugar and water that mixes easily into cool drinks and eliminates the problem of undissolved sugar granules sinking to the bottom. You can make this same recipe with limes.

Serves 4

¾ cup granulated sugar

¾ cup lemon juice (from 3 to 4 big, juicy lemons)

1 cup ice

1. In a small saucepan over medium-high heat, combine the sugar and ¾ cup water to create simple syrup. Stir occasionally until the sugar is dissolved.

2. Combine the lemon juice and the simple syrup in a pitcher. Add the ice and 2 cups of cold water, using more or less depending on the strength you desire.

3. Serve with lemon wedge garnishes (see How to Cut a Lemon Wedge Garnish, page 31) or keep in the refrigerator for up to a week.

(see How to Cut a Lemon Wedge Garnish, page 31)

× × × × × × × × × × × ×

Arnold Who?

Down South, the mixture of iced tea with lemonade in equal proportions is called a Half and Half. Legend has it that Arnold Palmer, the famous American golfer, ordered this drink in a bar in Palm Springs circa 1960, and it became forever associated with him—thus the "Arnold Palmer." Some people say an Arnold Palmer is actually a Half and Half with a jigger of vodka, so the nonalcoholic version is a "Virgin Palmer." Replace the vodka with beer and you get a "Hard Palmer."

×

#17 How to Chop an Onion
(or, *Basic Knife Skills*)

Next to washing dishes and toasting bread, chopping onions may be the most common task in the kitchen. Learn to do this cleanly and swiftly, and you'll have mastered the foundation of many recipes.

Slicing, dicing, and chopping onions (or anything) into uniform pieces isn't just for show, it's the only way to ensure even cooking. Otherwise, the small bits burn, and the big ones are nearly raw. Remember: Never, ever put an onion in the food processor; you'll wind up with an unappetizing mush! To prepare, dampen a dish towel, spread it out on the countertop, and set a cutting board on it. This will prevent slips and cuts to your hands. Make sure your knife blade is very sharp and longer than the onion.

1 Place the onion on the board and slice it down the middle vertically, through the root and stem. Lay each half cut-side down, and cut about ½ inch off of the stem end. Roughly peel both halves. Don't be dainty— onions are cheap, and you don't want peels in your food. Save all the trimmings to simmer for stock if you like.

2 Working with one half, still cut-side down, make several small, vertical slices from the cut end toward the root end, but don't cut all the way through. Leaving the

end intact holds the onion together.

3 Rotate the onion half 90 degrees and crosscut, stopping just short of the root, making small slices that will result in a dice. Cut to the last ½ inch of the root and discard it.

To mince: Use the same technique, but make three horizontal cuts as well, bracing the onion against your curled-under fingers (cutting toward the root) before rotating and crosscutting.

To slice: Simply cut the onion halves into half-moons, and don't crosscut.

To chop coarsely: Quarter the onion, then rock knife back and forth to slice into large chunks.

Minced

Sliced

Chopped

Chemical Warfare

You've no doubt heard scores of old wives' tales and "scientific" advice for slicing onions without tears. The most farfetched include holding a match between your teeth and actually chewing on a raw onion! The real trick is keeping irritants away from your face.

When you slice an onion, you break cells, releasing what's inside and allowing amino acid sulfoxides to form sulfenic acids. Enzymes once kept apart now mix together, producing syn-propanethial-S-oxide, a volatile sulfur compound that reacts with the water in your eyes to form sulfuric acid. The sulfuric acid burns, stimulating your eyes to release tears to wash away the irritant. Cooking renders the compound inactive, but here are some tips that will help with the burn:

• Use a knife that's super sharp and at least twice as long as your onion. Long, smooth strokes do less cell-wall damage, releasing fewer gases.

SYN-PROPANETHIAL-S-OXIDE

• Chill out: Less syn-propanethial-S-oxide evaporates from cold onions. Don't freeze them, though—thawed onions are mushy.

• Once you've handled an onion, don't touch your face. The sulfuric compound will irritate eyes, nose, and throat.

• Keep exposed cuts pointed away from you—the second you cut an onion in half, turn both halves face-down on the cutting board. Don't peel the side you aren't currently chopping.

• Turn on your vent hood or place a small fan on the countertop, directed away from you. Fumes that can't reach your face won't irritate your eyes.

××

How Do I Get This Smell off My Hands?

Second to tears, scented skin is the major drawback of handling onions. Here are some tips for overriding the odor:

• Some swear by rubbing their hands on stainless steel (there are even patented "soaps" made of the metal). The theory goes that the metal's self-restoring layer of chromium oxide, which protects its surface, prompts an oxygen exchange that might neutralize onion odor.

• One tried and true method is to cut a lemon in half and rub it over your hands and nails.

• Rub a handful of coffee beans over the fronts and backs of your hands, allowing the warmth of your skin to release their oils.

• Soak your hands in a bowl of tomato juice for at least five minutes. It works for "deskunking" dogs, and it works with onions, too.

• Rub your hands with baking soda. (Add a little moisture for the full effect.) It absorbs the odor and sloughs off the stinky cells from the skin's surface. ×

In the Middle Ages, onions were used as wedding gifts.

Knife Skills

Although you may teach yourself to chop well while holding your chef's knife like it's a hammer, what's called a "pinch grip" allows for more control over whatever you're hacking into bits with your chef's knife. (It's how the pros do it.) To start, pinch the top of the blade, near the handle, between your index finger and your thumb—use two fingers if it makes you feel better—and then wrap your remaining fingers loosely around the knife handle.

While precise measurements don't matter as much in a home kitchen, the exact dimensions of various cuts are something culinary students are expected to learn—and replicate, over and over again. To cut into the fixed dimensions below, start by making whatever vegetable you're using into a rectangle, and then go from there.

The American Culinary Federation gives exact dimensions for cuts as follows:

Batonnet (long stick): ¼" by ¼" by 2½"

Large dice: ¾" cube

Medium dice: ½" cube

Small dice: ¼" cube

Brunoise: ⅛" cube

Fine Brunoise: 1/16" cube

Regular Julienne (or matchstick): ⅛" square by 2" strip

Fine Julienne: 1/16" square by 2" strip

Most cookbooks, however, use "chopped" or "diced" simply to mean that you should be cutting your vegetable or meat into uniform pieces. If every piece is exactly the same, you'll have much better luck cooking your food evenly.

Knife Basics

Many of us are given, or we buy, a knife set at some point when setting up a kitchen, and it usually contains the basic knives you need:

Paring knife. A 3-inch blade for small jobs such as peeling garlic.

Utility knife. A slightly longer blade for bigger jobs like cutting up apples or slicing a cucumber into a salad bowl.

Serrated knife. Ideal for cutting bread but is also useful for thinly slicing soft vegetables such as tomatoes.

Chef's or cook's knife. A large blade—usually 8 to 12 inches—for big chopping jobs.

Of the basic knives, the chef's knife is the one you might want to buy separately to make sure you get a high-quality blade that suits your hand.

The Chef's Knife

The workhorse of the kitchen, the chef's knife is typically between 8 and 12 inches long and falls into two categories: German, with a curve at the front allowing for a rocking motion, and French, a straight version that requires an up-and-down slicing motion.

Blade. Usually made of high-carbon stainless steel. This strong metal helps maintain sharpness and prevents nicks in the blade.

Handle. Usually wooden or plastic, though higher-tech versions are all steel, lowering the possibility of harboring bacteria and increasing durability.

Heel. From the (blunt) end of the blade to the beginning of the handle. This is where you bear down with your palm when cutting through thick or hard foods.

Tang. Located inside the handle, this is the continuation of the blade's steel all the way through the end of the knife.

Rivets. The bolts that attach the handle to the tang. In good knives, they are smooth and do not protrude.

#18 How to Measure Flour

How important is measuring? Depends on what you're making. You can be pretty casual with most savory dishes, because a few more tomatoes, extra garlic, and a couple added glugs of wine won't break (and might *make*) a dish. Baking is a little different because of the chemical interaction of the wet and dry ingredients and the leavening agents. Pro bakers work solely by weight, but that's too fussy for most home cooks. (Although, if you're into precision, go get yourself a kitchen scale, stat.) You can generally get very good results by adhering to the measurements in a baking recipe, using this simple technique.

To get the most accurate quantities, liquid and dry ingredients should be measured using measuring cups designed for each. Here's how to measure flour to ensure best results with all your baking recipes. Note that this technique should also be applied to measuring out all dry ingredients, such as teaspoons of spices, salt, sugar, baking powder, and baking soda.

1 Dip a 1-cup dry measure into a container of flour and lift out an overflowing cupful.

2 Holding the measuring cup over the flour container, draw the flat (dull side) of a knife across the top of the cup to level it, letting the excess fall back into the container.

3 Put the measured flour into your mixing bowl. Don't shake the cup or it will settle the flour and make it denser.

It takes about 350 ears of wheat to make enough flour for a loaf of bread.

The Pancake Primer

A big platter heaped high with pancakes, edges crisp and golden, interiors fluffy and light—this is (almost) everyone's fantasy breakfast. If you've resigned yourself to the heavy, slightly off-tasting pancakes you get from packaged mixes, you'll be delighted to learn that tasty pancakes are just as easy to make without a mix! You're rewarded with better flavor, fluffier texture, and the freedom to tweak and customize to your heart's (stomach's?) content.

MILE-HIGH CAKES

Buttermilk and baking soda are the ingredients responsible for making pancakes puff, but adding a little baking powder as a backup can help ensure a quick rise. The other secret to getting height is a slightly thick batter; runny batter makes delicious thin pancakes, but not thick, tall ones.

FLOUR ARRANGEMENT

Buckwheat flour imparts an almost sourdough-like flavor and is beloved by many pancake fans. Interestingly enough, buckwheat is not actually wheat, it's a ground seed, and for pancakes it works best when mixed half and half with all-purpose flour. Whole-wheat flour also works best mixed with all-purpose, or the pancakes will be quite heavy and dense. To get more whole grains in your diet, however, there is another option: Whole-wheat pastry flour is so finely milled that it can take the place of all-purpose flour in many baked goods, such as pancakes, piecrusts, cookies, and quick breads (though not most cakes or yeast breads).

GOT BUTTERMILK?

Most people don't keep buttermilk on hand, so impromptu pancake breakfasts might find you scrambling for this key ingredient. Don't panic—there's an easy workaround: In a glass or ceramic cup (not a metal one), combine 1 cup milk and 1 tablespoon fresh lemon juice. Let it sit for ten minutes, and you'll have a slightly thickened, acidic milk that can replace buttermilk in your recipe. You can also whisk ½ cup milk with ½ cup sour cream or plain yogurt to make 1 cup

of buttermilk substitute for baking or cooking.

HOT HOT HEAT

Regulating the heat for pancakes is a tricky business, but with experience, you will quickly get the hang of it. Electric griddles and skillets have thermostats that set the ideal temperature, but for stovetop cooking, heat a large cast-iron skillet or griddle over medium-high heat for several minutes. (It's best not to heat a nonstick pan with nothing in it lest the coating be damaged.) The time-honored way to tell when the pan is hot enough is to sprinkle in a few drops of water off your fingertips. If the water bounces once or twice on the surface, the heat is ideal. If it sits and sizzles, it's not hot enough; if it instantly evaporates without bouncing, the pan is too hot. Turn off the heat and

cool the pan slightly before proceeding.

THE FIRST PANCAKE

The very first pancake is rarely perfect. Too much or too little oil or butter, a batter that is too thick or thin (adjust with a little more buttermilk or flour), or a pan that is too hot or too cold will all affect that first cake the most. The second pancake nearly always comes out better, so adjust whatever needs adjusting and eat the first one yourself (or share it with your kitchen helpers).

KEEPING THE CAKES WARM

If you're cooking a casual breakfast for just a few loved ones, you might just plate them right from the pan, so family members can eat as you cook. If you prefer to serve them all at once, turn the oven on to its lowest setting, usually 175 or 180 degrees Fahrenheit, and set a large, ovenproof plate in the oven. As each pancake is cooked, transfer it to the plate; they'll hold up well for up to about thirty minutes. The edges won't be quite as

(continued)

✕ ✕

What About Waffles?

The biggest difference between pancake and waffle batter is that waffles require an airier mix. The extra fluff often comes from butter or separated egg whites that have been beaten until soft peaks form. When folded in at the very end, they make for a lighter batter. ✕

crisp this way, but the pancakes will still be practically perfect when they come to the table, and you can't beat the presentation!

FLIP LIKE A PRO

If you've always admired people who can flip a pancake high and catch it effortlessly in the pan, know that the technique is mainly confidence. Once the first side is cooked, loosen the pancake with a spatula. Grasp the handle of the pan firmly (using a potholder if needed) and shake it back and forth a few times to make sure the pancake is loose. Then flip it upward with a sharp jerk of your wrist. Try to throw it high, a good 12 to 18 inches up. If you throw too low, you will end up with a pancake only half-flipped, folded back on itself, or caught on the edge of the pan.

Baking Basics: Biscuits and Quick Breads

Quick breads, unlike yeast breads, are simply mixed and baked, relying on the rising action of baking powder or baking soda combined with an acidic element such as buttermilk, yogurt, or sour cream. Quick breads can be savory, such as biscuits, or sweet, like a loaf of banana

Cake vs. Quick Bread

Both cakes and quick breads use baking powder or soda to rise, but cakes get tender lightness from beating butter, sugar, and eggs until fluffy. The best quick bread texture comes from not overmixing.

bread. Experienced cooks can make a batch of biscuits, start to finish, in about seventeen minutes, so they truly are quick.

ON THE RISE

Most quick breads get their lift from baking powder, a combination of baking soda and an acidic salt, such as cream of tartar or monocalcium phosphate, usually mixed into a base such as cornstarch. The liquid in the batter causes the chemicals in the baking powder to combine and release carbon dioxide gas bubbles. "Double-acting" baking powders have a second acid salt, such as sodium aluminum sulfate, which releases gas upon being heated, giving the bread a second, later lift when the batter goes into the hot oven.

Baking soda, meanwhile, works like that familiar childhood science experiment, when baking soda and vinegar combine with a rush to shoot off a bottle rocket or gush out of a papier-mâché

"volcano." The soda and an acidic component are combined just before the dough or batter goes in the oven; the chemical reaction gives off carbon dioxide, and those tiny bubbles of gas raise the bread. This is why quick breads are usually baked in a very hot oven, typically anywhere from 375 to 425 degrees Fahrenheit: The high temperature helps "set" the structure of the bread as the bubbles rise, trapping them inside so that the finished product is fluffy and tender.

DON'T WAIT TO BAKE

This leavening action also explains why quick bread batters cannot be mixed in advance and stored. As soon as the wet ingredients go into the dry ones, the batter should be poured directly into the prepared pan and popped in the preheated oven. If

Biscuit Variations

Biscuits are ideal for add-ins. Before adding the buttermilk, you can stir in 2 to 3 tablespoons of chopped fresh herbs such as chives, parsley, or rosemary. Or reduce the butter by half and add 1 cup grated Cheddar or Parmesan cheese. Or go in another direction entirely and add 2 tablespoons sugar and a large egg to make scones, best served warm with butter and jam.

quick bread batters hang around waiting to be baked, all the carbon dioxide will bubble out, and the resulting bread will be flat and tough. Nearly all savory quick breads are best the day they're made; keeping them overnight tends to make them tough and dry. Quick breads that contain sugar, eggs, and butter, however, will last longer.

GOOD FAT

Aside from Irish soda bread—which contains only flour, baking soda, salt, and buttermilk—most quick breads have a high proportion of fat to flour compared to yeast breads, which may have no fat at all. Whether it's butter, oil, lard, or vegetable shortening, the fat coats the molecules of the flour and helps prevent gluten from developing as the bread rises in the oven. When the gluten doesn't develop, the crumbs don't have as much elasticity, so instead of the chewy texture of a yeast bread, a quick bread will remain tender, coming apart easily when you tear or cut it.

Recipe BUTTERMILK BISCUITS

A standard Home Ec class recipe, buttermilk biscuits may seem intimidating, but once you learn how to make them, the effort pays off in the form of buttery, heavenly goodness.

Makes 8 to 12 biscuits

2 cups all-purpose flour (plus 2 to 3 tablespoons for shaping)

1 teaspoon salt

1 teaspoon baking soda

½ cup (1 stick) cold, salted butter

½ cup well-shaken buttermilk

2 tablespoons milk (optional)

1. Preheat the oven to 425°F and set out a baking sheet.

2. In a large mixing bowl, stir the flour, salt, and baking soda together with a wooden spoon.

3. Cut the butter into 8 pieces and drop them into the bowl. Use a fork or your fingers to "cut" or "rub" the butter into the dough, breaking it up into smaller and smaller bits as you combine it with the flour. (You can also use a pastry cutter for this job.) Stop when the flour mixture looks like a mass of crumbs, with no large lumps of butter visible.

4. Make a well in the center of the dough. Pour the buttermilk into the well.

5. Combine with the spoon, stirring just until the dough comes together into a clump.

6. Sprinkle 2 to 3 tablespoons of flour in a circle about 10 inches wide on a clean countertop or work surface, and then turn the dough out onto the flour along with any remaining dry bits left in the bowl.

7. Knead the dough briefly, folding and pressing it gently with the flat of your palms 3 or 4 times so that the shaggy mass becomes a smooth(ish) whole. Pat it gently into a sort of rectangle about ¾ inch thick.

8. Use a sharp knife to divide the dough into 8 to 12 squares. Lift the squares onto the baking sheet, gently rounding the edges—without overworking the dough.

9. If you like, use a pastry brush to lightly brush the surface of each biscuit with the milk. This helps make an evenly golden crust. Bake them for 10 to 12 minutes, until they are puffed and golden. Remove from the oven and serve immediately.

Recipe: FLUFFY PANCAKES

Short stack or silver dollar, blueberry or banana, pancakes are the classic and beloved weekend breakfast of champions.

Serves 6

2¼ cups all-purpose flour

2 tablespoons granulated sugar

1½ teaspoons baking powder

1 teaspoon baking soda

Pinch of salt

6 tablespoons unsalted butter, melted

1½ cups buttermilk

2 large eggs

Vegetable oil or butter, for cooking

1. Preheat the oven to 185°F and put a heatproof platter in the oven.

2. In a large bowl, whisk together the flour, sugar, baking powder, baking soda, and salt.

3. In a separate large bowl, whisk the butter with the buttermilk and eggs.

4. Heat a griddle or large frying pan over medium-high heat, and add 1 tablespoon of vegetable oil or butter to grease it. When the pan is hot (see "Hot Hot Heat," page 37), pour the dry ingredients into the wet and stir to combine.

5. Ladle about ½ cup batter into the pan to make 1 large pancake or 4 dollops of 2 to 3 tablespoons each to make silver-dollar pancakes. Cook until the edges start to look dry and a few bubbles begin to rise to the top, 2 to 4 minutes, depending on the size of the pancake. The cooked side should be just golden and not too brown.

6. Flip the pancake—you should then see it swell and rise as the gas bubbles released are trapped against the underside of the cooked surface. Cook 1 to 2 minutes more until just cooked through and golden on the second side. Transfer to the platter in the oven. Repeat with the remaining batter. Use caution when removing the platter from the oven because it will be hot!

Beginner's Bread: The Magic of Yeast

Do you dream of fragrant loaves of freshly baked bread, light in the middle and toothsome at the crust, warm from the oven, and slathered with creamy butter? Do you instead settle for spongy, gummy, plastic-wrapped store-bought bread? If your answer is "Yes, because baking bread is too complicated," you'll be pleasantly surprised to learn that a basic bread recipe has just four ingredients: flour, water, yeast, and salt. That's it. And once you understand how bread works, you can confidently master any bread recipe.

Flour. There are myriad types of flour, made from many grains from around the globe, but in the US, the most common is wheat flour. That category can be further broken down into enriched, blended, whole grain, bread, graham, bolted, cake, bleached and unbleached, and so on. Overwhelmed? Start with all-purpose flour, sold inexpensively at any supermarket in variously sized bags. And there you have your cornerstone.

Water. Water serves two functions in bread making: It activates the yeast and dissolves the ingredients into a uniform dough. More water means you get a stickier dough, which results in irregular holes, as in baguette or ciabatta. Skimp on the water, and you'll wind up with a dense, dry loaf.

Yeast. Yeast makes dough rise by "exhaling" carbon dioxide bubbles. The gluten in the flour stretches to accommodate them, like miniballoons, making the dough ball expand.

Instant or rapid-rise yeast, sold in packets at the supermarket, is inexpensive and easy to get your hands on. It quickens the process and minimizes steps, but some complain that flavor is sacrificed. Another option for the beginning baker is active dry yeast, which is a yeast that is dormant until you add water. Active dry yeast performs best if you "proof" it first—that is, combine it with slightly warm water and a bit of sweetener (to feed the yeast) until it turns bubbly and creamy. Artisanal bakers and pastry chefs use fresh yeast, mostly because of its flavor, but dried yeast produces excellent homemade loaves.

Salt. Salt adds flavor but also controls the yeast by slowing the fermentation process, keeping the bread matrix from overstretching and subsequently deflating. For a proper rise, you have to get the salt-to-yeast ratio right. Plain table salt will do, though some prefer the flavor of sea salt.

IT'S ALIVE!

Yeast are living organisms, in the kingdom Fungi (which also includes mushrooms). Here's how we know:

1. Yeast respires, a form of breathing. It takes in oxygen in the form of glucose, a simple sugar.

2. It eats and produces waste. After eating the sugar, it releases carbon dioxide gas, and, in anaerobic (air-free) environments, ethanol alcohol. Enzymes in the yeast turn starch into maltose, another sugar. This fermentation process is used in brewing beer, which is why certain breads have a beery taste, and accounts for why bread doesn't taste like flour-and-water paste!

3. And yeast reproduces. A single-celled organism, yeast reproduces through budding. This process happens when a smaller cell splits off from the edge of another cell.

When paired with salt, bread is a traditional offering of welcome in many cultures. In fact, the phrase "Bread and salt!" is a greeting in Russia, often uttered by a guest as an expression of gratitude and good wishes to a host.

✕ ✕

On Spoon Selection

Wooden spoons are ideal for stirring dough because they have a large surface area for mixing, they won't bend under pressure, and they feel good in your hand when moving around heavy dough and batters–they don't cut uncomfortably into your palm the way a metal spoon might. ✕

#19 How to Knead Bread Dough

Kneading is the process of combining water and flour (and any other ingredients) in a way that will result in springy, elastic dough and airy, nicely chewy bread. Many bakers use mixers equipped with dough hooks to combine the ingredients and stretch the resulting dough, but kneading by hand is the traditional way and is remarkably easy. (Of course, you don't *have* to knead to make bread—see the Four-Ingredient No-Knead Bread recipe that follows.)

1 Put your dough on a lightly floured surface. To avoid adding too much flour to your recipe, use as little flour as is effective to keep the dough from sticking.

2 Wash and dry your hands and remove any rings or dangling bracelets. Lightly flour your hands.

3 Gather the dough into a ball and start working it with the heel of your hand, pressing and stretching it until it has a little spring to it.

4 Fold the dough in half, rotate it 90 degrees, and repeat, continuing until the dough is smooth and stretchy, typically about 10 minutes (though this depends on the recipe).

Recipe: FOUR-INGREDIENT NO-KNEAD BREAD

This bread relies on fermentation from a very long rise, rather than kneading, to break down the proteins and form the strands of gluten that structure the loaf. Make it in the morning and let it rise all day, or make it before bed and let it rise all night. If you like, use half whole-wheat flour here instead, but increase the water to 2 cups.

Makes one (8-inch) loaf

3½ cups all-purpose flour

2 teaspoons kosher salt

¼ teaspoon instant yeast (see Note)

1¾ cups lukewarm water

1. Combine all of the ingredients in a large mixing bowl and mix thoroughly with a wooden spoon, stirring the dough about 20 times.

2. Once mixed, cover the bowl tightly with plastic wrap and keep covered for 12 hours at room temperature. Generously grease an 8-inch loaf pan.

3. Once the dough has risen, turn it into the loaf pan. It will be soft. Let rise again, covered with plastic wrap until it has doubled in size, about 2 hours.

4. Preheat the oven to 375°F.

5. Bake until it smells fragrant and has a golden-brown crust, 30 to 40 minutes.

NOTE: You can substitute ½ teaspoon active dry yeast for the instant. Proof it according to package directions before adding to the other ingredients.

Recipe: THE VERY BEST SANDWICH BREAD

Making bread is something of a project, so be sure you have a few hours to spare. Of course, most of that time is needed for the dough to rise.

Makes two (8-inch) loaves

2 cups warm water

2 tablespoons active dry yeast

2 teaspoons salt

2 tablespoons plus 2 teaspoons vegetable oil

⅓ cup granulated sugar

5½ cups bread flour, plus more for kneading

1. In a large bowl, combine the warm water, yeast, salt, oil, sugar, and half the flour. Mix thoroughly with a wooden spoon, and let rise in a warm place until it doubles in size, about 2 hours.

2. Turn the dough out onto a floured surface and gradually knead in the rest of the flour; continue kneading until smooth.

3. Put the dough ball into a large, lightly oiled bowl, and turn it several times to coat. Cover with a damp dish towel and leave it in a warm place until the dough doubles in size, about an hour.

4. Punch down the dough with your fist (this releases air bubbles), then let it rest for a few minutes. Meanwhile, lightly oil two 8-inch loaf pans.

5. Divide the dough into two equal parts. Pat each piece into an oval shape on a lightly floured work surface, and then fold the top and bottom over the middle like folding a letter. Put each loaf seam-side down into the prepared pans and cover lightly with plastic wrap. Let rise in a warm place until it's almost doubled, about an hour.

6. Preheat the oven to 350°F.

7. Bake for 35 to 45 minutes, until the crust is lightly browned and the loaves sound hollow when tapped.

Recipe: WHOLE-WHEAT SANDWICH BREAD

If you are looking to get more whole grains in your diet or simply prefer the toasty flavor of whole-wheat bread, this honey-sweetened loaf is the one to try.

Makes two (8-inch) loaves

2¾ cups warm water

2¼ teaspoons (1 envelope) active dry yeast

⅓ cup honey

¼ cup olive oil

3 teaspoons salt

4 cups whole-wheat flour

3 cups all-purpose flour, plus more for kneading

Non-stick cooking spray

1. Stir the warm water and yeast together in a large bowl. Let stand for 5 minutes.

2. Gently stir in the honey, olive oil, and salt.

3. Gradually add both types of flour while you stir. Mix until the ingredients are thoroughly combined and the dough begins to pull away from the sides of the bowl.

4. On a lightly floured surface, knead the dough until it is smooth and elastic (see How to Knead Bread Dough,

opposite). If the dough is sticky, add a bit more flour.

5. Put the dough ball into a large, lightly oiled bowl. Spray a sheet of plastic wrap with cooking spray, cover the bowl, and allow the bread to rise for about an hour or until doubled in size. Lightly grease two 8-inch loaf pans.

(continued)

6. Punch the dough down and divide it in half, using a sharp knife. On a clean work surface lightly sprinkled with flour, shape each piece into an oval, and fold the top and bottom over the middle like folding a letter. Put each loaf seam-side down in the prepared pans and cover with the oiled plastic wrap. Let rise again, until doubled in size, 30 minutes to 1 hour.

7. Preheat the oven to 375°F.

8. Remove the plastic wrap, and bake the loaves until the crust is lightly browned and the loaves sound hollow when lightly tapped, about 30 minutes.

#20 How to Make a Sandwich

Portable and tidy, with rich layers of meat, vegetables, and condiments tucked between slices of bread, the beloved sandwich allows the hungry to eat a quick and tasty, nutritious meal-in-one without the fuss of cutlery—anytime, anyplace.

1 Choose your bread. In general, consider sturdier or toasted breads for wet or saucy fillings, and softer breads when the contents are sturdy and harder to chew. For example, never put a Sloppy Joe on thin, white sandwich bread—it will soak through and get *too* sloppy. Conversely, for thick slices of roast beef, piled high with lettuce, tomato, and Russian dressing, a softer bread such as packaged sliced rye or white makes the sandwich easier to bite into.

2 If you want to, lightly toast the bread. For a wetter sandwich with juicy fillings such as tomatoes or dressing, or a very moist tuna salad, toasting keeps the finished sandwich from falling apart.

3 Spread something tasty on the bread. In some regions, practically every sandwich gets spread with an ultrathin layer of butter. This delicious coating of fat serves as a barrier to lock in juicy fillings and keeps the bread from drying out during hot summer picnics. I still love butter on a ham sandwich, but I've spread the love to other toppings, too.

4 Fill your sandwich. The range is almost overwhelmingly broad here—practically anything you can slap on bread fits the bill. See "Types of Fillings" (page 47) to get you started.

5 Enjoy your sandwich. Open-faced, triple-decker, cut into triangles, hot or cold—layer up and customize however you like. Creativity is most definitely rewarded.

What Makes It a Sandwich?

A Boston court, when confronted with the question in a case regarding a zoning law for "sandwich shops," ruled that it is commonly understood that a "sandwich" includes at least two slices of bread. As a fan of the open-faced sandwich, featuring items stacked atop a single slice, I beg to differ. But the ruling did get to the heart of the matter—a sandwich must involve bread, which serves as an edible container for fillings (meat, vegetables, cheeses—the possibilities are endless) and spreads (mayo, mustard, jellies, hot sauce, and so on), which add flavor and moisten the bread to prevent dryness.

A World of Bread Awaits

Sliced white or wheat bread. A perfectly acceptable choice as a foundation for your sandwiches, but there's a big world beyond Wonder. Explore and taste—you'll likely discover a new favorite.

Baguettes. Long, narrow French bread loaves. Cut it into shorter pieces, then split lengthwise and layer with slices of Brie cheese (no need to slice off the white rind, it's delicious!) and roasted red peppers from a jar. Or slather it with chocolate-hazelnut paste (such as Nutella), dot with sliced banana, and serve open-faced with coffee for a sweet breakfast.

Hard rolls. Also called bulkies, Vienna rolls, Kaiser rolls, and crusty rolls. Ideal for fried egg and cheese, with a little ketchup; pulled pork with pickles; or tuna salad with lettuce and a light layer of mayo.

Rye and pumpernickel. These flavorful old-world breads are made with rye flour as well as wheat, and are deli favorites for pastrami and corned beef, whitefish or lox, and toppings such as sauerkraut, Dijon mustard, and dill relish.

Flavored breads. Olive, onion, garlic, jalapeño, and so forth. These serve their purpose in a sandwich, plus bring intense taste to the table. Although you can certainly double-down with strong-tasting fillings such as fragrant cheeses, smoked or canned fish, and spicy or pungent condiments, these breads do a lot of the heavy lifting flavorwise and are delicious with just a simple schmear of goat cheese or mild deli meats such as honey-roasted or smoked turkey.

English muffins. These round, crusty flat rolls aren't just for breakfast! The nooks and crannies are excellent conveyors of spreadable fillings such as cream cheese or pimento cheese, and the sourdough flavor works well with milder items such as ham, Cheddar, or American cheese.

Flatbreads. Generally lower in calories than thicker breads, these chewy wraps are ideal with hummus, topped with sliced olives, or filled with cream cheese and cucumber. For a nutritious and delicious sandwich, fill a flatbread with grilled vegetables sprinkled with olive oil.

TYPES OF BREADS

Sliced white or wheat

Flatbreads

Hard rolls

Rye and pumpernickel

Flavored breads

English muffins

Baguettes

TYPES OF SPREADS

Mayonnaise. Creamy, eggy, and salty, much like butter it moistens and adds subtle flavor. I especially love it mixed with diced egg, canned tuna, or lunchmeats. (See recipe below to make your own.)

Mustard. Low in calories, piquant, and available in a wide variety of styles. On a burger, I'll take American yellow mustard, but on a cheese sandwich, give me seedy English mustard or German mustard accented with a burst of horseradish.

Ketchup. Sweet and vinegary, ketchup also brings the tang of tomatoes and salt to a sandwich. Best on hot sandwiches.

Barbecue sauce. Like ketchup, with smoke. Perfect for roasted pork and grilled chicken breast.

Avocado. Smash avocado onto bread with a fork and sprinkle with a little salt, and you have a moist, flavor-rich, nutritious spread full of healthy fats.

Secret sandwich sauce. One of my best-kept secrets is just mayonnaise and anything tangy. Try mayonnaise and a little ketchup, or mayonnaise and Dijon, or mayonnaise and steak sauce blended. The proportions are entirely up to you, but the blend is always delicious. For a little spiciness, try mayonnaise and a spoonful of chipotle in adobo.

Recipe: HOMEMADE MAYO

Most people don't even know what's in mayonnaise, that bewitching sauce originating in Mahon, Spain, let alone how easy it is to make from scratch. At its most basic, mayo has just four ingredients—though you should feel free to doctor it up with white pepper, paprika, mustard, hot sauce, or a minced garlic clove. (Before you start, see "Raw Eggs: Are They Safe to Eat?" page 29.) You can skip the whisking and make this in the blender, if you like, drizzling in the oil in a thin stream as the machine runs at a medium speed.

Makes 1 cup

2 large egg yolks

Juice of 1 lemon

½ teaspoon salt

1 cup mild-flavored oil, such as vegetable or canola

1. In a large mixing bowl, whisk together the egg yolks, lemon juice, and salt.

2. Continue to whisk while you pour the oil into the mix in a very slow stream. If you stop whisking or add the oil too quickly, it will separate and not thicken into an emulsion.

3. Keep whisking for 2 to 3 minutes until the mixture is creamy and thick. Taste and add a bit of salt or more lemon juice if you feel you need it. Serve at once and store extra tightly covered, in the refrigerator, for up to 5 days.

TYPES OF FILLINGS

Meats. Thinly sliced generally is best. Roasted meats such as turkey, ham, and beef are favorites, as are cured meats such as salami and mortadella. Try grilled steak, pork chops, or chicken breast, sliced horizontally with a sharp knife, for a variation. (A sandwich is an excellent use for leftovers.)

Vegetables. Hot or cold, veggie sandwiches rule. Try roasted vegetables such as peppers, onions, eggplant, or summer squash, and melt cheese on them if you like. Stack thinly sliced raw vegetables with bean sprouts or watercress, and then moisten with plenty of spread.

Eggs. Boil them for egg salad, dice them into tuna salad, fry and top with grated Cheddar—eggy sandwich possibilities abound. An excellent source of protein, you'll walk away satisfied.

Recipe: THE CLASSIC BLT

Ubiquitous in American culture, from the lunch counters of the 1940s to the trendy gastropubs of today, the BLT may be the single most popular sandwich after the hamburger. In a bacon, lettuce, and tomato sandwich, three ingredients vie to be top dog. I like them all equally. But I can't help thinking it should be called a BLTM because it wouldn't be the same without the mayo.

Makes 1 sandwich

3 slices thick-cut bacon

2 slices sturdy white bread, lightly toasted

1 to 2 tablespoons mayonnaise (preferably homemade, see Homemade Mayo, facing page)

2 to 4 leaves romaine lettuce

2 to 3 slices ripe tomato (preferably beefsteak)

Salt and freshly ground black pepper

1. In a medium-size skillet, fry the bacon until just crisp. Once cooked, transfer it to 2 layers of paper towels to drain. Lay another layer of paper towels on top and set aside.

2. Slather the lightly toasted bread with mayonnaise. On one slice, lay 1 or 2 leaves of lettuce, depending on their size, covering the bread completely.

3. Break the drained bacon strips in half and layer on top of the lettuce. Top with 2 to 3 slices of tomato, completely covering the bacon. Season the tomato with salt and pepper to taste.

4. Add another layer of lettuce, then top with the remaining slice of bread, mayo-side down.

5. Put the sandwich on a plate and slice in half diagonally. Flank with a pickle and potato chips, and serve.

#21 How to Refresh Stale Bread

Cutting costs on groceries is one of the surest ways to slash household expenses. And the first step to spending less on food is to not waste what you buy. This is obviously a big issue to tackle all at once, so let's start with the basics: bread. A backbone of the Western diet, bread unfortunately doesn't stay fresh long. Because stale bread is practically a given, a little culinary creativity is called for to make sure it doesn't end up in the trash. Here are some ideas to give new life to the staff of life.

Toast it. If your bagel, boule, or baguette is starting to harden, slice it and make toast. (Who doesn't love toast?) Bump this bread to the front of the meal-planning line and make grilled cheese sandwiches, BLTs on toast, cinnamon toast with tea, toasty garlic bread drizzled with olive oil, or mini-pizzas made with a slather of jarred marinara and grated cheese. You can make big batches of toast in the broiler on a cookie sheet.

Transform it. Make that stale bread into bread crumbs or croutons and give it a whole new life. Get started with recipes for French Toast Casserole, Panzanella (Bread Salad), and Meatballs, on pages 49–51.

Make it dessert. Bread pudding is a time-honored way to use up stale bread (see Banana–Chocolate Chip Bread Pudding, facing page), but there are simpler routes to dessert: Top sliced bread (try a baguette, an English muffin, or a bagel) with chopped bittersweet chocolate or a sprinkling of chocolate chips, and then toast until the bread is golden brown and the chocolate is melted. Spread the chocolate smooth and drizzle with extra-virgin olive oil and sea salt. For dessert crostini, thinly slice Italian or French bread, brush with oil, and toast under the broiler until lightly browned, about five minutes. Top with ricotta or goat cheese mixed with honey, mashed berries, or even caramel sauce.

If your loaf is a bit past its prime, don't despair. Here's how to soften bread that has hardened.

1 Preheat the oven to 325°F.

2 Put the stale bread in a clean paper bag and twist the end shut tightly.

3 Sprinkle the bag lightly and evenly with cool water, but don't soak it.

4 Heat the entire package in the oven (keeping it far away from the heating element or flame), allowing 5 minutes for small rolls and 20 minutes for full loaves. If needed, rewet the bag and repeat.

5 Serve the bread within 10 minutes, or it will harden again.

Aren't Carbs Bad for Me?

Carbohydrates, made up of starches, sugars, and fiber, provide us with the fuel we burn daily. Without them, our bodies can feel sluggish and our brains fuzzy. The higher the fiber and the lower the sugar, the better the carb.

Recipe: BAKED MEATBALLS IN TOMATO SAUCE

Hearty, flavorful meatballs deploy the frugal cook's secret weapon for stretching ground meat: cubes of stale bread soaked in milk. In fact, meatballs made without bread are heavy, dense, and dry, so it's an excellent way to use up stale bread and make a good dinner at the same time. Baking meatballs is much easier than frying them in batches, and they taste just as good.

Makes 2 dozen meatballs; serves 4

1 can (28 ounces) diced tomatoes

1 large onion

4 tablespoons butter

4 slices white bread, torn into large chunks

1 cup whole milk

1 large egg, beaten

1½ pounds ground chuck

½ cup freshly grated Parmesan cheese, plus more for serving

1 clove garlic, minced

1 teaspoon whole dried oregano

1 teaspoon salt

Hot cooked pasta (see page 55)

1. Put the diced tomatoes in a medium-size saucepan over medium heat. Peel the onion, slice it in half, and add one entire half to the pan along with the butter. Bring to a simmer, then reduce the heat to medium-low, and let the sauce simmer gently, stirring now and then, while you make the meatballs. Dice the rest of the onion finely and put it in a large mixing bowl.

2. Preheat the oven to 350°F. Line a rimmed baking sheet with foil (for easier cleanup).

3. Add the bread, milk, and egg to the onion in the mixing bowl. Stir and let sit for 3 minutes so the bread absorbs the moisture. Add the meat, Parmesan cheese, garlic, oregano, and salt, and mix thoroughly, ideally using slightly wet hands.

4. Form the mixture into 24 meatballs and place them on the baking sheet. Bake for 30 to 40 minutes, until browned and cooked through. (Break one open to check.)

5. Remove and discard the onion half from the tomato sauce. Add the baked meatballs to the sauce and toss to coat. Serve over hot pasta with additional Parmesan cheese.

Recipe: BANANA-CHOCOLATE CHIP BREAD PUDDING

Any kind of bread pudding works for me, but banana and melted chocolate take this dish from homey to fabulous. Serve it topped with freshly whipped cream (see Sweetened Whipped Cream, page 16) and shaved chocolate.

Serves 4 to 6

8 large slices stale white bread

3 tablespoons butter, melted

¾ cup chocolate chips

2 bananas, sliced

6 large eggs, beaten

2½ cups whole milk

1 cup granulated sugar

1 teaspoon ground cinnamon

2 teaspoons vanilla extract

1. Preheat the oven to 350°F.

2. Break the bread into small pieces and place them into an 8-inch square baking pan. Drizzle the melted butter over the bread. Sprinkle with the chocolate chips and banana slices.

3. In a medium-size mixing bowl, beat together the eggs, milk, sugar, cinnamon, and vanilla.

4. Pour the egg mixture over the bread, and lightly push down with your fingertips. Let the pudding stand for 10 minutes until the bread has soaked into the liquid.

5. Bake for 45 minutes, until puffy and golden and the top springs back when lightly pressed.

#22 How to Make Bread Crumbs

Make old bread the foundation of new dishes with easy, multipurpose fresh bread crumbs.

1 Tear the bread into chunks and pulse them in the blender or food processor to the desired consistency.

2 If you want dry bread crumbs, such as for coating chops or chicken breasts before frying or baking, first toast the bread chunks in a 375°F oven until dried out, about 10 or 15 minutes.

3 Season the crumbs with fresh or dried herbs, ground pepper, or powdered garlic.

4 Store the fresh bread crumbs in the refrigerator in an airtight container for up to a week or freeze for up to 6 months.

#23 How to Make Croutons

Give your soups and salads extra crunch, flavor, and substance with a sprinkling of homemade croutons.

1 Preheat the oven to 350°F.

2 Dice bread into large cubes, then toss them with enough extra-virgin olive oil to coat but not saturate.

3 Toast the cubes until dried and lightly golden, 20 to 25 minutes.

4 As soon as they come out of the oven, toss the croutons with salt and ground black pepper, or fancy them up with pesto, cayenne, onion salt, or lemon pepper.

5 Serve immediately or store in an airtight container for up to a week.

Recipe: PANZANELLA (BREAD SALAD)

Old-world Italian home cooks thought it was a sin to waste food, especially bread. This salad is my go-to when tomatoes are falling off the vine and I've got bread to repurpose. This salad becomes a full meal if you serve cooked sliced steak or chicken breast over the top.

Serves 4

2 pounds ripe tomatoes, cored and cubed

1 pound crusty bakery bread, such as a sourdough boule, torn into small pieces and lightly toasted for a few minutes in the oven

1 cup arugula leaves

12 fresh basil leaves, torn into large pieces

½ medium-size red onion, thinly sliced

¾ cup whole pitted olives

½ cup extra-virgin olive oil

4 tablespoons red wine vinegar

2 large or 3 small cloves garlic, minced

Salt and freshly ground black pepper

1. In a large bowl, combine the tomatoes, bread, arugula, basil, onion, and olives.

2. In a small bowl, whisk together the oil, vinegar, and garlic, and drizzle it over the salad.

3. Season the salad generously with salt and pepper, toss, and let stand for 15 minutes before serving.

Recipe: FRENCH TOAST CASSEROLE

This French toast improves on the beloved classic by having the stale bread soak overnight in its egg batter. In the morning, all you have to do is pop the pan in the preheated oven and you have a sweet breakfast for the whole family.

Serves 4 to 6

½ cup dark or light brown sugar

½ cup (1 stick) unsalted butter, melted

3 teaspoons ground cinnamon

8 slices stale bread

½ cup raisins

6 eggs

1½ cups milk

1 tablespoon vanilla extract

1. In a small mixing bowl, stir together the brown sugar, butter, and 1 teaspoon of the cinnamon. Pour the mixture into the bottom of a buttered 13-by-9-inch baking pan.

2. Arrange the bread slices on top, and dot with the raisins.

3. In a large mixing bowl, beat the eggs, milk, vanilla, and the remaining 2 teaspoons cinnamon. Pour the mixture over the bread. Cover the pan with foil and refrigerate for 4 to 8 hours or overnight.

4. Preheat the oven to 375°F.

5. Bake the casserole, covered with the foil, for 40 minutes. Uncover the pan, and bake for 5 minutes, or until the top is browned. Let stand for 10 minutes before serving.

#24 How to Make Pizza

Why go for delivery or frozen pizza when you can make bubbly, cheesy, completely customized pizza at home for a fraction of the cost? Premade dough is typically available for purchase at your local pizzeria, as well as at some supermarkets. Or make your own dough (see Foolproof Pizza Dough, page 52) for the ultimate treat. Homemade pizza can be a healthy, low-fat, high-nutrient supper, topped with tomato sauce, fresh vegetables, low-fat cheeses (such as a sprinkling of salty feta), or greens. Top your pizza with sausage, pepperoni, and extra cheese, and it becomes more of a "sometimes" food. Either way, it's a dinner that's sure to please.

1 Preheat the oven. A hot oven is the key to good pizza at home. Turn it up to 450°F or 500°F if your oven goes that high.

2 Sprinkle cornmeal on your baking sheet. Pat out your dough on a floured work surface to a pizza shape, stretching and pulling it gently to be as thin as possible. If you're having a lot of trouble, use a rolling pin, but wield it gently. Pizza won't roll out like piecrust. Just work slow and steady and it will gradually take shape.

(continued)

3 Add the tomato sauce, not too much (about 1 cup for a 12-inch pizza, 1½ cups for a 16-inch), and put the pizza in the oven. Bake this sauced crust for 7 to 9 minutes so that it is only partially baked. Edges should be a bit puffed and the sauce slightly dry.

4 Remove the pizza and layer on your toppings. Put the cheese on last so it can melt down over the toppings. And don't put on heaps of cheese (unless that's all you're using). Too much can bury the other flavors.

5 If you want to gild the lily, once you've added the toppings, brush olive oil and very lightly sprinkle salt or sesame seeds or fresh herbs on the outer rim of the crust. It will taste like a breadstick.

6 Return the pizza to the hot oven and bake until bubbling. Since the crust has already been parbaked in Step 3, the final baking time should be about 10 more minutes. Keep an eye on it. Times will vary depending on the toppings.

Recipe: FOOLPROOF PIZZA DOUGH

Makes two (12-inch) crusts

1 cup warm water (about 110°F)

2 tablespoons sugar

2¼ teaspoons active dry yeast (1 envelope)

2 teaspoons extra-virgin olive oil, plus more for brushing

3 cups all-purpose flour, plus more for kneading

2 teaspoons kosher salt

Cornmeal, for sprinkling

1. In a large bowl, combine the water, sugar, yeast, and oil. Let stand for 5 minutes.

2. Add half the flour and the salt and mix well to thoroughly combine. Add 1 additional cup of flour, reserving ½ cup, and mix with your hands until combined.

3. Turn the dough out onto a floured surface and knead it for 5 minutes, adding the remaining flour as necessary to form a smooth and elastic dough.

4. Transfer the dough to a large, lightly oiled bowl and turn it to coat. Cover with a damp towel and let rise in a warm place until it doubles in size, about an hour.

5. Punch down the dough and divide it in half. (If you like, you can store the dough for up to a week in a tightly sealed zip-top bag in the refrigerator or freeze it for up to 3 months.) Shape the halves into balls, place them on a cornmeal-coated baking sheet, lightly brush them with olive oil, and cover them with a clean, damp towel. Let the dough rest for an hour.

6. Working slowly, use your fingers and the heel of your hand to gently push and stretch the dough into a circle 12 to 16 inches wide. If you push and tug at it gently, it will gradually give way. But if you pull at it too firmly, it will tear. If it does tear, pinch it firmly back together.

⌗ ⌗

Creative Crusts and Pizza Shortcuts

Pizza recipes are really just suggested starting points—the proportions are up to you, and ingredients can be swapped in and out, or omitted as you like. Thinking creatively will help you make a meal in minutes from items you probably already have in your fridge or pantry. ⌗

Do I Need a Pizza Stone?

A pizza stone is a round stoneware, terra-cotta, or ceramic platter that sits under the pizza while it bakes. The microscopic pores in the pizza stone absorb steamy moisture from the baking dough while distributing heat evenly under the entire crust. The result is a perfectly cooked crust that won't burn before the toppings have cooked through. It's nice to have if you like a very crisp crust, but, like the pizza peel, it's not necessary. You can get excellent results using a baking sheet.

Recipe: QUICK NAAN PIZZA

India meets Italy with these simple and healthful entrées. Look for naan (Indian flatbread) in your grocery's Asian or ethnic sections, or in the gourmet deli and cheese section. These light, puffy breads make perfect quick crusts. If you have a jar of store-bought marinara or pizza sauce, it's even faster. If you don't have sauce, use canned tomato sauce (the smooth kind) or puree drained whole tomatoes in the blender with dried oregano.

Serves 2 to 4

1 cup bottled marinara or pizza sauce

2 large naan breads

8 ounces fresh small mozzarella balls

1 (14-ounce) jar roasted red peppers, cut into strips

Other toppings, such as cooked chicken cubes or crumbled cooked sausage

Fresh or dried basil, optional

1. Preheat the oven to 450°F.

2. Spread a thin layer of sauce on each naan bread. Dot with drained fresh mozzarella balls. Fill in the remaining space with pepper strips or other toppings as you like. If you have fresh basil, use your kitchen shears to cut strips from the leaves and sprinkle on top, or shake on some dried basil.

3. Bake on a pizza stone or directly on the oven rack, until the cheese is melted and bubbly, 8 to 10 minutes.

Recipe: BAGUETTE WHITE PIZZA

White pizza tastes gourmet, yet it requires minimal effort to make. Serve this cut into small squares as a starter, as a side dish with steak, or with an entrée salad as a substitute for garlic bread. You can make this with a stale baguette if you need to use it up.

Serves 6

1 baguette, cut in half lengthwise

½ cup (1 stick) butter, softened

Extra-virgin olive oil

Crushed garlic or garlic salt

16 ounces shredded mozzarella (about 4 cups)

1 cup ricotta cheese

Freshly ground black pepper

Minced fresh or dried oregano

1. Preheat the oven to 400°F and line a baking sheet with foil.

2. Take the two halves of baguette and cover the cut sides completely with a thin layer of soft butter. Pour on some high-quality olive oil, spreading it around with your fingers and sliding it over the butter.

3. Dot the bread with fresh, crushed garlic or sprinkle with garlic salt. Cover with shredded mozzarella cheese and dot with teaspoon-size dollops of ricotta cheese. Sprinkle with pepper and oregano to taste.

4. Bake on the prepared baking sheet until the cheese bubbles and browns, 10 minutes.

#25 How to Have Dinner Ready in Thirty Minutes
(or, Meal Planning and Nutrition)

A nutritionally sound meal is made up of macronutrients (fat, protein, and carbohydrates), plus a variety of micronutrients (vitamins and minerals). In other words, dinner should include a nice balance of fruits and vegetables, grains, proteins, dairy, and fats. Variety is the way to go—for health—because it keeps mealtime interesting.

The USDA recommends that 45 to 65 percent of daily calories come from carbohydrates, 10 to 35 percent from protein, and 20 to 35 percent from fats. No need to bring your calculator into the kitchen—just eyeball the plate, filling half with low-starch, low-fat fruits and vegetables (go easy on plantains and avocados) and the remaining half with a combination of lean meat or plant protein and healthful carbohydrates. Follow these steps and you are ready to make dinner in a flash, any night of the week.

1 Map it out. Planning meals helps you avoid the pitfalls of fast food and overspending. Think about it: When you're starved and need to grab something quick, you wind up ordering a pizza or buying premium-priced prepared foods at the store. If you've planned your meals for the week and shopped accordingly, you won't be caught empty-handed and hungry.

2 Prep your fresh food in advance. Spend 30 minutes preparing a week's worth of produce. Peel and slice carrots, core strawberries, wash and store lettuce (see How to Handle Lettuce, page 24), and cut heads of broccoli and cauliflower into florets. Store in airtight, lidded bowls in the fridge. Ready to be eaten raw in salads or with dips such as hummus and salsa, or sautéed or steamed in the space of 5 minutes, these foods are right for your budget and your health.

3 Make a roast. It can serve as a foundation for a week's meals. Bake a turkey or two chickens, pop a brisket in the slow cooker, or make a pork roast in a Dutch oven. Eat it right away for dinner, then refrigerate or freeze the leftovers for future sandwiches, stir-fries, salads, and soups.

4 Keep quick protein sources on hand. Eggs are cheap and nutritious, and they are easy to cook. Boil them and slice them over salads, stuff an omelet with veggies and a sprinkle of cheese for a hot dinner, or make quiche, if you are feeling ambitious. Canned beans, packed with protein, fiber, and vitamins, are cooked and ready; toss with onions, chives, peppers, and tomatoes, and dress with oil, vinegar, and salt and pepper, for a 10-minute salad.

5 Keep the freezer stocked. Leftovers, soups and casseroles, meat and fish all keep well for months in the freezer. Flash-frozen vegetables from the store—picked and frozen at their peak—can actually be more nutritious than fresh! Plus, they're cheap and long-lasting. With a full freezer, you are ready for anything.

Recipe: LINGUINE PRIMAVERA

Pasta primavera (or "spring pasta"), a vegetable-heavy Italian classic, is an easy, economical, meatless dish that's quick to prepare. Use as a main course, served with green salad and garlic bread (an excellent use for a slightly past its prime baguette or French bread!), or as a side dish for a meat or fish entrée.

Serves 4 to 6

1 pound linguine (for extra nutrition, use spinach linguine or whole-wheat linguine)

3 tablespoons butter

½ large onion, diced

2 cloves garlic, minced

2 cups chopped broccoli or cauliflower, or a mix (frozen is fine)

1 cup thinly sliced carrots

¾ cup sliced black olives

2 teaspoons Italian seasoning (or substitute 1 teaspoon dried basil and 1 teaspoon dried oregano)

¼ teaspoon freshly ground black pepper

⅓ cup dry white wine, cooking sherry, or chicken broth

1 large tomato, diced

1 cup freshly shaved Parmesan cheese

1. Cook the pasta according to package directions. (This should take about 10 minutes.)

2. While the pasta boils, melt the butter in a large skillet over medium heat. Add the onions, garlic, broccoli or cauliflower, carrots, olives, Italian seasoning, and black pepper, and sauté for about 5 minutes, until the onions start to soften.

3. Pour in the wine, sherry, or chicken broth, and continue to stir. Add the tomato and cook for a minute or two.

4. Drain the pasta and transfer it to a large serving bowl. Add the sautéed vegetables and toss well with the pasta. Sprinkle the Parmesan cheese over the top.

Variations

• For extra protein, add strips of cooked chicken, turkey, drained ground beef, or cannellini (white) beans when you add the tomato.

• For a rich tomato broth, skip the wine, sherry, or broth and substitute jarred marinara.

Procedures for Perfect Pasta

Since you learned to boil water on page 8, you should be a real pro at making pasta. All a box of dried pasta requires is a large pot of boiling water and a timer. Here are some tips to refine your pasta-boiling process:

• Fill a large stock pot with water and set it on the stove over high heat, until it comes to a boil. Before you put in the pasta, add generous amounts of salt to the water—this will ensure that the pasta is adequately salted.

• Follow the package instructions to determine how long to cook the pasta. Typically, pastas cook in 8 to 12 minutes. If you prefer your pasta slightly firmer—that is, *al dente*—remove it a minute or two before the package instructions indicate.

• When it's done to your liking, drain the pasta in a colander, then toss with sauce and any other additions, and serve. To fully infuse the pasta with its sauce, dump the drained pasta into the pot with the sauce and cook together for a couple of minutes.

#26 How to Make Soup

Soup is as old as cooking itself. With the invention of fire, the idea of combining foods, herbs, and flavorings in a pot to transform them into filling, nutritious, and easily digestible comestible was inevitable, and it has endured. Our word *soup* likely hearkens back to the Latin word *suppa*, meaning "bread soaked in broth." The old ways are often the best ways, and for ease, economy, and variety, soup is a star player at my family's table.

1 It all starts with stock. Make stock (a full-flavored broth), the basis for all soups, out of anything edible that imparts flavor and won't disintegrate. Use bones, woody vegetable trimmings, onion and garlic skins, whole herbs, lobster shells, fish parts, or limp vegetables. All you need is a large pot and enough water to cover your components. Bring to a boil, reduce to a simmer, and cook until you have flavorful liquid. (This can take as much time as you have—even a 20-minute simmer makes for a more flavorful base.) Skim the scum from the top and strain, reserving the broth. For added flavor, before adding stock to the pot, roast any bones or meat you are using until fragrant and sizzling or pour olive oil into your stockpot and fry the uncooked meat or bones until browned. (Remove the bone before puréeing, serving, or storing.) If you are using onions and garlic, chop and sauté them in the stockpot until transparent, then add the other ingredients.

2 Add your main ingredients to your broth. More refined soups will require a recipe, but soup's beauty is that it can be made with whatever you have in the pantry and fridge—leftovers, grains and pastas, veggies past their prime, almost any cut or variety of meat. If you're on a budget, buy whatever's on sale. Anything goes (almost) when you're making soup.

3 If you're using all vegetables and you like a creamy soup, puree it. This is easiest with a handheld stick blender (beware splashing hot soup!). If you're using a standing blender, blend the soup in small batches and hold the lid on with a dish towel to prevent any splashing. (Transfer each batch of the pureed soup to a clean saucepan.) After pureeing, enrich the soup with a little cream, Greek yogurt, sour cream, milk, or nondairy milk such as rice or almond. Start with a small amount, such as ¼ cup, and taste before adding more. A little bit of creaminess can go a long way; you want to enrich the flavor of the soup, not dilute it.

4 Finally, the finishing touches. Don't skip out on fresh herbs because they work wonders by brightening a soup's flavors. Try dill, parsley, oregano, basil, cilantro, or even mint for chilled soups. Chop them finely and add a tablespoon or two to the whole pot, or sprinkle a little on top of each serving. Other good toppings are a dollop of sour cream or yogurt or some shredded cheese. Cook a few slices of bacon to crispness and crumble them. Harness the power of croutons to make a bowl of soup into a meal. Make your own croutons if you've got a toaster (or an oven: See How to Make Croutons, page 50). Toast thick-sliced bread to a golden hue, brush with olive oil, and rub the surface lightly with a garlic clove. Cut into cubes and sprinkle on top.

Recipe:
CHORIZO AND BEAN SOUP

This warming sausage soup straddles the middle ground between soup and stew. Try it when time is limited but appetites aren't.

Serves 4 to 6

1 tablespoon olive oil

12 ounces dried chorizo sausage, diced

1 large onion, diced

4 stalks celery, chopped

5 large cloves garlic, minced

1 can (14 ounces) garbanzo beans, drained and rinsed

1 can (14 ounces) white beans (such as cannellini), drained and rinsed

4 cups chicken broth (preferably homemade)

½ cup white wine, cooking sherry, or beef broth

1 teaspoon dried thyme

1 teaspoon dried parsley

¼ cup fresh basil or Italian parsley, chopped

½ teaspoon dried chile flakes

1. In a large, heavy-bottomed stockpot over high heat, warm half the olive oil, then add the sausage. Cook until browned, about 5 minutes, then transfer to a dish and set aside.

2. Set the same pot back over medium heat and warm the rest of the olive oil. Add the onion and celery, and cook until softened, about 10 minutes. Add the garlic and cook until it's golden, another minute.

3. Reduce the heat to medium-low and add the cooked sausage and the garbanzo and white beans. Stir together to combine, until the beans are coated with the onions and oil.

4. Add the chicken broth and wine or beef broth, and bring to a boil. Reduce the heat to a simmer and add the dried and fresh herbs and the chile flakes. Simmer until slightly thickened, about 30 minutes.

✕ ✕ ✕ ✕ ✕ ✕ ✕ ✕ ✕ ✕ ✕ ✕

Does Alcohol Burn Off During Cooking?

Mostly . . . high temperatures evaporate most alcohol, leaving only the flavor behind. Test results vary regarding how much and how fast it is burned off, depending on whether you're flaming it in a skillet, baking, or simmering. No matter the method, however, the amount of actual alcohol that remains in a dish is usually quite insignificant. If you're very concerned, just leave it out. ✕

American families throw away about 14 percent of their food per year, adding up to about $600 per family in wasted groceries. Soup is the perfect recipe to absorb any extra produce left over at the end of the week.

Recipe: THE BEST CHICKEN SOUP

What makes a chicken soup the best? It might sound obvious, but: It's the chicken. My top choice is a free-range, organic kosher pullet. A pullet is a female too young to lay eggs; they generally weigh about 6 pounds at slaughter. Free-range chickens dine on insects and vegetation, adding to their flavor, and if they are organic, they haven't ingested hormones and pesticides. Any chicken, however, will make delicious soup—a whole broiler or even parts, if they are on sale.

Serves 6

FOR THE STOCK

3½- to 4-pound chicken

1 large yellow onion, quartered (unpeeled)

2 large carrots, cut into chunks (unpeeled)

2 stalks celery with leaves, cut into chunks

4 sprigs fresh parsley

4 sprigs fresh thyme

6 cloves garlic (unpeeled)

2 teaspoons salt

½ teaspoon freshly ground black pepper

FOR THE SOUP

1 cup finely diced carrots

1 cup thinly sliced celery

1 medium-size yellow onion, minced

1. To make the stock, put all the stock ingredients in a large soup pot. Add 2 quarts water, and bring the ingredients to a boil over high heat. Reduce the heat to medium-low, and simmer uncovered for 1 hour.

2. Remove the chicken and allow it to cool slightly. Remove all the breast meat and set aside. Return the carcass to the pot and continue to simmer, uncovered, for 2 to 3 hours (you can cook it for less time, but this makes a richer stock).

3. Strain the contents of the pot and discard all the solids—their flavor should have all transferred into the broth.

4. To make the soup, add the diced carrots, celery, and onions to the chicken stock. Simmer until the vegetables are tender, about 15 minutes.

5. Chop the reserved chicken breast meat into bite-size pieces, add it to the pot, and heat through.

Variations: There are as many styles of chicken soup as there are cultures on earth. Here are some suggestions:

• Chicken noodle or rice. Add raw or cooked noodles or rice to the boiling soup and simmer until the starch is cooked or heated through as necessary.

• Chicken-vegetable. Zucchini, turnips, parsnips, potatoes, or green peas are all excellent additions. For ease, use frozen mixed vegetables.

• Egg drop. Use a ratio of 1 beaten egg to every 2 cups pure chicken broth. Whisk the egg into the hot broth, top with sliced scallions, and serve.

• Chicken-barley. A filling and nutritious whole grain, barley requires extra salt and pairs well with fresh mushrooms. Add ½ cup medium-size pearl barley with the vegetables and cook until tender, 15 to 20 minutes.

• Matzoh ball. These are dumplings made with unleavened matzoh meal; packaged mixes make them super simple. Cook the matzoh balls as you would most pasta, boiling separately and adding to broth upon serving.

✕ ✕

Does Chicken Soup Cure Colds?

Nothing cures the common cold, but chicken soup can help the symptoms. Old-world moms knew this, which is why it's called Jewish penicillin. Researchers say that chicken soup acts as an anti-inflammatory by slowing the movement of white blood cells, which cause congestion. The steam also temporarily clears a stuffy nose and offers liquid and salt to combat dehydration; in addition, because it's easy to eat and digest, soup provides calories for energy when you're weak. ✕

#27 How to Grill Vegetables

D on't use that grill just for burgers and steaks. Grilling is a quick way to cook a lot of veggies, and it brings out an abundance of flavor. Try spring and summer veggies such as asparagus, eggplant, zucchini, and corn, or even cool-weather produce such as yams, leeks, and fennel.

A Guide to Cooking Methods

Vegetables are the most health-promoting foods of all. Skip the veg, and you'll miss the benefits of their fiber, antioxidants, and good-for-you phytochemicals. Many adults don't eat nearly enough vegetables, and although many profess to dislike them—I suspect a childhood experience with overcooked, mushy, or canned vegetables that hardly resemble their original form is to blame—even veggie fans often don't cook them because they never learned how. The good news is there are many ways to cook veggies to their best advantage, and all of them are simple enough for novice cooks.

1 Make sure your vegetables are clean and thoroughly dry. Dampness will cause sticking.

2 Chop, season, and marinate your vegetables. A light coating of oil and spices does the trick, or use bottled, oil-based salad dressing in a pinch.

3 For dense vegetables, like potatoes, yams, and winter squash, cube and parboil them for 5 minutes first, then skewer or slice and finish them on the grill.

4 For smaller or skinny pieces, like asparagus stalks, string beans, or broccoli florets, line the grill with foil first or thread them onto kebab sticks.

TIP: When making kebabs, skewer vegetables of similar thickness and density together to ensure uniform doneness.

5 Preheat a gas grill on high heat with the lid closed for 10 minutes.

6 Lightly oil the rack. Arrange the pieces on the grill and cook for 3 to 5 minutes, turning the vegetables until browned and softened. Don't overcook or char when grilling vegetables. Move the pieces around often to avoid blackening. If you're cooking small pieces, you can also use a vegetable grill pan to keep the pieces from falling through.

⸙ ⸙

Mellow Out

In general, the longer you cook strong-tasting vegetables, the stronger the resulting flavor and odor becomes. Here are some guidelines to mellow assertive flavors, which should help get vegetable skeptics on board. With all of these cooking methods, start with cleaned and trimmed vegetables, torn or chopped into uniform pieces for even cooking.

• Cook only until tender; don't boil or stew.

• Add salty toppings such as Parmesan cheese or soy sauce.

• Mix a little lemon juice with any butter or olive oil to make a tangy sauce.

• Add a touch of sweetness with a squeeze of honey when dressing or cooking vegetables with butter.

#28 How to Sauté Vegetables

For this preparation, you'll need a large, heavy-bottomed skillet. Use nonstick if you are shooting for a low-fat meal because you'll need less oil.

1 Use enough oil or butter to coat the pan. For heart-healthy sautéing, use olive, canola, or coconut oil, which hold up well under high temperatures.

2 Before adding the vegetables, heat the pan over medium-high heat until it is sizzling hot. You want the shortest cook time possible, and a preheated pan allows your vegetables to slide around without sticking.

3 Let the vegetables brown lightly in the hot pan for a moment or two, then add a couple of tablespoons of water or broth. As the liquid evaporates, the vegetables will cook through more evenly.

4 For extra flavor, add minced garlic or grated fresh ginger during the last 30 seconds to 1 minute of the sauté. Season with salt and pepper, maybe a touch more butter or olive oil and some soy sauce or chili flakes, and serve at once.

#29 How to Steam Vegetables

For this method, you will need a steamer basket. These are inexpensive and available at any home goods or grocery store.

1 Put a steamer basket into a saucepan with a lid, and add an inch or two of water. (The water should just reach the bottom of the basket, but not quite touch it.)

2 Put the vegetable pieces into the basket, cover the pan, and bring the water to a boil over high heat.

3 Once boiling, reduce the heat to medium. Throughout cooking, check to make sure the pan doesn't boil dry. Add more water as needed, but make sure whatever you add is hot.

4 Cook until vibrant in color and just tender when pierced with a fork, anywhere from 3 to 30 minutes, depending on the vegetable.

5 Remove the vegetables from heat, season, and serve immediately to prevent additional softening.

×××

Making Meatless Meals

There are many good reasons to be a vegetarian or a vegan: health, thrift, the environment, ethics. Many people who choose not to eat meat or other animal products cite a combination of these motivators. Because American tradition has long defined a square meal as one with meat as its cornerstone, the question becomes: "How do I get the nutrition I need on a plant-based diet?"

Well-planned vegetarian and vegan diets are nutritionally adequate for all people in all stages of life, so long as care is taken to include adequate protein, iron, vitamin B$_{12}$, omega-3 fatty acids, iodine, calcium, iron, and zinc—nutrients sometimes lacking in animal-free diets. (See suggestions on page 89.)

#30 How to Roast Vegetables

Caramelized and intensely flavorful, roasted vegetables are an easy and delicious crowd-pleaser. Keep in mind that roasting makes veggies shrink. A pound of vegetables may feed four when steamed, but you'll need half again as much if you're roasting them.

1 Preheat your oven to 425°F. (You may need to adjust the heat, depending on your vegetable's size and density. Quick-cooking veggies like asparagus can take the higher heat; firmer stuff like potato chunks and squash cubes may need a lower oven, such as 350°F or 375°F, so they cook through.)

2 Line a roasting pan with foil coated with cooking spray (to ensure easy cleanup).

3 Toss the chopped vegetables with oil or an oil-based salad dressing before putting them in the pan. Leave space in between to allow hot air to circulate, so they'll cook evenly on all sides. If the vegetables look crowded, use a second pan.

4 Don't undercook! Roasting can take a while. Cauliflower florets or butternut squash chunks may need as long as 40 minutes to get nicely browned and tender, whereas asparagus stalks or green beans may be ready in 10 minutes. Shake the pan occasionally to shift the vegetables around and let them brown. Vegetables are done when they're browned and a little shriveled on all sides and tender inside.

#31 How to Blanch Vegetables

Cooking vegetables in hot water got a bad name for many people who were subjected to mushy, overboiled cauliflower or tasteless green beans in their youth. But cooking vegetables in salty hot water can bring out the flavor beautifully, if you don't overcook. Blanching lets vegetables have a brief dip in boiling water, then they are rinsed in cold water so the cooking stops before the mushiness starts. This is a great method for green veggies such as string beans and broccoli because it keeps the color bright.

1 Bring a large pot of water to a rolling boil. Add a tablespoon of salt; some chefs say the best cooking water tastes "salty like the sea."

2 Prep the vegetable into serving pieces: top and tail green beans, break cauliflower or broccoli into florets, shell the peas.

3 Put the vegetable pieces into the boiling water and cook for 2 to 3 minutes. Take out a piece with a fork and run it under the cold tap and sample it. When the vegetable is crunchy-tender, pour it into a colander and rinse under cold water to stop the cooking.

4 Dress immediately with olive oil or a little melted butter, salt and pepper, and maybe a squeeze of lemon.

#32 **How to Chop Broccoli**

Tasty, affordable, always available, and good for you, broccoli is every home cook's dream vegetable. It also takes well to almost any cooking method—blanching, steaming, roasting, sautéing. . . . Whatever your mood, broccoli should be your go-to green. Breaking a head of broccoli into nice bite-size pieces—a daunting task for novice cooks—is key for easy eating as well as even cooking.

Heads Up

Choose broccoli heads with firm, compact clusters of small florets. The individual flowers that make up the florets should be dark green or have a purple cast to them. Reject heads on which the florets are yellowish-green, enlarged, or opened, or if the stalks are rubbery, limp, or wilted.

Storing and Freezing

For best results, plan to use or freeze fresh broccoli soon after buying it. To store, mist the heads with water, wrap loosely in damp paper towels, slide the bundle into a zip-top bag, and don't seal it. (Fresh broccoli requires air circulation.) It will keep for up to a week.

To freeze, cut washed, raw broccoli into florets and chop the peeled stalks (see instructions, following). Steam or blanch the broccoli for one minute to parboil it (this improves its quality after freezing), then plunge it into ice water, drain, and seal in airtight containers or closed zip-top bags with all the air pressed out. This cooked frozen broccoli can be added to soups or stir-fries at the last minute, or it can be thawed and heated in the microwave for a quick supper side dish.

Cooking Fresh Broccoli

Cook only what you'll eat right away. Given that fresh broccoli cooks up in just a few minutes, there is no point in making enough for leftovers, which get mushy and are not as flavorful. If you need to save time, wash and cut it in advance. If you do have leftovers, cooked broccoli should be sealed in an airtight container or closed zip-top bag and kept in the refrigerator for no more than two days.

1 Rinse, don't soak, broccoli in cool water just before preparing. Remove any leaves attached to the stalk.

2 Trim the stalks off each head, leaving about an inch of stalk below the florets.

3 Peel off the woody, outer layer of the stalks with a paring knife or vegetable peeler.

4 Slice the head of the broccoli in half lengthwise.

5 Hold the halves together and slice the head crosswise to the desired size.

6 Finish chopping by cutting each floret off the head in a downward motion, leaving a little stalk on each cluster. If the individual florets are bigger than you'd like, slice them in half lengthwise.

#33 How to Make Mashed Potatoes
(or, How to Do Anything with a Spud)

A pillar of the world's cuisine, potatoes come in about five thousand varieties with anywhere from five to ten types available at most American supermarkets. For the best results when cooking with potatoes, the right tuber is key. Potatoes for mashing should be fluffy and somewhat dry, and never gluey, whereas salad potatoes need to be firm enough to hold their own against dressings without dissolving. Potatoes for scalloping can't fall apart during slicing and need heft to convey luscious, creamy sauce.

The Right Spud for the Job

Practically speaking, potatoes fall into two categories: starchy and waxy. A third, middle-ground type—the all-purpose—offers versatility when storage space is a factor.

Starchy. Oblong in shape, with a rough, corklike skin, these are the top choice for baking, mashing, and french fries. Also called floury potatoes, their high starch content makes them less dense, so they break down more during cooking, resulting in a smoother texture. Mashed potatoes will be smoother, baked potatoes fluffier, and fried potatoes will steam from the inside, offering light interiors with crispy exteriors. When pierced with your fingernail, or sliced, this type excretes a milky liquid (that's the starch). Look for these names in your produce section (depending on where you live): baking potatoes, Idaho potatoes, russets, Norgolds, Goldrushes, Cal Whites, German Butterballs, baking whites, and Norkotahs.

Waxy. Also called boiling potatoes, these can be round or oval in shape, with a thin, smooth, and waxy skin. These potatoes are best for casseroles, soups, roasting, and salads. If you can scrape off the skin with your fingernail, your potato is waxy. High in sugar and moisture, but low in starch, they are firm and toothsome, holding their shape when sliced and cooked. Look for these names in your produce section: yellow potatoes, salad potatoes, Yellow Finns, fingerlings, new reds, La Sodas, and Australian Crescents.

All-purpose. These potatoes fall in the middle, combining dryness and firmness, and can work in most recipes in a pinch. Slightly fluffy when baked, they will also hold their shape when boiled and can be used for mashed potatoes, though they offer a less silky texture. Look for these names in your produce section: Yukon Golds, Katahdins, Kennebecs, Superiors, and Peruvian Blues.

Yes, They Are a Vegetable

The belief among my Irish husband's people is that humans can survive eating only potatoes, supplemented by dairy for vitamins A and D. True, they contain vitamins, minerals, phenols, and lots of fiber in the jacket, but high-starch diets alongside sedentary lifestyles are linked to diabetes and heart disease. Preparation method makes a difference, too. Fried or mixed with high-fat dairy, potatoes are more of a treat than a vegetable.

(continued)

Freshness Matters

When buying potatoes, look for spuds that are firm to the touch, with no give when squeezed. Reject any with sprouts or "eyes" because this means they have begun to go to seed, and those with green patches, which are a sign of prolonged exposure to light or extreme temperatures. When handling potatoes, take care not to bruise them or it will lead to rot. Store in a cool, dark, and dry place for a long shelf life.

Green Under the Skin?

That's chlorophyll, which alerts us to the presence of solanine, a natural but poisonous glycoalkaloid found in plants in the nightshade family. This substance defends potatoes against insects and biological disease, and it is toxic to humans. It tastes bitter and can cause nausea, diarrhea, and if eaten in very large quantities, nerve damage or paralysis. Bottom line: If all of the green can be peeled away and discarded, the rest of the potato can be eaten. When in doubt, however, toss the offending spud.

1 Choose your potato. Pick a type from the starchy or all-purpose categories, avoiding the waxy category. Any will do, but a Yukon Gold has the added bonus of that golden-yellow color, reminiscent of the potato's best friend—butter.

2 Prepare the potatoes for boiling. Peel them with a vegetable peeler. Quarter them, place them in a very large bowl, and rinse them with cold water to remove excess starch. Transfer the potatoes to a large pot.

3 Boil the potatoes. Cover the potatoes with cold water, salt them to your taste (1 teaspoon of salt for every 2 quarts of water is the way my family likes it), and set over medium-high heat to bring them to a boil. Starting in cold water helps your potatoes cook more evenly because the temperature rise is slow. If you throw your tubers into hot water, the outsides will cook first, while the interior will still be raw. Once the water comes to a boil, reduce the heat to a simmer. The potatoes are ready when they are tender when pierced with a fork. Cooking time depends on the size of the potato chunks and the size of your pot, so check on your potatoes every 5 to 10 minutes or so.

4 Dry the potatoes: Once they are cooked, carefully pour the water out of the pot, cover it, and set it back over the lowest heat setting on your stove for about 5 minutes. This will cook off the excess water, ensuring lighter mashed potatoes.

5 Bring on the flavor! This is where you choose your mashing tool and use it to combine the potatoes with your favorite seasonings, creamy ingredients, or broth. Make sure anything cold, like milk or butter, is warmed before adding and that your potatoes travel from stovetop to tabletop pronto.

After rice and wheat, potatoes are the third most important food crop in the world. The tuber was first domesticated in the Andes mountains of South America.

The Best Tool for the Job

There's more than one way to mash a potato. Here are the options:

Fork. In a pinch, crushing cooked potatoes with a fork will do. Use a pressing motion, rather than a stirring motion, for the fluffiest texture and be careful not to overwork the potatoes or they will turn gluey.

Wire masher. Looks something like an electric coil. The mashing surface is relatively small, so the potatoes will stay light in texture because it doesn't destroy all the delicate starch granules. Best for those who like small chunks in their mash.

Flat masher. A flat disk with holes punched out. Same principle as a fork, but less labor-intensive. The results will be more uniform, but slightly heavier in texture than with a wire masher.

Potato ricer. This gadget looks like a giant garlic press, with a lever and small holes through which a cooked potato is forced. Silky-smooth in texture, riced potatoes will be heavier because no air is incorporated as it is with the up-and-down motions of the other methods.

Whisk. After crushing the cooked potatoes using one of the gadgets above, you can whisk the mash (with additions like butter and cream) for a minute or two in order to incorporate some air and fluff them up.

Electric mixer. Beat crushed potatoes (along with butter and cream) with a hand mixer and your result will be whipped potatoes—light, fluffy, and filled with air. Restaurants use this method for economy: More air means less potato per serving. This style holds up well in a chafing dish, at a steam table, or piped out of a pastry bag if you're being fancy.

Food processor. STOP! This appliance (as well as the blender) strikes fear in the heart of starchy vegetables everywhere. The rapidly spinning blade smashes every last starch granule, leaving you with a gluey mess.

Recipe: THE BEST MASHED POTATOES

Now that you know the ropes, here's a foolproof recipe for a rich, fluffy mash that elevates any dinner to special-occasion status.

Serves 4

1½ pounds Yukon Gold potatoes, peeled and quartered

1 teaspoon salt

¼ cup heavy cream

3 tablespoons butter, at room temperature

Milk, for mashing

1. Wash, peel, and quarter the potatoes, as per Step 2 in How to Make Mashed Potatoes (see page 63) and then soak them. After a long soak, as long as overnight, discard the cloudy water and transfer the potatoes to a large pot. Cover them completely with cold water, then add the salt.

2. Bring the potatoes slowly to a boil over medium heat, then reduce the heat and let them simmer, uncovered, until they're fork-tender. Carefully pour off the water, then dry them in the pot as per Step 4 in How to Make Mashed Potatoes, being careful not to let them scorch.

3. In a small saucepan over low heat, warm the cream and butter together until the butter melts. Do not allow the mixture to boil. Pour the cream and butter over the potatoes and mash them using your tool of choice. If desired, whip the mashed potatoes with a whisk or hand mixer, adding milk a tablespoon at a time, if needed, for the consistency you like. Do not overbeat, or your potatoes will turn gummy.

#34 How to Cook a Steak

Seems simple enough, but because it involves so many variables—the cut, timing, temperature, and seasoning—cooking a steak takes practice. Quality meat isn't cheap, so the stakes are high, so to speak. Here's how to make sure you'll never have to serve (or eat!) chewy, tasteless, or dry steak again.

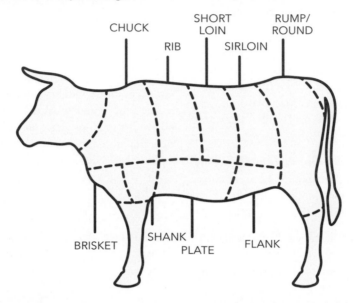

Start with Good Meat

Consult your butchers. They're experts and will steer you to the best cuts at the best price. Always buy the best grade you can afford (prime, choice, and select, in that order) and inspect the meat closely: Look for pinky-red. Avoid deep red and never buy gray or greenish meat, or steaks that are spongy or slimy, in ripped packages, or have old sell-by dates. Choose steak that's firm to the touch, with a fine texture, and look for marbling—the thin threads of white fat running through the meat.

What's in a Name?

The most tender meat comes from the least-exercised parts of the cow. Connective tissue is tough, so instead buy cuts from the short loin, tenderloin, or rib sections. Top choices:

New York strip, T-bone, porterhouse, rib eye, and tenderloin or filet mignon. Flank steak provides great value and beefy flavor, though it tends to be less tender.

✕ ✕ ✕ ✕ ✕ ✕ ✕ ✕ ✕ ✕ ✕ ✕ ✕ ✕ ✕ ✕ ✕ ✕ ✕ ✕

Protein Primer

Proteins are a combination of amino acids that are essential to our bodily functions–like muscle development and repair and metabolism–and must be obtained through food because they aren't manufactured by our bodies. For healthy individuals eating a balanced diet, 10 to 15 percent of our calories should come from protein. There is no danger from consuming too much protein, except for those with kidney or liver disease who should be planning their meals under the care of doctors and nutritionists. ✕

1 Marinate. Take your steak out of the fridge, place it in a flat, wide bowl and brush it with olive oil or clarified butter. This adds moisture and flavor, and prevents it from sticking to the grill or pan. Sprinkle with salt (ideally kosher)—use a heavy hand, you're seasoning the whole steak, inside and out—plus freshly ground black pepper. If possible, plan ahead and allow it to come to room temperature for about 1 hour (cold steaks take longer to cook, and the longer the cook time, the tougher the steak). If you like, marinate the seasoned steak in a zip-top bag with a couple of tablespoons of olive oil, the juice of a lemon, and a minced garlic clove.

2 Prepare the flame. The goal is to cook your steak at a high temperature for not much time. Therefore, a grill is best. Before you set meat to flame, heat the grill on high for 20 to 30 minutes.
If you don't have a grill, use your broiler. Position your rack about 5 inches from the flame and preheat the broiler to high. Meanwhile, heat a large, empty cast-iron skillet or grill pan over high heat on the stovetop for about 5 minutes. (Open a window or turn on the hood fan—your kitchen is going to get smoky!)

3 Lay your prepped steak on the grill. For a ½-inch-thick steak, let it lie for 3 minutes, then flip it with tongs. (For a 1-inch-thick steak, 4 to 5 minutes is good.) Don't poke at it! Piercing a steak releases juices. Once you've flipped the steak, grill it for another 1 or 2 minutes for medium-rare.

If using a broiler, coat the bottom of the heated cast-iron skillet with a little oil, lay in the steak, then slide it under the broiler. Cook for 3 minutes, then using tongs, flip it and cook it for another 3 minutes—this timing will work well for a steak about ½ to ¾ inch thick. Test for your preferred timing and try not to overcook.

4 Test for doneness. The amount of time to cook a steak is partly a learned art, but don't overcook it or even the best meat can taste like shoe leather. Go for just a few minutes and check it; you can always throw a steak back in the pan but you can't uncook it. Press the middle of the steak with your finger (quickly—it's hot!). If it feels jelly-like, it's too rare. If it just springs back when you press it, it's medium-rare. If it's firm or hard, it's well done (and probably dry). If you're nervous, make a small cut in the center to see if the steak is done the way you like it. You'll let some of the juice escape, but losing some juice is better than overcooking a good steak "just to be safe." If it's not done enough, return it to the grill or broiler for another 1 to 2 minutes. Keep in mind that the steak continues cooking for a minute or two after being removed from the heat.

5 Let it rest for five to ten minutes. The temperatures of the center and edges will begin to equalize, allowing the juices to distribute evenly. If you cut it right away, all the juices will pour out the edge and onto the plate, resulting in a less flavorful steak.

#35 How to Cook Lamb Chops

Think lamb chops are fancy and only for gourmet cooks? Think again. This super-simple frying-pan method always yields juicy chops. Choose rib chops, about 1 inch thick, for this method. They're the ones with the long bone "handle" and a circle of meat at the end. Perfect finger food! You'll need two to three chops per person.

1 Sprinkle both sides of the chops with salt and freshly ground black pepper.

2 Put 2 tablespoons of oil in a large, heavy-bottomed skillet and set it over high heat. You want it very hot. To test, add a teaspoon of water to the pan—it should evaporate almost immediately.

3 Lay in the chops—if they don't sizzle, the pan's not hot enough. Cook them for 4 minutes per side. Don't touch them or disturb them while they cook,or you won't get a nice crust. When done, they should still be pink in the middle.

4 Remove the chops from the pan and serve.

Recipe: SMOTHERED PORK CHOPS

You can fry a pork chop in a similar way to a lamb chop (adding a minute or two per side), but pork chops particularly like gravy. Thick chops especially are inclined to be dry because most pork is pretty lean these days, so chops take well to being cooked in sauce.

Serves 4

½ cup all-purpose flour

1 teaspoon salt

½ teaspoon freshly ground pepper

4 boneless pork loin chops, ¾ to 1 inch thick

2 tablespoons vegetable oil, or more as needed

2 cups milk

1 unsalted chicken bouillon cube, optional

1. Preheat the oven to 350°F. Put the flour, salt, and pepper in a zip-top bag, and then toss the chops in it. Shake well to coat the chops. Put bag aside.

2. Heat the vegetable oil over medium-high heat in a Dutch oven or heavy ovenproof pot with a lid. Brown the chops well, about 2 minutes per side, adding a little more oil if needed.

3. Sprinkle 2 tablespoons of the seasoned flour over the chops and add the milk and a half cup of water, stirring gently to combine. If desired, crumble the bouillon cube into the milk and stir to combine.

4. Cover the pot and bake until the gravy is thickened and the chops are cooked through, 45 to 60 minutes. Alternatively, you can cook them over medium heat, covered, on the stovetop, but check them occasionally and add a little more liquid, if needed—the sauce tends to boil a bit harder on the stovetop.

#36 How to Cook Chicken Breasts

Boneless, skinless chicken breasts make excellent meal staples, but many shy away after having eaten one too many that were rubbery and tasteless. The method here finishes them moist and just cooked through, avoiding that stringy dryness that gives chicken a bad name. Serve with a vegetable side, add slices to a salad, or toss with pasta.

1 Pound each breast lightly (sandwich it in plastic wrap or waxed paper) with a rolling pin or can of beans until it is an even thickness throughout. (Wash the pin or can well with hot soapy water.)

2 Put ⅓ cup flour in a large mixing bowl, and then stir in a teaspoon each of salt and pepper. Lightly dredge the chicken breasts in the seasoned flour until just lightly dusted.

3 Heat a large, heavy-bottomed skillet that has a tight-fitting lid over medium-high heat. Once hot, add a tablespoon each of olive oil and butter.

4 When the butter is sizzling, reduce the heat to medium, then add chicken breasts in a single layer. Cook for 2 minutes, allowing one side to lightly brown.

5 Flip the chicken, reduce the heat to low, and cover the pan. Set a timer for 12 minutes.

6 After 12 minutes, turn off the heat, but don't uncover the pan. Set the timer for 8 minutes.

7 Uncover and serve.

#37 How to Roast a Chicken

Roasting a chicken is actually far simpler than the succulent, crispy-skinned, dramatic end result might lead your guests to believe. In fact, a roast chicken is such a thrifty, delicious, and satisfying cornerstone to a meal that you shouldn't save it for only special occasions. Serve it sliced as a main course, then use the leftovers as an ingredient in other dishes such as curried chicken salad, wrap sandwiches, and white pizza. I often roast two or more whole six-pound birds weekly. This technique using a hot skillet in a very hot oven cuts the cooking time and makes a very crisp skin.

1 Preheat the oven to 425°F.

2 Check the cavity for any giblets or other parts—often housed in a plastic bag. Using your hands, rub 1 stick of butter, softened to room temperature, all over the chicken, making sure to get it into every crack and crevice. Tuck rosemary sprigs—8 to 10 whole ones—under the breast skin and into the cavity. Halve two lemons and push them into the cavity. Sprinkle the whole chicken liberally with salt and freshly ground black pepper, and also sprinkle salt into the cavity with the lemons and rosemary.

3 Put a large, dry, empty cast-iron skillet on the stovetop and heat it over high heat for 5 minutes. When it's hot, put the prepped chicken carefully into the hot skillet. It will sizzle loudly! With a potholder or oven mitt, carefully lift the skillet into the oven. Bake the chicken for 1 hour, until the thickest part of the thigh reads at least 165°F on an instant-read thermometer and the skin is crisp and browned.

4 Remove the chicken from the oven, and tent it with foil. Allow it to rest for 15 minutes, then slice and serve.

TIP: Peel and wash vegetables such as carrots, onions, celery, potatoes, yams, parsnips, and turnips, and cut them into like-size chunks. Toss with olive oil and put them on a baking sheet, in a single layer. Sprinkle with salt and pepper. Roast the vegetables on a different rack while your chicken roasts, and you'll have a complete meal when they're done.

Bake stuffing (or dressing) in a casserole dish, not inside the bird. In order for stuffing to be safe to eat, it needs to reach 165 degrees Fahrenheit. To achieve that, you'd have to overcook the poultry.

To Baste or Not to Baste?

In a word, not. Basting only flavors the skin; it doesn't penetrate to the meat, so the old myth that it moistens the bird isn't true. Remember the roasting rule: The longer the cook time, the drier the meat. Each time you open the oven to baste, it cools down, and then you have to leave the bird in longer. Skip it.

#38 How to Brine a Bird
(or, the Chef's Secret)

Brining, or soaking in heavily salted water prior to cooking, is a way of increasing the moisture-holding capacity of poultry, resulting in tender cooked meat. Salt changes the structure of the muscle tissue, allowing it to swell and absorb water along with any flavorings dissolved or infused in the water. Brining is especially beneficial for turkey, but you can also soak chicken, game hens, or any poultry, to delicious effect.

Keep It Cold

Because brining doesn't preserve meat, the poultry and the brine must be kept cold to inhibit bacteria growth. Both meat and its soaking liquid must remain colder than 40 degrees Fahrenheit, so you'll need a cooler large enough to hold bird and brine or a container that will keep the bird submerged and will also fit into a refrigerator. Plan ahead and clear space if needed.

If using a cooler, it is important to thoroughly clean and sanitize it before and after use. A solution of 1 tablespoon of chlorine bleach to 1 gallon of water will do. Rinse thoroughly with clean water after sanitizing. Next, you must keep the poultry and brine cold without diluting the mixture: Put the bird and brine directly into the cooler, then add zip-top bags filled with ice or reusable gel packs to keep them cool. Monitor the temperature using an instant-read thermometer.

1 Make your brine. Start with ½ cup table salt (or 1 cup kosher salt) per gallon of water. Stir the salt so it dissolves. You need enough brine to fully submerge your bird.

2 For each gallon of brine, squeeze in the juice of one lemon and toss in the squeezed rinds as well; add aromatics as desired. You can squeeze in lemon juice and also toss in the rinds; add 1 tablespoon black peppercorns or ¼ cup hot sauce; or a handful of potent dried herbs such as rosemary or oregano leaves.

3 Let the bird soak in its bath. The real purpose of brining is to let the salty moisture penetrate the meat, and that takes a long time.

BRINE SOAKING TIME TABLE

Whole chicken (6 pounds)	6 to 12 hours
Chicken or turkey parts	2 hours
Whole turkey	24 hours
Turkey breast	8 hours
Cornish game hens	2 hours

⚔ ⚔

Brine Warning!

Do not salt brined meat before cooking. As with commercially packaged kosher chicken, the meat is already salty. If your recipe advises sprinkling with salt and freshly ground black pepper, pepper alone will do. ⚔

XXX

How Do I Choose a Chicken to Roast?

Once you learn to roast a whole bird, it can really change your game in the kitchen—it's more economical, often more flavorful, and definitely impressive.

- Look for Grade A chickens—they have the highest meat-to-bone ratio.

- Pass on chicken with torn packaging, old sell-by dates, "off" odors, or grayish skin.

- Skin and flesh color should range from pinkish to white to yellow.

- Top choice: pullet or roaster. These have a lot of fat under the skin. Look for a 5- or 6-pounder.

- Other good choices include broiler/fryer—these are younger, smaller birds, usually 2½ to 3 pounds, with more flavorful albeit a smaller amount of meat. Cornish game hens, usually 1½ to 2 pounds, are similar to roasters, but a smaller breed (typically, a serving is a whole bird). Moist and meaty. X

#39 How to Braise Beef

Filling and comforting, slow-cooked beef offers the ultimate satisfaction to meat-and-potatoes lovers. A pot roast or stew warms the kitchen on cold or rainy days, and it fills the house with a fragrance that whispers wholesome abundance. A one-dish dinner with the components of a square meal, braises are simple, nutritious, and budget friendly crowd pleasers.

Tough to Tender

Braising is simply a method of cooking foods over low heat for a long time, partially submerged in liquid. Cooked incorrectly, pot roast or stew cuts are so tough and dry they are practically inedible, but braised, these meats yield fork-tender, juicy morsels. The cheaper, less tender cuts contain a lot of collagen, the connective tissue that holds muscle fibers together. When cooked slowly in the presence of moisture, collagen dissolves into gelatin, allowing meat fibers to separate. This is the essence of tenderizing tough cuts of meat. The gelatin will set as it cools.

Go Dutch

To braise meat, you'll need a slow cooker, Dutch oven (a large, heavy cast-iron pot),

or other heavy pot with a tight-fitting lid. If using the oven (with the heat set at 325 degrees Fahrenheit), make sure your pot is ovenproof. You'll still need to use the stove for the searing step (see facing page). Either way, the lid is key because the steam in the pot helps cook and tenderize the meat.

Advanced Braising

Once you've mastered the basic concepts of braising, and long, slow cooking, branch out and experiment.

Change up your meat: Beef with bone (like short ribs) will yield extra flavor from the marrow.

• Chicken breast or bone-in chicken parts

• Game, such as bone-in rabbit or venison

• Lamb or mutton

• Pork, with or without bones

• Sturdy seafood such as monkfish, shrimp, lobster, eel, octopus, or squid

Play around with veggies: Anything goes (almost), but firm, hearty ones work best.

Beets	Tomatoes
Endive	Turnips
Leeks	Yams
Parsnips	

Liquid gold: Water will work, but why not add flavor?

• Beer or stout

• Tomato or vegetable juice

• Wine—red or white

• Stock or broth (shortcut: dissolve bouillon cubes in hot water)

Herbs and spices:
Season to taste.

Basil	Oregano
Bay leaves	Parsley
Cilantro	Rosemary
Garam masala	Sage
	Thyme

1 Choose your cut. Tough cuts of beef such as round, brisket, rump, chuck, and flank are often economical, and they hold up the best to long braises. For the best bargains, tell your butcher you want pot roast or stew meat, and he'll point you to what's best and cheapest that day. Because they come from ends of cuts, their availability and price change regularly.

2 Sear the meat. It's a myth that searing locks in juices, but you should still do it. Browning the meat in oil produces new and complex flavor compounds as the sugars and proteins in the meat react under high temperatures and the surface color deepens. Your braise will have richer flavor, and the meat will have an appealingly brown (rather than gray) hue.

3 Add liquid. Whether you use water, wine, broth, or anything else (see Advanced Braising, above), the meat must be mostly submerged to attain a proper braise, but not drowned or you won't get a nice, thick sauce.

4 Cook it low and slow. Collagen softens in low, moist heat, but muscle fiber firms under high heat because proteins unfold and form new linkages. The higher the cooking

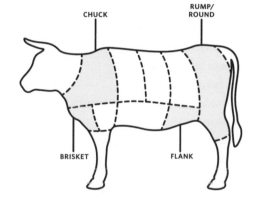

temperature, the tougher the muscle fibers become, shrinking in length and width, becoming tight. Whether braising on the stovetop or in the oven, don't let the liquid boil—reduce the heat to a gentle simmer and cook it for a long time.

5 Add veggies. To make your roast or stew into a one-pot supper, add veggies to the braise in the last 45 minutes or hour of cooking. Chop them into uniform pieces so that they'll cook evenly.

6 Finally, don't leave your braise cooking for *too* long. Check it during the last hour of cooking—going past the fork-tender stage can yield dry, stringy meat.

Recipe: BASIC BEEF STEW

Beef stew usually falls into one of three categories: with brown gravy, broth or wine, or a tomato-based sauce. Here's an old-fashioned brown version.

Serves 6

⅓ cup all-purpose flour

1 teaspoon salt

¼ teaspoon freshly ground black pepper

2 pounds stewing beef, cut into cubes

¼ cup olive oil

½ cup beef broth, wine, or beer

4 cups boiling water

1 tablespoon red wine vinegar

1 tablespoon Worcestershire sauce

1 teaspoon brown sugar

2 large onions, sliced

6 stalks celery, destringed and cut into chunks

3 bay leaves

6 medium-size carrots, peeled and cut into chunks

10 small red potatoes, peeled and halved

1. In a shallow dish, mix together the flour, salt, and pepper. Roll the beef cubes in the mixture to coat, shaking off excess.

2. Pour the oil into a medium-size Dutch oven and heat on the stovetop over high heat. Working in batches, carefully cook the meat until each piece is browned.

3. Once all of the beef is cooked, pour in the broth. With a wooden spoon, scrape the sides and bottom of the Dutch oven to loosen any cooked-on bits.

4. Layer the beef cubes back in the Dutch oven and add the boiling water. Stir, then add the vinegar, Worcestershire sauce, brown sugar, onions, celery, and bay leaves. Reduce the heat to low, cover, and simmer until the meat is fork-tender, about 3 hours.

5. Add the carrots and potatoes, and simmer until all vegetables are fork-tender, about an hour.

#40 How to Make a Pot of Chili

One of those rare comfort foods that is packed with good-for-you ingredients, chili can be a soup or a stew, with as many personalities as there are cooks. Purists insist that chili shouldn't contain beans, tomatoes, or grains because they didn't appear in the original recipes prepared by chuck wagon cooks for settlers in the West and Southwest. Modern cooks and vegetarians, however, like to lighten things up with all manner of legumes and veggies, as well as grains such as bulgur or quinoa. The good-natured debate over what goes into a pot of chili—everything from ground beef and shredded pork to cinnamon and chocolate powder to beans and hot peppers—rages on. I say make it your own, using these tips, tricks, and shortcuts. First, learn the basic guidelines, listed below, and then you'll be able to improvise as you see fit.

1 Always brown meats before adding liquid to the pot for richer flavor.

2 If your recipe calls for chopped fresh chiles, but you like your chili less spicy, pierce a whole fresh chile pepper several times with a knife tip and let it simmer whole in the sauce, instead of adding it chopped at the beginning. Fish it out and discard before eating.

3 Let the flavors mingle. Make chili in advance, refrigerate it, and reheat it later.

4 When possible, use fresh herbs. If you must use dried, make sure they haven't been sitting in the back of your pantry for more than a year.

5 Use broth instead of water in your chili or when cooking dried beans.

✕ ✕ ✕ ✕ ✕ ✕ ✕ ✕ ✕ ✕ ✕ ✕ ✕

What Makes White Chili White?

The absence of tomatoes, red peppers, and red meat. As with regular chili, there are as many styles as you can dream up, but most white chilis include chicken or other poultry, green chiles, and white beans, and some are thickened with masa or cornmeal. ✕

TYPES OF CHILI MEAT

Ground beef

Stew meat

Italian or pork sausage

Boneless pork shoulder

Combos

Bone-in short ribs

Ground poultry

The Meat of the Matter

You can make a pot of chili, from familiar to fancy, with any meat that gets better with a slow simmer.

- **Ground beef.** Use ground beef for fattier, more flavorful chili or ground sirloin or chuck for chili that tastes more like steak.

- **Stew meat.** You can also use brisket or other economy roasts, and cut them into cubes yourself. Remember, low and slow makes these cuts tender. Don't boil them. (See How to Braise Beef, page 72.)

- **Bone-in short ribs.** You'll have to eat around the bone, but the marrow and connective tissue add depth to the flavor.

- **Ground pork or Italian sausage.** Pork is delicious and goes well with classic chili spices. Italian sausage is pre-spiced, so you can cut down on some of the ingredients and steps.

- **Boneless pork shoulder.** Richly flavored and perfect for simmering. Cook it like cubed beef.

- **Venison.** Use it because you love the gamy flavor or because your uncle who hunts has a freezer full of it. Balanced with beans, it's great for chili.

- **Combos.** You don't have to use only ground beef. Try cubed beef and pork, or lamb and beef. You can also add some smoky flavor with chopped, smoked bacon cooked along with the cubed or ground meat. Experiment!

- **Poultry.** Use any you have on hand, from chicken parts to turkey breast to whole stewing chicken. Usually used in white chilis, but it's a great option when you're looking to fortify with lean protein.

✕ ✕

"Never Salt Beans Until They're Cooked"—Science Fact or Science Fiction?

Science fiction. Salt them early and often! The old saw says that salt will keep tough skins from softening. In fact, the skins of unsalted beans absorb so much water that the interior puffs up and breaks the skins. Salted bean skins will remain intact. What makes beans hard is age. Really old beans can simmer for hours and never get soft.

Why? Because calcium and magnesium in the skins act as barriers, supporting the structure and keeping them firm. By soaking beans overnight in salted water, you allow sodium ions to switch places with some of the calcium and magnesium ions, which makes the skins and interiors soften at the same rate. ✕

Don't mix up the meat dish and the vegetable—chili with an *i* is the spicy meat stew, while chile with an *e* refers to the pepper. The powder, because of its use in the stew, is spelled with an *i*.

Recipe: BEGINNER'S CHILI

Chili is a great dish for beginning cooks. The mix and balance of ingredients is very forgiving, so it's hard to ruin a pot of chili! For a square meal, ladle it over pasta or rice and serve with a green salad, or spoon into large tortillas, adding shredded lettuce, cheese, and salsa to make burritos. For a game-day favorite, layer corn chips into pasta bowls with chili, cheese, chopped onion, and hot sauce.

Serves 6

2 tablespoons vegetable oil

1 pound ground sirloin or chuck

1 large onion, chopped

2 large cloves garlic, finely chopped

1 (14½-ounce) can diced tomatoes, undrained

1 (8-ounce) can tomato sauce

1 tablespoon dried chili powder

1 teaspoon ground cumin

¼ teaspoon salt

¼ teaspoon freshly ground black pepper

2 cups cooked kidney beans (or 1 [16-ounce] can), rinsed and drained

1. Set a large (at least 3-quart), heavy-bottomed pot over high heat and pour in the oil. Add the ground sirloin and, stirring constantly, cook until it begins to brown and crisp at the edges, about 7 to 10 minutes.

2. Add the onions and garlic, and cook until onions are transparent, but not browned, about 10 minutes.

3. Add all of the remaining ingredients except for the beans. Allow the mixture to come to a boil, then reduce the heat to medium-low and simmer for 20 minutes.

4. Add the beans, and simmer, uncovered, for an additional 20 to 30 minutes, stirring occasionally, allowing the chili to reduce to your desired consistency.

X X X X X X X X X X X X

Next-Level Chili

Once you can master the basics, change it up.

- Make it vegetarian or vegan: Instead of using meat, in Step 1, brown 1 large onion, chopped, 1 celery stick, chopped, and 1 red bell pepper, diced. Add 1 drained can of chickpeas, pintos, or cannellini along with the kidney beans.

- Add 1 teaspoon unsweetened cocoa powder or ½ cup dark coffee for depth.

- Simmer a cinnamon stick in the chili (remove before serving).

- Stir in 1 tablespoon peanut butter for a richer flavor.

- Add 2 chopped chipotle chiles in adobo or 2 tablespoons barbecue sauce for a smoky flavor. Brighten a dull chili with 2 tablespoons red wine vinegar.

- Bring on the umami! That's the meaty-savory flavor that makes people's mouths water. Add 1 to 2 tablespoons soy sauce, 1 tablespoon chopped anchovies, or 1 teaspoon Marmite (a British condiment made of brewer's yeast) to the pot. X

#41 How to Fry Chicken
(or, How to Pan-Fry Anything)

Of all the possible foods that can be fried (shrimp, potatoes, candy bars), chicken is the star. If you've ever gone to the trouble of battering and frying chicken—or any food, for that matter—only to watch breading or batter fall off in the oil, or suffer soggy coating that should have been crisp, then you understand that it takes know-how. Fried food isn't the healthiest, so in my family, we view it as a "sometimes" treat. If I'm going to splurge, I want my fried food to shine, with juicy interiors and golden, crunchy outsides. Here's how to make that happen.

The Technique

Pan-frying is a dry-heat cooking technique in which food is partially submerged in oil in a pan, on a stovetop, with the aim of a crisp crust and a moist interior. The food is cooked both by contact with the pan and by the hot oil. In deep-frying, food is fully suspended in hot fat and cooked simultaneously on all sides.

Won't It Be Greasy?

Not if you do it right, which is to use very hot oil. Frying at too low a temperature is what makes fried food greasy. A good rule of thumb is 350 degrees Fahrenheit for deep-frying. Use a deep-fry thermometer, one of the most useful, least-expensive frying and roasting tools, and also try dropping in a cube of bread before you add the food you're actually frying. The bread should sizzle and brown quickly in the oil, not lie limply, soaking up grease.

Beat the Crowds

Crowding is the biggest no-no when frying. Putting food in hot oil causes the temperature of the oil to drop. Adding too much at once can drastically reduce the temperature, and it can't recover quickly enough to build up sufficient steam to push back against the oil and keep it from infiltrating the food. Leaving space between pieces also allows hot, dry air to circulate, forming crisp crusts. So fry in small batches. It is worth the extra time, so you're not left with a pile of soggy, greasy food.

1　When battering or breading food to fry in hot oil, the most important thing is to eliminate moisture. Before frying chicken, some soak it in beer, some in buttermilk, and some in brine. To get rid of residual droplets, allow the marinated chicken to dry on a baking rack for up to 10 minutes, and if it's still not dry, dab the chicken with a paper towel or clean dish towel.

2　There are three steps to breading food for pan-frying:

a. Dredge it in flour.

b. Dunk it in beaten egg.

c. Coat it with breading, such as panko, cracker crumbs or toasted bread crumbs (see How to Make Bread Crumbs, page 50).

3 The flour bonds the egg to the food, and then breading clings to the egg during frying. Although you always want to shake off any excess egg or crumbs, you want to make sure not to miss a spot. If you fail to coat a small area with egg, hot oil uses that as a gateway, seeping under the crumb layer, causing it to peel away during frying.

4 Crisp pan-fried food requires sizzling hot fat. Use a frying thermometer and about an inch of oil per pan. The oil's depth should be no more than half the food's height. Too little oil, and the cook time will be too long, resulting in tough meat. Too much oil, and it could boil over or result in greasy food. Heat the oil to 350°F.

5 Use a large, heavy-bottomed and deep saucepan. Avoid nonstick pans because they do not withstand high temperatures. Try a test run; it's a rule of thumb among experienced cooks that the "first" of some fried foods, such as the first fritter, won't be perfect. Put one item in first and see if the oil is hot

enough, or too hot, and how long it takes to brown one side before flipping (usually 2 to 4 minutes, depending on the food). If it's perfect, well, that's a little treat for the chef before you continue frying the rest. Timing will vary greatly depending on what you're cooking. Keep a close eye and flip when the first side is golden brown. Pierce the first piece with a knife and be sure it's cooked through. If so, continue with that timing. If not, you may need to lower the heat slightly to prevent excessive browning and cook for a little longer.

6 Be prepared to turn up the heat after adding the food. The oil might be at the perfect temperature, but adding a batch of food may lower it significantly. Counter this by turning up the flame to high just as you add the food, then lower it again moments later as you continue cooking.

7 Have a paper towel–lined platter ready to receive the cooked food. Put down 3 or 4 layers for best grease absorption.

Recipe: BUTTERMILK FRIED CHICKEN

N ow that you've got the technique in hand, here's a classic recipe for buttermilk-marinated, down-home-style fried chicken.

Serves 6 to 8

4 chicken legs, halved into drumsticks and thighs

4 whole chicken breasts, halved

2 cups buttermilk

2 tablespoons salt

2 teaspoons freshly ground black pepper

2 cups all-purpose flour

1 teaspoon paprika

Safflower, sunflower, or peanut oil

1. In a large zip-top bag, combine the chicken parts, the buttermilk, and half the salt and

pepper, and marinate in the refrigerator for 6 to 8 hours.

2. Combine the flour and remaining salt, pepper, and paprika in a large brown paper grocery bag (not a lunch bag) or a plastic shopping bag (be sure there are no holes in the bottom).

3. One piece at a time, lift the chicken parts from the buttermilk, drop into the bag containing the flour mixture, and toss until coated. Set each piece aside.

(continued)

4. Prepare two skillets by adding oil to a depth of ½ inch and heat over medium-high heat. When the oil is sizzling hot (350°F), use tongs to lay breast pieces in one skillet, and legs in the other, working in small batches to avoid crowding.

5. Fry on the first side for about 10 minutes, then turn the pieces over and fry for another 20 to 25 minutes. Turn the chicken occasionally so it browns on all sides. It's done when the crust is golden and the juices run clear when pricked with the tip of a knife. Remove to a paper towel–lined platter and eat hot or at room temperature. (Once refrigerated, the crust won't be the same.)

#42 How to Cook French Fries
(or, How to Deep-Fry Anything)

F rench fries, doughnuts, onion rings, mozzarella sticks, chicken legs, and cod fillets. . . . Most of us enjoy these crispy morsels at burger joints, state fairs, and chain restaurants, but we rarely cook them at home. It's no wonder—deep-frying works best when you have a special appliance for the task; it can be messy, and there are safety issues to consider. Done right, however, deep-frying can yield surprisingly greaseless, delectably piping-hot morsels made just the way you like them.

The French Fry–An International Favorite

The French call them *pommes frites,* the Dutch call them *frieten,* and the English call them *chips.* Beloved from Belgium (where they were actually invented) to Australia to Canada, fry lovers coat them in ketchup, drench them in gravy, pair them with fish fillets, douse them in vinegar, shake on garlic salt, and dip them in mayonnaise. From planklike steak fries to whip-thin shoestrings, fries are a treat almost everyone enjoys.

Pick Your Potato

For frying, you need a starchy potato such as a russet, Long White, Norkotah, or Gold Rush. You can also use all-purpose types such as Kennebec or Yukon Gold. In hot oil, the texture of starchy potatoes stays mealy and dry, making sure the inside of the fry stays fluffy and light.

Can Your Oil Take the Heat?

To deep-fry any food—be it potatoes, chicken, zucchini, or Oreos—you'll need fat with a very high smoke point, which means it can be heated to high temperatures. If the oil isn't hot enough, breading disintegrates and food acts like a sponge, absorbing the surrounding oil. And greasy deep-fried food tastes awful! Heat a low-smoke-point oil to a high temperature, and it will break down, causing fishy and "off" flavors, doubly ruining your food. There are many choices of high-smoke-point fats (see "Fats for Deep-Frying," facing page), so pick the right flavor for your dish.

Deep-Fryer: Fun, but Optional

Deep-fryers are very handy, but not crucial. There are electric fryers that look like big stockpots with a plug, restaurant-style fryers for countertop use, and stovetop deep-fryers fitted with a lift-out basket. These can be good investments if you plan on doing a lot of frying, but to avoid the expense, you can simply use a large pot or Dutch oven and scoop out fried foods with a slotted spoon.

Safety First!

The key to deep-frying at home is safety. Boiling hot oil is dangerous, reaching temperatures of more than 400 degrees Fahrenheit. It can boil over, starting a fire or burning you. Set deep-fryers on flat surfaces, far from the edge of countertops, and follow manufacturers' instructions. Use back burners on the stove. Don't fry while wearing loose-fitting clothing or floppy sleeves. And remember, *never* douse a grease fire with water. Always have a fire extinguisher nearby, or smother a fire with a lid, flour, or cornmeal.

1 Cut the potatoes with a large, very sharp knife in order to create smooth surfaces. Jagged cuts allow oil to seep into crevices instead of forming a seal against the oil, resulting in spongy, greasy fries. Cut them into uniform pieces to ensure equal browning. Too thin, and the whole fry will be crispy and lacking a fluffy interior. Too thick, and the crust will be overcooked, leaving the inside raw. Aim for ¼- to ½-inch strips.

2 If you like, rinse the potatoes in cold water before cooking. Some people feel this washes off the excess starch and makes a crisper fry; others think it's fussy and unnecessary. Try it and see if you care either way!

3 Whether rinsed or not, potatoes should be quite dry before you fry, for both safety and optimal cooking. Pat the surface with several clean paper towels to dab up any excess moisture.

4 Working in small batches, so each fry can be surrounded on all sides by hot oil, par-cook the potatoes in the hot fat at a temperature of 325°F. Use the temperature setting on your fryer or set up your pot with a frying thermometer. Cook them until they're blond and limp (3 to 5 minutes), then remove them with a slotted spoon or skimmer.

5 Put the par-cooked fries in a bowl lined with paper towels and let them rest for 15 minutes to 2 hours.

6 When ready to serve, reheat your oil to 375°F. Again, working in small batches, repeat the frying process, allowing each batch to fry until golden brown and crispy (4 to 7 minutes), then drain on fresh paper towels. Salt, and then serve very hot. No matter how well cooked, a cold fry is not what you want.

Fats for Deep-Frying

In general, the lighter in color and the more refined an oil is, the higher the smoke point. The most popular fats for deep-frying are vegetable or canola oils, which have mild flavors and are inexpensive—good if you're using a quart of it for frying. You can filter the cooled oil through a paper towel–lined strainer and pour it back into the bottle to save for deep-frying later, but let your nose be your guide: If the oil smells at all funny when you reopen the bottle, the food will taste the same way. Discard it and start fresh.

#43 How to Cook a Pot of Beans

I t's true, you can always use canned beans, which are not so different in flavor when they are used in cooked dishes. But in salads and sandwiches, canned are far inferior to home-cooked dried beans—and they cost more to boot. The main barrier, for the time-starved, is the soaking step. Not only is this effortless, but also, there's a shortcut that gets beans on the table same-day. Here's how to make perfect beans and leave the cans in the pantry.

Why We Soak

Many think the soaking step is just to reduce the gas that beans cause in poor chili-lovers like me and my family. That's partly true—it may help eliminate indigestible complex sugars, though some food scientists disagree!—but that's not the only reason. Mainly, beans are dirty! During commercial packaging, beans aren't washed because residual moisture causes them to sprout (they're seeds) or to mold and ferment. Rinsing and soaking clears the beans of dirt, pebbles, insects, pesticides, and chemical fertilizer.

1 Rinse the beans in a colander and pick them over for pebbles, sticks, and debris.

2 Soak the beans. The larger the bean, the longer the soak. (Small beans and legumes, like lentils, don't require soaking.) And the longer the soak, the shorter the cooking time. Soak beans in roughly three times their volume of cool water for 6 to 8 hours before cooking. Dried beans can be soaked too long, which can cause them to ferment, changing their flavor and making them less easily digestible.

For a quicker soak, put them in a pot with cold water to cover by 2 to 3 inches. Bring them to a boil, and then, with the pan off the heat, allow them to remain in the water for 1 to 2 hours. They are now ready to cook.

3 Drain the beans, or, preferably, lift them out of the soaking water with a slotted spoon, leaving any grit in the bottom of the bowl. Then, put them in a pot with enough water to cover.

4 Loosely cover the pot, with the lid set slightly askew, and simmer gently over low heat until the beans are creamy and tender, 1 to 2 hours. One pound of dried beans, which is about 2 cups, will yield 6 to 8 cups of cooked beans, depending on the type. Taste them occasionally to test for doneness.

#44 How to Cook Rice

If you eat a lot of rice in your home, a rice cooker is well worth a spot on your countertop. In as little as 20 minutes or up to 12 hours or more later, you lift the cover to find hot, perfectly cooked rice, tender but with separate grains. It's a little kitchen miracle. If rice is only an occasional food, however, cook it on the stovetop using the absorption method, which means you put in just as much water as the rice needs to absorb.

Whatever rice you choose, do not use "converted" rice, which is parboiled and dried to cook faster, robbing it of flavor.

Rice in Season

A stock cube is an easy way to add flavor to a pot of rice. But you can add other flavors as well. Try replacing the water with homemade chicken stock or coconut milk. Cook a minced onion in the rice pot in a little butter until the onion is tender but not brown, and then add the rice and liquid. Add spices or dried herbs along with the water and salt. Rice is very forgiving, so let your taste buds be your guide.

1 Choose your rice: white, brown, jasmine, basmati, and so on, as well as long, medium, or short grain. The only ones to avoid for cooking rice this way are risotto rice, such as Arborio or Carnaroli, which is grown to have the excess starch that makes a risotto creamy, and wild rice, which is technically a seed and needs to be boiled in a lot of water and drained, as if it was pasta.

2 Decide how much you need. One cup of rice will yield 2 to 3 cups of cooked rice. Brown rice will give you about 2 cups. Basmati will fluff right up into 3 cups. Long-grain white rice will give you about 2½ cups. If you're cooking to serve 4 people, 1½ cups uncooked rice is reasonable.

3 Measure the rice and water into a pot with a lid. The basic rule of thumb is 1 part rice to 2 parts water, good for long-grain white rice, but you'll have to adjust for other kinds. Brown rice needs a little more—1 cup rice to 2¼ or 2½ cups water, and short grain needs a little less, 1 cup rice to 1¾ cups water. Try your preferred rice with the 1:2 ratio with water and see if it cooks up the way you prefer.

4 Add salt, about ½ teaspoon per cup of rice. Rice without salt is bland. If the bouillon cube package says that 1 cube makes 2 cups broth, then 1 cube should be okay for 2 cups water and 1 cup rice. Some cooks add a tablespoon of butter or olive oil, but it's not necessary.

5 Bring the pot to a boil over high heat. If you used a bouillon cube, stir it into the boiling water so it doesn't sit there intact as your rice cooks. If you're just using salt, no need to stir.

6 Decrease the heat to low and cover the pan, and don't touch it. It should not be boiling hard; the lid should not jiggle. Don't stir it; don't take the lid off. Let it cook for 15 minutes (25 to 30 minutes for brown rice). Then remove the pan from the heat and let it sit until any steam is absorbed and the rice is tender without being mushy, 8 to 10 minutes.

7 Take off the lid and fluff the rice with a fork to separate the grains. Serve at once.

#45 How to Roll a Burrito
(or a Wrap)

The burrito is a cousin to the taco—both involve folded-up tortillas stuffed with fillings. In fact, in Mexico, some call burritos *tacos de harina,* or "flour tacos." Literally translated, *burrito* means "little donkey," probably because burritos resemble the rolled-up bundles they transport. American burritos typically hold some combination of beans, rice, meat, lettuce, salsa, guacamole, cheese, and sour cream. But a burrito can be made with whatever's on hand to meet any diet or taste. They're so easy to prepare—consider them your go-to for quick weekday lunches and dinners.

The Wrap-Up

Burrito's wrapper—the tortilla—is an unleavened bread, usually made with flour, salt, water, and fat. (Some of the puffier, Tex-Mex-style tortillas are leavened with baking powder.) For the health-conscious, they now come in fiber-rich whole wheat, along with rice, quinoa, and other gluten-free flours. For a flavor boost, try the spinach, sun-dried tomato, chipotle, and jalapeño varieties. Read the label for ingredients and look for wrappers without added preservatives for best flavor.

All Rolled-Up: Burritos, Wraps, Sushi Rolls, and Egg Rolls

The Earl of Sandwich knew that stuffing tasty fillings into an edible container was a brilliant way to prepare a low-mess, portable meal. Joining, and I'd say surpassing, the beloved sandwich in the annals of smart culinary design are the burrito, the summer roll, sushi rolls, and the wrap.

These delectable rolled meals offer the upgrade of a completely sealed envelope for the meats, vegetables, and condiments inside, making them even more suitable for lunches and meals on the go.

1. Prepare your fillings. (This step can be done in advance.) Wash and chop lettuce and tomatoes or other veggies. Cook or warm up some rice. Prepare whole beans seasoned with spicy sauces, or warm refried beans. Fry or sauté ground beef, strips of chicken breast or steak, or fish such as tilapia or monkfish. Grate cheese. The key is to have all ingredients ready for stuffing when the tortillas are warm.

2. Go big! I recommend 12-inch tortillas or larger to allow a good stuffing of ample fillings for a full meal; this also helps to prevent leakage.

3. Spray a large, heavy-bottomed skillet with cooking spray and set it over high heat to warm. Lay in tortillas one at a time, heating for 30 to 45 seconds per side. Don't overbrown or dry them out. You want them to be slightly puffy and pliable. Lay them flat on a plate to be filled.

4 Spoon rice on first to form an absorbent layer. Make a rectangle, leaving about 3 inches of space around the perimeter. Don't pile it too thick, or you won't be able to roll it.

5 Add layers of beans and meat on top of the rice rectangle.

6 Lock it down. If you're using sour cream or guacamole, layer it in next. They'll act like glue to secure loose ingredients such as shredded cheese, lettuce, jalapeños, and chopped cilantro.

7 Dress it up. Add diced and shredded toppings along with saucy condiments for the finishing touch.

8 Secure the perimeter. With the rectangle of layered ingredients oriented vertically, fold the tortilla's left side just over the ingredients, leaving uncovered tortilla to the right. Then fold the bottom up about 1 to 2 inches. (If you're wrapping it up and transporting it to lunch or a picnic, fold in each end to help keep the fillings sealed tight.) Finally, finish rolling the burrito tightly from left to right. It'll look something like a sleeping bag. If done properly, your hands (and shirt!) should stay clean while munching.

> The humble sandwich—cousin to the wrap—was born under curious circumstances: The fourth Earl of Sandwich, John Montagu, was a gambler who famously ate a piece of beef between two slices of toasted bread so he didn't have to leave his game.

Other Filling Ideas

Pretty much anything can go into a wrap—when you're bored with the standard rice and bean base, don't forget these other combinations! Simplicity can be good, but the bigger the wrap, the more you can stuff in, so experimentation is key.

- Caesar salad with grilled chicken

- Baba ganoush spread, hard-boiled egg, cucumber, tomato, tahini, parsley

- Spinach salad with honey mustard, dried cranberries, red onions, and chickpeas or turkey

- Falafel with hummus, olives, pickled cabbage, and harissa

- Prosciutto and arugula with fig spread and goat cheese

- Tuna salad with lettuce, celery, tomatoes, and capers

- Curried chicken salad or cauliflower with golden raisins and romaine lettuce

- Kale with sausage and feta

- Roasted red peppers with white bean spread and spinach

- Mushrooms, caramelized onions, and polenta

- Muffaletta: olive spread, cold cuts, lettuce, and tomato

- Tomato, mozzarella, basil, and chicken

- Lemon Greek yogurt spread, asparagus, and pancetta

- Black beans, corn, and zucchini with salsa and smashed avocado

- Pulled pork with BBQ sauce and cole slaw

#46 How to Make Maki
(or, Making Sense of Sushi)

A maki roll is the sushi you're probably most familiar with—those neatly cut rolls sold in Japanese restaurants, deli salad bars, and even supermarket cold cases. They're usually made with toasted nori (the green seaweed wrapper that holds them together), rice, and filling.

Don't I Need Special Equipment?

Not really! I recommend a bamboo sushi mat, known as a makisu mat, which is very inexpensive and easily found in Asian markets.

A makisu mat holds the ingredients together while rolling and makes the sushi roll tight and firm so it holds together when you cut it into rounds. If you don't have a mat, you can roll sushi using a clean dish towel.

1 Lay a makisu mat (or whatever you are using to roll) on a clean work surface. Lightly toast a sheet of nori over a gas flame, holding it over the heat for a few seconds using a pair of tongs, or put the nori sheet in a toaster oven for 15 to 20 seconds. This softens it enough to roll without breaking, and toasting improves the flavor.

2 Place the sheet of toasted nori on top, shiny-side down, rough-side up. The rice will stick to the rough side.

3 Using a wet wooden paddle or spoon or a rubber spatula, apply a very thin layer of rice (no more than a ¼ inch thick) to the entire sheet, leaving a 1-inch strip bare at the top, for sealing the roll shut. Work around the remaining three sides and edges, then move to the middle. Wet the paddle again, as needed, working slowly and gently. If you tear the nori, the roll will fall apart during cutting.

4 Place a thin line of ingredients, about one third of the way up from the bottom.

5 Before rolling, use your fingers to gently moisten the exposed strip at the top of the nori. Then dot several grains of rice about ½ inch apart across the wet strip to glue the roll shut.

6 Holding the bottom edge of the mat or dish towel with your thumbs, lift the nori and roll it away from you, keeping the ingredients together and pushing to press the rice into place.

7 Allow the sushi roll to rest for 3 or 4 minutes before cutting so that moisture can seep into the nori, softening it so that it's less likely to tear. Using a very sharp knife dipped in water, cut the roll into six pieces.

8 Serve with soy sauce, wasabi, and pickled ginger.

To minimize damage to the fish as it is cut, Japanese knives have a thin carbon steel blade that is sharper than stainless steel knives.

Am I a Vegetarian If I Eat Fish?

Labels aside, any path toward mindful, healthful eating deserves kudos. But here are the most commonly accepted parameters and definitions of vegetarianism:

Pescatarian. Abstains from red meat and poultry but eats dairy products and seafood.

Flexitarian. Generally abstains from meat and animal flesh, eats dairy products, and may or may not eat seafood. Occasionally eats meat and poultry in a conscious way.

Ovo-lacto vegetarian. Eats eggs and dairy products, and may or may not eat seafood. Does not eat red meat or poultry. *Ovo-vegetarians* eat eggs, but not dairy and eschew meat and poultry. *Lacto-vegetarians* eat dairy but not eggs, and eschew meat and poultry.

Vegan. Eats only plant-based products. Does not eat animal flesh, dairy, eggs, seafood, or any product made from animals, including broth or gelatin. Because it is made by bees, honey is a topic of debate.

Raw vegan. Eats only an unprocessed diet of vegan food, none of which has been heated to more than 115 degrees Fahrenheit, the belief being that high temperatures affect nutritional value and render some compounds in foods harmful to the body.

Macrobiotic. Eats unprocessed vegan foods, such as whole grains, fruits, and vegetables. Emphasis on the vegetables.

#47 How to Cook with Tofu

I n many ways, tofu is a perfect food: low in fat, high in protein, derived from plant sources so it's heart healthy and cholesterol free. It can add creaminess to smoothies, turn a stir-fry into a meal, and stand in, marinated and grilled, as a steak. Time and time again, I hear "I like tofu when I eat it in restaurants, but I don't know how to make it." These basics will set you on the right road.

First developed in China around 200 BCE, tofu is a nutritional powerhouse, with all 8 essential amino acids, 10 grams of protein per half cup, and loads of calcium, potassium, and magnesium.

Types of Tofu

• **Silken tofu.** Usually called for in soup, sauce, and dip recipes. It won't hold its shape, so it's not ideal for stir-fries or grilling. More often than not, you'll find it in a brick pack, unrefrigerated.

• **Regular tofu.** This is the most common type and is divided into different firmness levels, including: soft, medium, firm, and extra-firm. It typically comes packed in water and is found in the refrigerator case. Even when extra-firm, this tofu is somewhat soft and benefits from

pressing. This is the type to use for stir-fries, casseroles, and stews.

• **Brick tofu.** As you'd expect, the package looks like a brick. Because the goal is to offer the firmest tofu possible, it's packed with very little water and comes in a plastic wrapper that almost looks vacuum-packed and is sold in the refrigerator case. This style is best used when a recipe calls for clean slices or cubes that won't fall apart.

It's easy to make most styles of tofu firmer if you want drier tofu to ensure crispy edges when frying, or solid chunks or "steaks" for an entrée.

1 Place a block of medium or firm tofu at the end of a cutting board.

2 Place a second cutting board or a heavy, flat plate on top, sandwiching the tofu in a makeshift press. Position the tofu near the edge of the kitchen sink, so that the liquid will run down the drain.

3 Prop the back end of the bottom cutting board up a few inches, using a stable baking tray or casserole dish to angle it.

4 Place something heavy, like a book, on the top cutting board or plate.

5 Allow the weight to press the liquid from the tofu over the course of an hour or two.

6 Once the tofu has drained, it will be quite firm and easy to slice into cubes, or steaks. Marinate the chopped tofu in a mixture of your choice (wet or dry), refrigerated, for several hours. Drain the marinated tofu before cooking.

7 If frying the tofu, to ensure a golden, crispy crust, dredge the cubes in cornstarch before cooking in very hot oil.

8 Be patient—allow your tofu to cook on all sides until nicely browned. It will be flavorful and crunchy on the outside, with a piping hot, creamy interior.

Protein Sources for Nonmeat Eaters

Whether or not you follow a plant-based diet, there are many sources of protein beyond meat.

Artichokes
Asparagus
Avocados
Beans
Beet greens
Broccoli
Coconut milk
Eggs
Greek-style yogurt (higher in protein than regular yogurt)
Hummus
Kale
Lentils
Low-fat cottage cheese
Low-fat, part-skim cheeses like mozzarella, Cheddar, and Swiss
Nut milks
Nuts and nut butters
Peas
Powdered whey protein (for shakes and smoothies)
Quinoa
Seeds (such as sunflower and pumpkin)
Seitan (dough made from seasoned wheat gluten)
Skim milk
Soy products (including soy nuts, soy butter, soy milk, and tofu)
Spinach
Veggie burgers

Recipe: IMPOSSIBLE-NOT-TO-LIKE TOFU STIR-FRY

The tofu in this recipe is firm and crisp, and it absorbs the flavors of the marinade and the vegetables with which it's cooked. The beauty of the recipe is that you can choose whatever vegetables you and your family prefer—it's quite accommodating, as is tofu itself. Serve on top of brown, white, or jasmine rice, or on top of buckwheat soba or whole-wheat pasta. Flank with a salad of lettuce, radish, and cucumber, topped with peanut dressing, for extra nutrition and flair.

Serves about 4

1 (16-ounce) package extra-firm water-packed tofu

½ cup lemon juice

½ cup soy sauce

½ cup brown sugar

2 teaspoons crushed garlic

1 teaspoon minced fresh ginger

½ teaspoon freshly ground black pepper

1 teaspoon toasted sesame oil

½ cup plus 1 tablespoon cornstarch

½ cup vegetable stock

2 tablespoons peanut oil

2 cups chopped vegetables (broccoli, onions, snow peas, bell peppers, carrots, celery)

1. Drain and press the tofu (see How to Cook with Tofu, page 88). Once firm and dry, cut it into large, uniform cubes.

2. In a medium-size saucepan, combine the lemon juice, soy sauce, brown sugar, garlic, ginger, pepper, and sesame oil, and cook over low heat until the sugar is dissolved. This mixture will be your marinade.

3. Combine the tofu cubes and one third of the marinade in a zip-top bag, and refrigerate for 4 to 6 hours.

4. When ready to cook, pour the marinated tofu cubes into a colander and let drain. Once drained, combine the tofu in a clean zip-top bag with ½ cup cornstarch. Seal the bag and shake to coat.

5. In a saucepan, combine the remaining marinade with the vegetable stock. Bring to a rolling boil, then reduce the heat to medium and cook, stirring, for 4 minutes.

6. In a small mixing bowl, whisk 1 tablespoon of the cornstarch with 1 to 1½ tablespoons cold water until there are no lumps.

7. Slowly add the cornstarch slurry to the sauce, whisking continuously until it begins to thicken, then reduce the heat to low.

8. Heat the peanut oil in a large heavy-bottomed sauté pan over high heat. Add the tofu to the hot oil, working in batches to allow ample space between cubes. Resist the urge to touch your tofu cubes until the edges are brown and crisp on one side, about 6 minutes—then use tongs to flip. Once browned on all sides, set the tofu aside.

9. Using the same pan, sauté the vegetables, adding more oil if needed. The vegetables are done when they are bright in color and fork-tender.

10. Return the tofu cubes to the pan with the cooked vegetables. Top with the reserved sauce and serve.

✕✕✕✕✕✕✕✕✕✕✕✕✕✕✕✕✕✕✕✕✕✕✕✕✕✕

Smoke Points and Oil Types

Some oils withstand high temperatures better than others. The *smoke point* of oils and fats refers to the temperature at which they break down and start to fail as lubricants. When oil breaks down, it will fill your kitchen with smoke, and foods will start to stick to the pan and absorb an "off" taste.

Extra-virgin olive oil tastes great in vinaigrette, but it has a low smoke point. Some better choices for high-temperature frying are safflower oil, sunflower oil, peanut oil, refined canola oil, and coconut oil. Lard and beef fat are what our grandmothers might have recommended. ✕

#48 How to Repurpose Common Leftovers

(or, Giving Meals a Second Career)

'd almost feel sorry for the uneaten portions of my meals, if I didn't know they were headed for greatness in Round Two of their culinary lives. To cope with leftovers in a creative way, and to avoid eating the same meal many nights in a row, repurpose the main ingredients into new dishes that are exciting in their own right. Here's how to use up the leftovers most Americans are confronted with on a regular basis.

Roast Chicken

• Chop it up and make your favorite chicken salad.

• Sandwich it between tortillas with Cheddar cheese for quesadillas.

• Bake it on a pizza crust with mozzarella and ricotta for white pizza.

• Buy a ready-made piecrust and some jarred gravy and mix it with crisp-cooked chopped veggies for chicken pot pie.

Roast Turkey

• Layer it on a sandwich using cranberry sauce and mashed potatoes as a condiment.

• Simmer it with potatoes and peas in store-bought curry sauce.

• Chop it into canned cream of mushroom or cream of broccoli soup, and then serve over wide egg noodles.

• Mince it and stir it into chili (see Beginner's Chili, page 77).

Hamburger Meat

• Make a cottage pie. Sauté leftover meat with butter and onions. Add some cooked peas and carrots, and throw in some leftover gravy or beef stock to moisten. Spoon into a casserole dish, top with mashed potatoes, and bake.

• Mix it into macaroni and cheese for a one-dish meal.

• Make a taco salad. Line a bowl with tortilla chips and layer on cooked ground beef, lettuce, onions, tomatoes, sweet corn, jalapeño peppers, Cheddar cheese, and salsa.

• Sauté tomatoes, onions, garlic, and bell peppers. Add cooked rice and cooked ground beef. Layer into bowls and top with shredded cheese.

Mashed Potatoes

• Mix 1 cup mashed potatoes with a beaten egg, some olive oil, some finely chopped onion, and some fresh herbs. Mold into pancakes and fry.

• Make mashed potato soup. Sauté mushrooms and onions in butter. Add leftover mashed potatoes and chicken stock until it's a chowderlike consistency. Stir in some shredded cheese. Top with sour cream and scallions.

(continued)

Spaghetti Sauce

• Use as a pizza sauce on a store-bought or homemade crust (see Foolproof Pizza Dough, page 52).

• Make pizza burgers by using garlic bread as the bun and spreading spaghetti sauce over the meat patty. Melt mozzarella cheese on top under the broiler.

• Make stuffed peppers by topping and coring green bell peppers and stuffing them with a combination of cooked ground beef, cooked rice, and spaghetti sauce. Put them in a casserole dish, cover them with foil, and bake at 350°F until the peppers are soft, about 30 minutes. Uncover, top with mozzarella cheese, and bake until melted.

• Make a quick minestrone soup. Sauté onions and celery in a large pot with a little olive oil. Add the leftover spaghetti sauce, then pour in beef stock, cooked vegetables, and canned beans.

Cooked Vegetables

• Use them to top a homemade or store-bought cheese pizza.

• Make a no-crust quiche (see No-Crust Vegetable Quiche, facing page).

• Make quick vegetable soup. Sauté onions and garlic in olive oil in a soup pot, then pour in beef, chicken, or vegetable stock. Add lots of chopped cooked or frozen veggies, plus chicken or turkey, if you have it.

• Make a stir-fry. Fry strips of chicken or steak in vegetable oil with desired seasonings, then throw in your cooked vegetables for the last minute of cooking.

Recipe:
FRIED SPAGHETTI OMELET

O h, the delicious comfort of a fried spaghetti omelet. In a way it's a pasta dish, in another it's a quiche, and in still another it's an Italian egg foo yung! This dish is a brilliant way to put leftover pasta to work, of course, but I sometimes make fresh pasta just to make this recipe. Don't be shy about layering on your favorite toppings!

Serves 3 to 4

6 tablespoons butter

4 cups cooked spaghetti (or other pasta)

3 large eggs

⅔ cup milk

⅔ cup freshly shredded Parmesan or Pecorino Romano cheese

3 tablespoons chopped fresh flat-leaf parsley

Freshly ground black pepper

Salt

1. In a large, heavy-bottomed skillet, melt the butter over medium heat. Add the pasta and fry it gently in the butter, tossing a couple of times to coat.

2. In a medium-size mixing bowl, whisk together the eggs and milk. Stir in the cheese, parsley, and freshly ground black pepper to taste. (I use a lot.) Pour over the fried pasta.

3. Cook the omelet over medium heat until a golden crust forms on the bottom. Flip it over, and cook the other side until it forms a golden crust (a few more minutes). Slide the omelet out onto a platter.

4. Salt to your taste, cut into wedges, and serve hot with more cheese for sprinkling, if you like.

Recipe: NO-CRUST VEGETABLE QUICHE

Take away the crust, and a quiche is an exceedingly easy entrée that comes together in minutes. It's also one of the tastiest ways around to use up leftover cooked vegetables. Broccoli and Cheddar is a classic combo, but this recipe works just as well with extra mushrooms, peppers, wilted greens, and even potatoes!

Serves 4 to 6

6 large eggs

1 cup milk

¼ cup finely chopped onion

2 tablespoons unsalted butter, melted, plus more for greasing the pan

½ teaspoon salt

Freshly ground black pepper

1 cup chopped cooked vegetables

½ cup shredded Cheddar cheese

½ cup shredded mozzarella cheese

1. Preheat the oven to 400°F. Butter a 9-inch pie plate, and set it aside.

2. In a medium-size mixing bowl, whisk together the eggs, milk, onion, melted butter,

salt, and a generous grind of black pepper. Gently fold in the chopped vegetables.

3. Pour the mixture into the pie plate and sprinkle the cheeses evenly over the top.

4. Bake until set and golden brown on top, about 20 minutes.

#49 How to Start Canning

Thrifty homemakers and practitioners of traditional arts know that canning, or "putting up," food is an excellent way to capitalize on what's fresh and abundant during rotating harvest cycles and to stock a fridge or pantry with delicious treats made by hand. In canning, food is preserved by being processed and then sealed in airtight containers (at home, they are typically jars). A broad range of methods can be deployed when preserving foods this way: pasteurization, boiling, steaming, refrigeration, and freezing among them. Any shelf-stable preserve such as jam, jelly, marmalade, or curd has been temperature-treated in some way to kill microorganisms and render inactive enzymes that could cause spoilage. Food is then vacuum-sealed to prevent air, and the microorganisms that come with it, from entering the container and recontaminating food.

Learning to can—like learning to sew, knit, cook, clean, build shelves, or paint a room—is a valuable skill that offers great rewards. Safe canning practices can get rather involved, so before you get started, visit instructional websites like those of the National Center for Home Food Preservation (nchfp.uga.edu), the Centers for Disease Control and Prevention (cdc.gov), and the Federal Food Safety blog (foodsafety.gov). Your local library will have books describing what you need to buy and do in order to preserve foods you've grown or found at rock-bottom prices at the height of freshness at your grocery or farmers' market.

Botox's Evil Twin

Clostridium botulinum. This potentially deadly microorganism can cause a disease called botulism that can affect the central nervous system. The bacteria is anaerobic, meaning it can grow in low-oxygen conditions, such as in an improperly sealed can or jar, and particularly

(continued)

in low-acid foods, such as canned green beans. Botulism can cause nerve and brain damage, paralysis, and even death in those with weakened or compromised immune systems.

Why Risk It?

Done properly, canning is a fun and cost-effective way to store foods—and homemade jams and salsas make excellent gifts. With meticulous sterilization practices and the proper equipment, home canning poses almost zero danger, particularly when canning high-acid foods like tomatoes or pickles. Proper canning techniques include choosing only fresh foods to process, washing them thoroughly, adding acids such as lemon juice or vinegar to naturally low-acid foods, using noncompromised jars and brand-new lids, and vacuum-sealing them in a boiling-water or pressure canner at the right temperature and for the correct period of time.

The Freezer: An Easier Way to Homemade Jam

You can make preserves to be stored in your refrigerator or freezer. Although they don't last as long as the shelf-stable variety, the cold and the use of acids like lemon juice extend the life of your food, keeping bacteria and microorganisms at bay. So, if you have an embarrassment of fruit after a spree at the U-pick farm or a gift from your green-thumb uncle, these shortcut methods are perfect as a simple first stab at home food preservation.

✕ ✕

What's Nonreactive Cookware?

Nonreactive cookware allows you to cook foods that are acidic (citrus, tomato sauce, wine) or alkaline (eggs, dairy, asparagus) without reactivity between the food and the cookware. Problems with reactive cookware include breakdown and discoloration of food (eggs can develop a grayish tinge), metallic or "off" flavors, the leaching of ions from the cookware into the food, and staining or pockmarking of the pan.

Nonreactive materials include glass, stainless steel, ceramic, enamel, and hard anodized aluminum. Reactive materials include (non-stainless) steel, cast-iron, copper, and aluminum. These materials conduct heat evenly and are excellent for boiling water, frying burgers, or making stock. But if you're working with acidic or alkaline ingredients, stick to nonreactive cookware. ✕

Recipe: STRAWBERRY FRIDGE PRESERVES

One perk of refrigerator jam is that, because it doesn't get canned, the fruit stays close to its natural state, so it tastes fresh. Try this recipe with fresh strawberries (not frozen)—it will stay delicious for up to three weeks. I particularly like this one because it's fruitier than it is sweet. Add a spoonful to oatmeal or yogurt, or spread it on toast.

Makes about 2 cups

1 quart (4 cups) strawberries

1½ cups granulated sugar

Juice of 1 lemon

1. Wash, hull, and halve the strawberries.

2. In a very deep, nonreactive pot, bring the berries and sugar to a boil over high heat, and let cook for 5 minutes. Using a large, flat spoon, skim any foam from the top.

3. Reduce the heat to a simmer and add the lemon juice. Allow the mixture to cook for 10 minutes, stirring frequently.

4. Remove the pot from the heat, and use a slotted spoon to remove the solid berries to one or more clean lidded jars, filling about halfway. Return the pot to the burner and simmer over low heat until the liquid is reduced by half; depending on the heat, this can take between 10 and 15 minutes. Once reduced, use a ladle to distribute it evenly among the jars.

5. Allow the jars to cool completely, cover them securely, and refrigerate.

Recipe: NO-COOK PEACH AND RASPBERRY FREEZER JAM

For long-term preservation without the effort of vacuum-sealing, rely on your freezer. The freezer method of jam making is exceptionally easy because it doesn't even require turning on the stove. The secret is "jam sugar," which is available wherever you buy canning supplies in the autumn. It contains enough pectin to break down the structure of the fruit without the need for heat.

Makes about five (8-ounce) jars

2 cups (about 6) washed, peeled, and thinly sliced peaches

2 cups washed and hulled raspberries

1½ cups granulated jam sugar

3 tablespoons lemon juice

1. In a large mixing bowl, stir the peaches, raspberries, sugar, and lemon juice together until well blended. Let stand for 10 minutes, then crush the mixture lightly using a potato masher to release the juices.

2. Ladle the jam into clean jars and let set uncovered for an hour.

3. Cover tightly and freeze. The jam should last about 1 year in the freezer.

TIP: To peel peaches easily, dunk them in boiling water for a minute, then remove and rinse them in cold water. You should be able to slough off the peel by hand.

Pectin: Jam's Secret Ingredient

Pectin is a natural compound found in all fruits; it causes jams, jellies, and preserves to "set," or gel. Most commercial pectins are extracted from citrus fruit and contain no artificial substances. With cooked preserves, pectin shortens the cooking time, allowing fruits and vegetables to retain more freshness and brighter color.

Pectin requirements differ from fruit to fruit, and among commercially packaged pectin, there are differences between brands and forms, so use the type your recipe specifies. Because pectin reacts with sugar, don't omit or use a substitute for sugar without substituting "light" or "low-sugar" pectin to go with it, or the set of the jam will be off.

#50 How to Make Perfect Piecrust

Someone who makes a good piecrust is said to have a good "hand" with pastry. And how people adore (and envy) the person with a good pastry hand! In fact, perfect piecrust is within everyone's grasp, once you learn its secrets (see Double-Crust Apple Pie, page 98).

Get Your Chill On

Cold fat, cold water, cold hands. The flakiness that we so admire in a piecrust happens when the cold fat, be it butter, shortening, or lard, coats the individual flour grains without melting and soaking into them. Many pastry pros use a marble work surface to roll out the dough, because marble is naturally 8 degrees Fahrenheit colder than the surrounding environment, helping keep the pastry chilled. Cool hands have the same effect.

Fat for Flavor

A crust made with lard or shortening is decidedly the most flaky, but not quite as tasty as an all-butter crust. Many bakers like to use half butter, half lard or shortening in their crusts to get the best of both worlds.

1 Measure the butter, lard, or shortening, cut it into pieces, and put the pieces in the freezer for 30 minutes while you gather your other ingredients.

2 Fill a cup with cold water and drop in a few ice cubes. Measure the water you need for the pastry directly from this cup (avoiding the cubes).

3 "Cut" the chilled butter into the dry ingredients. Grasp a butter knife in each hand, then pull them vigorously in opposite directions until the butter disappears into the flour. Sprinkle ice water into the flour mixture until the dough begins to clump.

4 After the piecrust dough has come together, quickly gather it into a ball, wrap it in plastic wrap, and chill it in the refrigerator for 30 minutes to an hour before rolling. (Too much longer and you'll have to let it warm up a bit at room temperature before you can roll it.)

5 Sprinkle your work surface with a couple tablespoons of flour. Place the pastry ball in the center, pat it into a disc, and start

rolling it out gently with a rolling pin lightly dusted with flour. Start in the middle of the disc, and use short, firm strokes. For a professional-looking crust, roll forward only, rotating the crust a quarter turn between each stroke to make a smooth, even circle about 12 inches across and about ¼ inch thick.

✕ ✕ ✕ ✕ ✕ ✕ ✕ ✕ ✕ ✕ ✕ ✕

The Best Apples for Pie

The trick is to find an apple that won't dissolve into mushiness but isn't so crisp that it won't soften much at all. Super-crispy varieties such as SweeTango and Honeycrisp are bred to be eating apples, so don't cook with them. Look for deeply flavorful apples that aren't too watery (avoid Red or Golden Delicious for baking) and make sure they have a pronounced tartness. Best choices include Granny Smith, McIntosh, Macoun, and Northern Spy. ✕

Baking's Heavenly Triumvirate

Any good baker knows that baking is as much about science as it is intuition—chemistry is key. Here are a few truths about baking's big three.

BUTTER

• Butter, shortening, lard, and margarine can be substituted in equal parts. The difference? Taste. Butter adds a richer flavor than margarine, and shortening doesn't have any flavor at all. Commercial lard tends to be flavorless, but home-rendered lard can have a more meaty flavor. Caution: Don't attempt to substitute "light" butter spreads because they will ruin the texture of your finished product.

• Don't swap in liquid fats, like canola oil or peanut oil, when butter (or another hard fat) is required for creaming.

• In croissants, piecrust, and puff pastry, the flakiness comes from the butter being chilled. In these applications, the butter is "cut" in rather than being creamed.

• If a cake sinks in the center, you might have used too much butter, preventing it from rising properly.

SUGAR

• Sugar not only sweetens baked goods but also adds tenderness to delicious cakes, piecrusts, and cookies.

• You can generally swap out one granulated sugar for another. Replace white sugar with palm sugar, cane sugar, turbinado sugar, or coconut sugar. You can even substitute brown sugar, but it will darken the color of your baked good.

• Sugar helps baked goods brown. If you have a too-pale yellow cake, or straw-colored blondies, lack of sugar could be the culprit. Too brown or burnt? Too much sugar.

EGGS

• Eggs bind, add texture, leaven, and help pastries achieve a golden-brown color. Egg yolks lend moisture and richness. The protein in egg whites forms a fluffy structure that traps air. When whipped, they add lightness and volume.

• The more you beat egg whites, the stiffer the protein strands become and the more structure they provide. Caution: No fat can touch beaten egg whites or the structure will break down and they won't stiffen. Use clean tools.

Recipe: DOUBLE-CRUST APPLE PIE

There are few desserts that go right to the heart like a freshly baked pie, and apple pie is the queen of American pastries. The classic piecrust in this recipe makes one double-crust pie or two open-top pies. You can also use it for quiches or savory tarts.

Makes one (9-inch) pie

FOR THE CRUST:

2 cups all-purpose flour

1 teaspoon salt

11 tablespoons unsalted butter, cold

⅓ cup ice water

FOR THE FILLING:

6 to 8 medium-size apples (see "The Best Apples for Pie," page 97), peeled, cored, and thinly sliced

½ cup granulated sugar

2 tablespoons all-purpose flour, plus more for rolling

1 teaspoon ground cinnamon

2 tablespoons lemon juice

1. Make the crust. In a large mixing bowl, combine the flour and salt. Cut in the butter until the mixture resembles fine crumbs.

2. Sprinkle the water over the flour and stir with a wooden spoon just to combine.

3. Turn the pastry (and any remaining flour in the bowl) out onto a clean work surface and gather it together into a ball. Divide it in half, pat each half into a thick disc, and wrap each in plastic wrap. Chill in the refrigerator for at least an hour.

4. When ready to bake, preheat the oven to 400°F.

5. Lightly flour a clean countertop and rolling pin. Roll out one of the pastry discs to a circle 12 inches wide and about ⅛ inch thick. Roll it very loosely around the rolling pin and transfer the pastry to a deep 9-inch pie pan.

6. Sprinkle more flour on the work surface and roll out the other pastry disc slightly thicker, to a circle 10 inches wide. Set aside.

7. To make the filling, put the sliced apples on the piecrust in the pan and sprinkle evenly with the sugar, flour, cinnamon, and lemon juice. Gently transfer the remaining piecrust to top the pie, and use a fork to press down all around the edges. Use a paring knife to trim off any excess crust around the edges, and then use the tip of the knife or a fork to poke air holes all over the top of the pie.

8. Bake for 50 minutes, or until the crust is golden brown and the apples are tender. To test, poke a paring knife into the center of the pie to make sure the apples offer no resistance. If the pie needs a few more minutes, you can cover the crust with foil to keep it from browning too much. Cool slightly before slicing to allow the juices to set.

#51 How to Peel an Apple

If you have well-honed knife skills (and a well-honed knife), a paring knife is the old-time way to do it. But for most of us, a knife takes off too much apple along with the skin. Instead, use a sharp vegetable peeler.

1 Start near the stem end of the apple.

2 Pull the peeler toward you as you rotate the apple away. Ideally, you'll take the skin off in one or two long peels, turning the apple as you work toward the blossom end.

✕✕✕

Pie Topping Options

Pies don't have to be topped with pastry. Make a crumb or streusel topping by combining 1 cup all-purpose flour, ¾ cup light brown sugar, 1 teaspoon cinnamon (if you like), and 6 tablespoons salted butter, melted. The mixture will look like wet sand. Use your fingers to mix it, pinch it into big crumbs, and sprinkle it all over the surface of the pie before baking. To make an oatmeal crumble topping, reduce the flour to ¾ cup and add ½ cup rolled oats to the mixture. ✕

#52 How to Cream Butter, Sugar, and Eggs

Once you've got this step down, all you need is some flour to make a basic, down-home cake. There's a technique to wedding this trio, though. The secret to perfect creaming—the first step of so many baked goods—is to take your time and whip lots and lots and lots of air into the butter. Air is nature's leavening agent; the more air, the lighter the pastry.

1 Bring your ingredients to room temperature to allow everything to blend well and to prevent uneven baking.

2 Measure out the butter, according to your recipe, and put it in the bowl of your stand mixer or in a stable mixing bowl to be used with your hand mixer.

3 Measure out the sugar according to your recipe, and set it aside.

4 Ready your beater and whip the butter on a high speed. Do this for a long time, then do it some more. You want tiny air pockets to form—the more the better.

5 Reduce the speed to low and add the sugar to the butter a little at a time, until they're combined.

(continued)

6 Increase the speed, and whip the butter and sugar until thoroughly creamed, lightly fluffy with no visible sugar crystals in the mixture.

7 Reduce the speed to low and add the eggs one at a time. Beat the eggs into the creamed butter and sugar until they are thoroughly combined and the mixture turns pale yellow.

8 Now that these three ingredients are creamed, you can add in your remaining ingredients, a little at a time.

Pound cake is so called because the original ingredients required were a pound each of butter, sugar, eggs, and flour.

Recipe:
VERY BEST BLONDIES

Blondies are sometimes described as "brownies without cocoa," but I think of them more as a love child of the brownie and the chocolate chip cookie. They are always super popular, so I suggest making these your signature dish for potlucks, parties, and bake sales. Using a healthy dose of vanilla puts these over the top.

Makes 24 blondies

½ cup (1 stick) unsalted butter, melted, plus more for greasing the pan

1 cup all-purpose flour, plus more for dusting the buttered pan

1 cup brown sugar, firmly packed

1 egg

2 teaspoons vanilla extract

½ teaspoon salt

½ teaspoon baking powder

⅛ teaspoon baking soda

⅓ cup butterscotch or chocolate chips, optional

1. Preheat the oven to 350°F. Butter and flour an 11-by-7-inch baking pan.

2. In a large mixing bowl, whisk together the melted butter and brown sugar until smooth, then beat in the egg and vanilla.

3. In another bowl, combine the flour, salt, baking powder, and baking soda. Add the dry ingredients to the butter and sugar mixture, stirring just until no streaks show. Add the chips, if using, and mix lightly to combine.

4. Pour the batter into the prepared pan, and spread it evenly, using a rubber spatula dipped in water. Bake for 30 to 40 minutes, or until a toothpick inserted into the center comes out clean. The top should have a crispy, crusty layer.

5. Remove the pan to a baking rack and let cool completely before cutting into squares (otherwise the blondies will tear and crumble).

Recipe: RICHEST BROWNIES

There are many types and styles of brownies, all of which I'll eat and enjoy: fudgy brownies; chewy brownies; cakelike brownies; flavored brownies featuring espresso, cinnamon, or chili powder, or add-ins such as walnuts or white chocolate chips; frosted brownies; or bare brownies.

But these are my favorite. Rich and dark, they're like a hybrid of brownies and fudge. These are super easy to make, but quality cocoa makes all the difference.

Makes 24 brownies

1 cup (2 sticks) unsalted butter, melted, plus more for greasing the pan

½ cup all-purpose flour, plus more for dusting the pan

1 cup granulated sugar

1 cup light brown sugar

1 cup cocoa powder

½ teaspoon salt

4 large eggs

2 teaspoons vanilla extract

1. Preheat the oven to 350°F. Butter and flour (or use cocoa) an 11-by-7-inch baking pan.

2. In a medium-size bowl, combine the flour, granulated sugar, brown sugar, cocoa, and salt.

3. In a separate large mixing bowl, beat the eggs with a whisk or hand mixer until they are pale yellow and fluffy. Beat in the melted butter, a little at a time. When combined, add the vanilla, and mix until smooth.

4. Add the dry mix to the wet mix, mixing just until combined. Do not overwork the batter.

5. Pour the batter into the prepared pan and smooth it out with a rubber spatula dipped in water.

6. Bake for 40 to 50 minutes. Check for doneness by inserting a toothpick into the center of the pan. If it comes out clean, they're done. The top should have a crispy, crusty layer.

7. Remove the pan to a baking rack and let cool before cutting into 24 bars (otherwise the brownies will tear and crumble). Frost with Cream Cheese Frosting, if desired.

Recipe: CREAM CHEESE FROSTING

Makes about 2 cups

½ cup (1 stick) unsalted butter, at room temperature

4 ounces cream cheese, at room temperature

1 teaspoon vanilla extract

2 cups confectioner's sugar

1. With a hand or a stand mixer, beat the softened butter until fluffy and smooth, about 2 minutes.

2. Add the cream cheese and beat for 2 more minutes, until fluffy. Beat in the vanilla.

3. Working slowly, add the confectioner's sugar to the butter mixture, beating at a medium speed, until the frosting is smooth.

#53 How to Make Cookies

Cookies are America's most popular dessert, and with thousands of possible variations—from white chocolate raspberry to banana-espresso-chocolate chunk—there's truly something for everyone to appreciate.

(continued)

Baking is essentially chemistry, but with information and practice, anyone can master it. In days of yore, we learned how to make cookies at the elbow of sensible aunts and grandmothers who tried until they got it right. Nowadays, the secrets are more commonly learned from books, so here's my advice for how to make mouthwatering cookies that would make those aunts and grandmothers proud.

1 Precise ratios of wet and dry ingredients are important—if you add too much flour to the dough, you'll get tough cookies.

2 Don't overwork the dough (another recipe for toughness), but make sure it's thoroughly mixed or the finished product will be too crumbly. (If you mixed the dough properly and the cookies still crumble, your recipe might need more eggs for binding.)

3 Always preheat the oven, as directed. (You will end up with a doughy mess otherwise!) Position racks and baking sheets near the middle of the oven, not too close to the top or bottom.

4 Whether rolling, molding, or just dropping the dough from a soupspoon, make all of your cookies the same size to ensure uniform baking.

5 If your cookies don't brown properly, you may not have used enough sugar.

6 If they brown too much, it might be your cookie sheet: Avoid dark and shiny baking sheets. Opt instead for dull-finished, heavy-gauge aluminum sheets. If your cookies always seem to burn, your oven might run hot. Check often and adjust cooking time and temperature according to your experience.

7 If making batches, and reusing baking sheets, allow them to cool in between, running the bottoms under cold water as needed.

8 Unless your recipe says otherwise, transfer smaller cookies from the baking sheet to a wire rack immediately because the heat of the sheet continues to cook them.

9 If your cookies get hard or too crisp soon after cooling, store them in an airtight container with a slice of bread to soften them.

10 Use your nose! It's as valuable as your timer when baking. As soon as the cookies start to smell done, check them. They probably are. If you like them chewy, take them out immediately so long as they look set and not wet in the center. They'll firm up as they cool.

× × × × × × × × × × × ×

Newfangled Cookies

Who says a cookie has to be a disc? For parties or special treats, try these shapes:

- **Pat the dough into muffin tins.** They come out thick, a bit cakelike, and require a longer bake time. Top these rounds with a scoop of ice cream.

- **Make cookie "bowls."** Chill cookie dough, then roll cold dough out to a ⅛-inch thickness, as you would pie dough. Flip over a muffin tray, spray the "bumps" with cooking spray, drape circles of dough over each one, and bake. Let them cool on the pan for 15 minutes, then loosen them with a butter knife, carefully flip them over onto wire cooling racks, and let stand for half an hour.

- **Make chocolate chip cookie brownies.** Line a muffin tin with cupcake papers. Fill them one-third full with brownie batter, then fill the next third with chocolate chip cookie dough. (Leave the top third empty.) Bake and remove wrappers for double-layer decadence. ×

Recipe: SUPREME CHOCOLATE CHIP COOKIES

Perfect chocolate chip cookies are a delicious medley of contradictions. There's the thrill of crispy edges giving way to the gooey interiors. There's the contrast of salty and sweet. The cakiness of the cookie dough flanking the chocolaty candy of the chips. This recipe delivers on all fronts, and the cookies are dangerously addictive thanks to an unexpected finishing touch: a sprinkling of kosher salt on top. The real secret is letting the dough sit overnight, so the butter permeates the flour: It's an old bakery trick that will make your cookies taste like a pro baked them.

Makes 2 dozen large cookies

3½ cups all-purpose flour

1¼ teaspoons baking soda

1¼ teaspoons baking powder

1½ teaspoons salt

1¼ cups (2½ sticks) unsalted butter,
    room temperature

1¼ cups light brown sugar, firmly packed

1¼ cups granulated sugar

2 large eggs

2½ teaspoons vanilla extract

16 ounces chocolate chips

Nonstick cooking spray

Kosher salt, for topping (optional)

1. Mix the flour, baking soda, baking powder, and salt together into a large mixing bowl.

2. In a separate large mixing bowl, using a hand or stand mixer, beat the butter for 1 minute. Add the sugars and cream them with the butter (see How to Cream Butter, Sugar, and Eggs, page 99) until light and fluffy.

3. Add the eggs and vanilla and beat on high until fully combined, 1 to 2 minutes.

4. Add the dry ingredients to the wet ingredients, beating on low for the shortest amount of time required to fully combine. Remove the bowl from the stand mixer, if using one, and stir in the chocolate chips using a rubber spatula dipped in hot water.

5. Cover the dough tightly with plastic wrap, and refrigerate it for at least 8 hours and up to 24 hours.

6. When you're ready to bake the cookies, preheat the oven to 350°F and prepare several large baking sheets by spraying them with nonstick cooking spray. Using a tablespoon, ladle out 6 large dough balls—a generous ⅓ cup each—per sheet. If you like the salty-sweet thing, sprinkle the dough very, very lightly with a few crystals of kosher salt.

7. Bake the cookies until golden brown and just set in the center, 16 to 18 minutes, watching carefully so as not to overbrown them. Once done, remove the baking sheet from the oven, place it on a wire rack, and cool about 15 minutes. Then, transfer the cookies directly onto wire racks to continue cooling (although they're excellent when warm). Make sure the baking sheets cool between batches.

Variations: Mix in any of the following (at the same time as you add the chocolate chips) for an indulgent treat:

- ½ cup chopped toasted walnuts
- ½ cup M&M's
- 1 cup mini-marshmallows
- ½ cup mini–Reese's peanut butter cups
- ½ cup peanut butter chips
- 1 cup finely chopped pecans
- ½ cup mashed banana
- ½ cup coarsely chopped Junior Mints

#54 How to Frost a Birthday Cake

You can celebrate a birthday without balloons and streamers. One can even imagine a birthday without a party. If hard-pressed, a birthday could even survive the absence of the "Happy Birthday" song. But if it's my birthday, there'd better be a cake. And I mean a good one. That's why, in my house, I make all the birthday cakes, including my own (see Yellow Birthday Cake with Chocolate Frosting, page 105).

Let's be honest here, though—as important as flavor is, and it is *very* important, a birthday cake needs a wow factor. Towering height, gorgeous swirls of frosting, and those dramatic, colorful layers of cake and filling. Although folks often outsource birthday cakes to a bakery, thinking such a creation is beyond their reach, you can make celebration-worthy cakes at home.

1 To achieve a bakery-style look and to increase the height of a cake, you can split each cake layer and fill the space between with frosting, jam, or custard.

2 Using a large serrated bread knife, slice through the middle of the layer using a sawing motion.

3 Using your hands, gently lift the top of the layer off, slipping a rimless baking sheet between the layers. Repeat if you have more than one layer. If your layers aren't quite flat on top, trim a bit more.

4 Now, frost the layers. Put a dab of frosting in the middle of your cake plate to anchor the bottom layer to it.

5 Scoop about ½ cup of frosting onto the middle of the bottom layer, and using a rubber spatula or a small offset spatula, spread it

outward, extending beyond the edges. Add more frosting as you go, as needed for a generous filling layer.

6 Stack on the other cake layer, cut-side down. Press the layer with your palms to make it level. Either repeat the previous step, if making multiple layers, or prepare to frost the cake.

7 First create a "crumb coat," a preliminary layer of frosting that seals in crumbs and makes the cake easier to frost. Spread a thin layer of frosting, about 1 cup, over the sides of the cake, working in sections. Incorporate the frosting squeezing out from between the layers. It doesn't have to look perfect—this is just a first coat to hold down the crumbs. Smooth a thin layer of frosting over the top. For a more finished professional look, refrigerate the cake for a half hour. (If it looks fine and you're not bothered, simply proceed.)

8 Smooth another 2 cups of frosting onto the cake, starting on the sides and finishing with the top. If you like, dip the spatula in warm water to prevent streaks in the frosting and achieve a polished look.

9 For a super-polished look, refrigerate the cake again, then add a third layer of frosting. (If you don't want to, use all the remaining frosting in Step 8.) If you like swirls, swirl the top with the back of a teaspoon, twisting your wrist to make a little wave in the frosting. For a flat look, use a bench scraper (also called a dough scraper or bowl scraper) and slowly turn the cake on a cake stand as you hold the scraper still against the frosting, pulling it smooth as you turn.

Cake Frosting Tips

· All frostings aside from whipped cream should be room temperature before spreading. Cakes must be cool to avoid melting.

· Before frosting, edge the cake plate with strips of waxed paper. Once the frosting sets, peel them away carefully for a clean finish.

· Allow 4 cups of frosting for one 8- to 10-inch two-layer cake.

Recipe: YELLOW BIRTHDAY CAKE WITH CHOCOLATE FROSTING

Here's my strongest recommendation for this or any layer cake recipe: Beat the living daylights out of the butter and sugar. Cream it for no less than 12 minutes with a hand or a stand mixer. It'll seem like forever, but trust me, it gives the cake a velvety texture that will make everyone think it came straight from a bakery.

For this yellow cake, the buttermilk and vanilla extract really brighten up the flavor. If you don't have buttermilk, stir 2 tablespoons of lemon juice into 2 cups of whole milk, and let it stand while you're creaming the butter. This is already a very big three-layer cake, so I don't split and fill these layers; it's not necessary with this super-moist, dramatically tall confection.

(continued)

Makes one (8-inch) three-layer cake

FOR THE CAKE:

1 cup (2 sticks) unsalted butter, at room temperature, plus more for greasing the pans

4 cups cake (or all-purpose) flour, plus more for dusting the pans

1½ teaspoons baking powder

1 teaspoon baking soda

1 teaspoon salt

2 cups granulated sugar

1 tablespoon vanilla extract

4 large eggs, at room temperature

2 cups buttermilk, room temperature

FOR THE FROSTING:

1 cup (2 sticks) unsalted butter, softened

1 pound (about 4 cups) confectioner's sugar

⅓ cup cocoa powder

1 teaspoon vanilla extract

1 to 2 tablespoons heavy cream or milk, or more if needed

Sprinkles, or other decoration, optional

1. Preheat the oven to 350°F. Butter three 8-inch round cake pans and sprinkle lightly with a little flour, shaking to coat.

2. Make the cake: In a medium-size bowl, sift together the flour, baking powder, baking soda, and salt.

3. Put the sugar and 1 cup of the butter in a mixing bowl or bowl of a stand mixer and beat at medium-low speed for 3 to 4 minutes, scraping down the bowl several times to incorporate all the sugar. Then turn the mixer to medium and keep beating until the butter and sugar have tripled or quadrupled in volume and are light and impressively fluffy, for several minutes. Don't lose heart. Let your mixer do its work.

4. Beat in the vanilla, then add the eggs, one at a time, letting each one incorporate well before adding the next. You may need to give each egg a minute or two.

5. Add one third of the buttermilk to the butter and sugar mixture, letting it incorporate well, then add one third of the flour mixture. Repeat until the buttermilk and flour mixture are incorporated fully.

6. Divide the batter among the prepared cake pans and smooth with a rubber spatula. Bake until golden and fragrant, 20 to 22 minutes, testing with a skewer at the 20-minute mark. You don't want the skewer totally dry—that means the cake is overcooked. As soon as you get a few moist crumbs stuck to the skewer but no wet batter, take the cake out of the oven.

7. Cool for 10 minutes in the pans, then run a knife around the edges and flip the rounds carefully onto cooling racks and cool completely.

8. Make the frosting: In a large, clean mixing bowl, beat the cup of butter on medium speed until smooth, then gradually add in the confectioner's sugar.

9. Beat in the cocoa and vanilla, then add a tablespoon or two of cream or milk and continue beating until the frosting is smooth and fluffy, 3 to 4 minutes. If you feel the mixture is too thick, add another tablespoon of cream or milk, but beat well after each addition to fully combine so you don't overly thin it.

10. Assemble and frost the cake (see How to Frost a Birthday Cake, page 104) with a generous amount of frosting between each layer. Sprinkles on top may be optional at your house, but not at mine.

TIP: The point of slowly adding the wet and dry alternately in Step 5 is to keep the volume high. Too much wet or dry all at once would break down all the beautiful air bubbles you've beaten into the butter, sugar, and egg, deflating the mixture.

The largest birthday cake ever made weighed more than 128,000 pounds! It was made in Alabama.

#55 How to Make Ice Cream
(Without a Machine)

The response I get when I serve ice cream and sorbet to guests, and casually mention it's homemade, is deeply gratifying and worth the minimal effort it takes to pull it off. I also like the control I have over the balance of flavors, ingredients, and add-ins. Because they're all-natural with quality ingredients and lower sugar, I feel good about serving my icy desserts to my family.

For most people, making ice cream at home is an occasional event. Investing in specialized equipment might not be worth the money, particularly if storage space is at a premium. But almost every kitchen has a hand mixer or stand mixer—and that's all you need to make this super simple and perfectly sweet, creamy frozen treat.

1 To make a quart of ice cream, start with 2 cups heavy cream. Using a hand mixer and a large mixing bowl or a stand mixer, whip the cream to heavy, stiff peaks (see How to Whip Cream, page 15).

2 In another large mixing bowl, combine 1 can (14 ounces) of sweetened, condensed milk with your desired flavors and add-ins, and mix thoroughly with a rubber spatula.

You can flavor the ice cream with anything you like, but here are some ideas to get you started.

Butter pecan: 3 tablespoons melted butter, 1 cup toasted pecans

Rocky road: ¾ cup (or more) chopped almonds or walnuts, 1 cup mini-marshmallows, ½ cup chocolate syrup

Hazelnut and chocolate: ½ cup chocolate chips, ½ cup toasted hazelnuts, ½ cup Nutella

Fresh peach: 3 ripe peaches, peeled, chopped, and tossed with 1 teaspoon lemon juice and 2 tablespoons granulated sugar

3 Fold the whipped cream into the condensed milk mixture, working slowly, adding a little at a time. Don't overmix or you'll push the air out of the whipped cream.

4 Pour into a 1-quart plastic container, such as a food storage or takeout container, and freeze for at least 8 hours, ideally stirring a few times to break up any ice crystals.

✕ ✕ ✕ ✕ ✕ ✕ ✕ ✕ ✕ ✕ ✕ ✕ ✕ ✕ ✕ ✕ ✕

The Rock in Rocky Road

Many ice cream makers rely on rock salt, a very coarse, inedible variety of unrefined salt. (It's the same kind that is sprinkled on icy roads and sidewalks, but it's usually available at a food-grade level in the salt section of your supermarket, labeled "rock salt.") The rock salt slurry that surrounds the freezing cylinder allows the contents to freeze at a lower temperature, speeding up the process. ✕

#56 How to Make Sorbet in a Bag

This method relies on the same science as the ice cream ball (see "Machine-Made: Ice Cream Makers," facing page), that is, the chemical reaction between rock salt and ice that quickly freezes the ingredients. The technique is so simple that kids can do it, and the time involved from start to finish is about 10 minutes.

Sorbet made this way tends to be icier, rather than smooth, and features more crunchy crystals, like an Italian ice. Go super simple with bottled fruit juice, or amp it up by pureeing and straining fresh fruit and adding special touches like citrus zest or finely chopped herbs. To make 1¼ cups of sorbet, try this technique.

1 Pour 1 cup fruit juice or puree into a sturdy, quart-size zip-top bag and seal tightly. Don't completely fill the bag; you need room for expansion. NOTE: Adding alcohol changes the freezing point so it will result in a softer, less dense texture; this is a recipe that works best without any add-ins.

2 Combine 2 cups ice, 1 cup rock salt, and 1 cup water in a sturdy, gallon-size zip-top bag.

3 Insert the smaller bag into the larger bag, taking care not to spill the water mixture. Shake the bags vigorously, then lightly massage the juice inside the ice-water mixture. Repeat until the juice's consistency becomes sorbetlike, 8 to 10 minutes.

Do this step outside or in a space that's easy to clean up, such as in a deep sink or over a tile floor. Mishaps are not unheard of! It's perhaps not the most practical way to make a frozen dessert, but kids love it; it's like an edible science project for them.

4 Carefully remove the smaller bag, scoop out the frozen dessert, and either serve immediately or transfer to an airtight container and freeze for use within a month.

Recipe: SIMPLY SUPER STRAWBERRY SORBET

Ice cream's sophisticated cousin, sorbet is elegant in its simplicity. It's a concentration of one or a few flavors, offered in a cold, refreshing form. Generally low- or nonfat, and made without dairy, sorbet is a healthful way to indulge guests—or yourself. You can make it in an ice cream machine, but a food processor works just fine.

Serves 6

1½ cups granulated sugar

2 quarts fresh strawberries, washed, hulled, and halved

Juice of 1 small or ½ large lemon

1. In a medium-size saucepan, combine the sugar with 1½ cups water and bring it to a boil. Reduce the heat and simmer until the sugar completely dissolves, then remove it from the heat and let cool.

2. In a food processor, combine the strawberries, sugar syrup, and lemon juice, and blend it until smooth.

3. Using a wire-mesh sieve, or cheesecloth laid into a colander, strain the mixture to remove lumps and seeds if you like an ultrasmooth sorbet. You can skip this step if you like texture.

4. Line a 9-by-13-inch metal or Pyrex baking dish with plastic wrap, leaving some overhang on each side, and pour the mixture on top. Place the tray in the freezer and freeze until firm, anywhere from 2 to 8 hours.

5. Lift out the frozen fruit puree using the rim of plastic wrap. Break the frozen fruit puree into pieces, using a kitchen mallet, meat tenderizer, or the heavy handle of a knife. Working in small batches, process the frozen pieces in the food processor to smooth and blend.

6. Serve immediately or freeze the sorbet in an airtight container for up to a month.

Machine-Made: Ice Cream Makers

Laundry can be done by hand, but a washing machine makes the process faster and less laborious. It's the same with ice cream. A gadget or machine is nice to have, though not strictly necessary. Let's break them down by type.

ICE CREAM BALL

Looks like a soccer ball, and it's meant for playing and roughhousing. Fun on picnics, since it allows you to combine two summer activities—playing ball and making ice cream. Spoon fruit, milk, and other ingredients into a metal chamber, then put ice and rock salt into a chamber surrounding them to bring down the temperature to freezing. The motion of the ball mixes the ingredients and churns in air. Makes a quart or a pint at a time, depending on which model you choose.

FREEZER BOWL

Works like the ice cream ball, with an ice cream chamber surrounded by another chamber filled with a saltwater solution designed to reach and hold low temperatures. Fill it, put it in the freezer for half a day to overnight, then insert the bowl into the electric part of the maker, in which the mixing is done. Most designs make a quart of ice cream, just right for the average family. This is the go-to model at our house. (Essentially, this is a small modern version of the old-fashioned ice cream makers of my youth that made a gallon of ice cream by electrically turning the paddle inside a large metal container surrounded by ice and salt.)

HAND-CRANK MACHINE

Similar to the freezer bowl, ingredients go in an inner chamber, with ice and salt in a surrounding chamber. As with all old-fashioned household machines, elbow grease gets the job done. A hand crank is attached to an interior paddle that aerates the ice cream, dissolves ice crystals, and ensures smooth and even freezing.

SELF-CONTAINED COMPRESSOR FREEZER (AKA AUTOMATIC ICE CREAM MACHINE)

If you make a lot of ice cream and have the counter space, this may be your best bet. Double the size of a bread box, this houses a built-in freezer, allowing it to run continuously at a consistent, freezing temperature. No need to cool ingredients, exert physical labor, or add salt and ice.

#57 How to Make a Pot of Coffee

The best way to make coffee is a surprisingly controversial subject. Aficionados have lots of advanced ideas from farming to brew methods. But can you make a good cup of coffee with an everyday drip pot? Most definitely. It may not be the top choice of coffee snobs, but there's no denying that drip is the most common way Americans get their fix. You can set it and forget it, and if you do it right, you end up with an excellent cup of joe.

1 Get a clean start. If you use your coffeemaker every day, you'll need to clean the unit every few weeks and the carafe daily to avoid the bitter taste of old coffee (see How to Clean a Coffeemaker, below).

2 Use fresh, cold, filtered water and freshly ground beans that have been stored (not for too long!) in an airtight container.

3 Choose the right grind for your filter. For flat-bottomed paper filters, use a medium-size grind (close to the texture of fine sand). For conical filters, go with medium-fine (a little finer than salt). Plastic or metal reusable filters do best with a medium-coarse grind (similar to sea salt).

4 Pay attention to the ratio. A good place to start is 2 tablespoons ground coffee per 6 ounces water (1 cup on a typical coffeemaker). Experiment to find your preferred ratio.

5 Decant it while it's hot. If your drip coffeemaker has a glass carafe atop a hotplate-style heating element, don't let it just sit there and scorch. As soon as the cycle is complete, pour the coffee into an airtight thermal carafe. Leaving it on the burner, exposed to air, makes it bitter and burnt-tasting in very short order.

6 If you like milk in your coffee, warm it first. Cold milk will make your brew's temperature plummet on contact, and who wants lukewarm joe?

#58 How to Clean a Coffeemaker

All you need is the all-natural miracle cleaner: distilled white vinegar. When you smell a hint of stale coffee as you are adding water, it's probably time to clean. If you have hard water, clean it every couple of weeks anyway. Otherwise, every month or so.

1 Pour a mixture of half white vinegar and half cold water into the tank.

2 With no coffee in the basket, run the coffeemaker through a regular cycle.

3 After one cycle, cool the vinegar and water mixture and run it through a second time.

4 Discard the vinegar water and clean the carafe with dish soap and water, rinsing very thoroughly.

5 Fill the carafe with cold water, and, again with no coffee in the basket, run the plain water through a cycle to rinse out traces of vinegar or soap. Repeat until you no longer smell the scent of vinegar.

The Buzz on Caffeine

Caffeine levels vary by varietal, and blends will include a combination of beans with lower and higher concentrations. Keep in mind that milk displaces coffee, so a 20-ounce black coffee will typically have more caffeine than a 20-ounce latte. How long the grounds come into contact with the water also has an impact on caffeine levels: Espresso typically has less caffeine per ounce than drip coffee.

It's in the Water

If your coffee tastes flat, your chlorinated or fluoridated tap water may be to blame. Or if your well water is too hard or soft or slightly sulfurous, the coffee won't be as good as it could be. Always use filtered water for best results.

Proportion Is Key

The ratio of coffee to water is to some degree a matter of personal taste. My mother prefers her coffee a pale clear brown (my Irish husband calls it "bogwater"), whereas I like mine almost muddy dark, to be tempered with a lot of hot milk. But a good standard brewing proportion is 8 cups of water (as measured on the coffeemaker's carafe, usually 48 ounces) to a level ½ cup of ground coffee.

Bring on the Beans: Arabica vs. Robusta

The type of beans you buy does matter. The two main species grown are arabica and robusta. How they are classified depends on the region, climate, and elevation at which they grew. Those factors determine quality. Arabica coffee, which contains less caffeine, is more highly regarded than robusta coffee. Robusta is more bitter with less coffee flavor, but has better body than arabica. Cheaper and more abundant, robusta is used in instant coffee blends.

(continued)

✕ ✕

Baristas Share Their (Coffee) Tips

• Grind your own beans, fresh. The flavor is worth the extra effort.

• Keep beans and grounds in airtight containers in cool, dry, dark places. Don't freeze or refrigerate them! The beans will pick up odors.

• Use cold water to brew, regardless of the style of coffeemaker. For a French press or pour-over, fill your kettle with cold water for best flavor.

• If you like the scent and taste of cinnamon, vanilla, or cocoa, blend them with the beans and store in a sealed container. For subtle aromatics, use whole spices such as cinnamon sticks, vanilla beans, and cardamom pods instead of extracts and powders.

• Before pouring in the java, warm the mug with a few inches of boiling water. Wait a moment, then toss it. This helps maintain the temperature of your drink.

• Use an instant-read thermometer to test a pot of coffee the second it's finished brewing. If the temperature isn't between 195 and 205 degrees Fahrenheit, your brew will be bitter. Invest in a new unit. ✕

Regional Accents

The climates of the many coffee-growing countries and regions vary. The impact of this difference on coffee beans is unquestionable and affects signature traits such as body, acidity, and flavor. There are too many varieties to list, but it's worth trying a range of them to see what you like best. For example, Hawaiian Kona tends to be full-bodied, with a mild acidity and a sweet, winelike, mellow flavor. It's also generally among the most pricy. On a tight budget? Try Colombian beans, which boast a medium-full body, medium acidity, and a rich, caramel flavor.

The Roast

High-quality coffee beans from well-regarded regions are usually roasted lightly so as to maintain the signature flavors of the beans. As beans darken, their flavors are eclipsed by the flavors created by the roasting process itself. In darker roasts, the "roast flavor" is so dominant that it can be difficult to distinguish the origin of the beans, so lesser-quality beans are often used. As with all things coffee, it's a matter of personal taste.

#59 How to Brew a Cup of Tea

Yes, it's a simple four-step process: Boil water. Tea bags in. Pause. Tea bags out. But these tips will help you make a perfect, full-flavored cup each time. So many little things can go wrong, however. Was the water at a full rolling boil? Did you "scald" the teapot by pouring in some boiling water to take the chill off for a moment or two? Is your tea fresh, or has it been sitting in a cupboard for a year or two?

Don't Be Bitter

Tannins are compounds that occur naturally in tea, as well as in nuts, wine, cheeses, cranberries, and chocolate, and they are responsible for dark coloration, bitterness, and astringency. The bitterness of tea also depends on whether it's been fermented—the process through which leaves are crushed, exposing the cells to oxygen and causing them to oxidize and darken—and on brew time. In short, less fermentation means a milder cup, and longer brewing means more tannins are released, resulting in more bitter of a flavor. Therefore, lighter teas and less steep time mean less bitter tea. I prefer black tea, steeped for ages, so I temper my brew with plenty of milk and sugar. If you add milk to your tea, the tannins

target the proteins in the milk rather than those in your mouth, resulting in a much less astringent taste.

Stash It

No health-related concerns govern the storage of tea, but preserving flavor is a concern. Invest in airtight, light-proof containers for storing your tea and label them with the type of tea and the date you purchased it. Tea leaves keep a long time, but not indefinitely. A good rule of thumb is one year for loose tea and six months for tea bags. Store them sealed in a zip-top bag in the freezer and they'll keep twice as long.

A Gentle Pick-Me-Up

By dry weight, tea in fact contains more caffeine than coffee, but it requires less tea to brew a cup, so a cup of tea has less caffeine than a cup of coffee. When boiling water is poured over tea leaves, most of the caffeine is released in the first 30 to 90 seconds. At this point, the tea is at its most stimulating. Allow it to steep longer, and more tannins and L-theanine (an amino acid linked to relaxation of the nervous system) are extracted. These help cancel the effects of the caffeine, turning the beverage from stimulating to soothing. One study in the United Kingdom found black tea drinkers were able to de-stress faster than those who drank a fake tea substitute because their blood contained lower levels of the stress hormone cortisol.

Here's to Your Health

Tea contains flavonoids, antioxidants that are found in many fruits and vegetables as well as beverages such as wine and beer. Flavonoids may help combat the cancer-causing effects of free radicals, or damaged cells, and research suggests that people who drink two cups of tea or more a day have less heart disease, lower risk of stroke, and lower levels of "bad" cholesterol. Polyphenols and other compounds in the tea plant are also natural antimicrobials, promoting dental hygiene by killing harmful bacteria in the mouth.

1 Heat the water. The better the water, the better the tea. If your tap or well water is hard (has a high mineral content), use filtered, spring, or bottled water. Bring the water to a rolling boil for every type of tea except pure white—for this delicate flower, heat just to the point of boiling.

2 Heat your teapot and your cups by pouring in a few inches of boiling water, swirling it around, then pouring it out.

3 Measure your tea. For each 6 ounces of water, use 1 teaspoon of loose tea in a tea ball or sachet, or one tea bag. In the British Isles, most people add another "one for the pot" to make the flavor a little stronger.

4 Pour the boiling water over the tea and let it steep. How long you let it sit depends on variety and personal taste, but here are "ideal" steeping times.

White: Tea bag—1 minute, loose tea—3 minutes

Green: Tea bag—2 minutes, loose tea—4 minutes

Oolong: Tea bag—3 minutes, loose tea—5 minutes

Black: Tea bag—4 minutes, loose tea—6 to 7 minutes

5 To serve, remove the tea bag, tea ball, or sachet, and allow the tea to stand and cool for a minute or so. It's most common to offer lemon slices, milk, and sugar to guests, but there's no law on the books forbidding maple syrup, stevia, orange slices, cinnamon sticks, or even peppermint candies!

⤬ ⤬

Just the One

Suppose you don't want to make a pot and only want one perfect delicious cup of tea for yourself? It does help to "scald" the mug or cup by swishing it out with boiling water for a moment or two, before you pour that water down the drain and start fresh. For best results, be sure to let your mug of tea brew for 4 to 5 minutes before adding milk or sugar. ⤬

Your Cup of Tea:
A Guide to Types and Varieties

All tea comes from the exact same species of plant, *Camellia sinensis,* a bush whose leaves are turned into a seemingly endless variety of tea—black, green, and white. The range of types and styles is determined by where the bush is grown, the level of maturity at which the leaves are picked, and how the leaves are processed after harvesting. For instance, some varieties of tea leaves are left in a climate-controlled room to oxidize—a process called fermentation—in order to darken them and draw out specific flavors. Note that herbal teas, also called tisanes or infusions, are a totally different matter and can be made from any herb, fruit, or spice.

Black tea. Fully fermented. The most common type, the tea is reddish in hue with a fruity and flowery aroma. Varieties include Darjeeling and Ceylon, or blends such as English Breakfast.

Oolong tea. Semi-fermented. The name translates to "black dragon," but the brew is in fact a golden-brown because the fermentation process is stopped when the leaves are merely yellowed, and not fully darkened. This tea has a unique, delicate flavor, and you're likely to be offered it in Chinese restaurants.

Green tea. Unfermented. Green tea leaves are heated as soon after harvesting as possible to prevent fermentation. This process preserves the highest level of vitamins, minerals, and antioxidants. Yellowish-green in color, and the flavor is herbal and grassy.

White tea. Unfermented. Preserved using the same process as green tea, but only the buds of the plant, not the leaves, are used. White tea is more delicate in flavor than green, and it lacks the grassy tones.

#60 How to (Mostly) Decaffeinate Tea

It's impossible to remove 100 percent of the caffeine from tea or coffee—even commercially decaffeinated varieties still contain some caffeine—but this neat trick will remove up to 80 percent of the caffeine in your cup. If you have sensitivities, though, stick to herbal.

1 Put a tea bag or sachet or tea ball filled with tea leaves into a mug or tea pot.

2 Pour in boiling water.

3 Steep for 30 to 90 seconds—no more than that! Pour off the steeped tea.

4 Refill the cup or pot with fresh boiling water and re-steep to your taste.

In the British Isles, there's a little running joke that whoever pours the tea for a group is called "Mother," regardless of gender. The volunteer reaching for the teapot might say, "I'll be Mother."

#61 How to Make Iced Tea

Leaving tea and water to brew in the sun, though picturesque, is unfortunately not a safe practice. Water heated only by the sun won't top 130 degrees Fahrenheit, and to kill harmful water-borne bacteria, it must reach 195 degrees Fahrenheit and stay there for 3 to 5 minutes. Instead, make it in the fridge, cold-brew style.

1 Combine 8 cups cold water with 6 tablespoons loose-leaf tea or 12 standard-size tea bags in a covered pitcher.

2 Refrigerate for 24 to 36 hours, until it's ruby red in color.

3 Strain out the tea leaves with a fine-mesh sieve or remove the tea bags, and serve.

X X X X X X X X X X X X

Cloudy to Clear

Cloudiness in iced tea won't affect the taste or harm you, but it's not as pretty. To keep your tea from clouding, never stick hot tea in the refrigerator—bring it to room temperature first. Hard water (water that naturally has a lot of dissolved minerals in it) will interact with the tea's natural tannins and cloud it. Use bottled water if your tap water is hard. If your iced tea does cloud, pour in some boiling water and let it rest. This should clear it up. ✕

Recipe: SOUTHERN-STYLE SWEET ICED TEA

It seems so simple, yet there are so many potential mishaps when making iced tea, including it turning cloudy or tasting bitter. Here's how to brew true-flavored, crystal-clear, Southern-style sweet tea. If you love a glass full of clanking ice cubes, brew your tea stronger than recommended to compensate for the dilution ice will cause as it melts.

Makes 2 quarts

6 black tea bags
⅛ teaspoon baking soda
1 cup granulated sugar

1. Put the tea bags and baking soda (my mom would say "a big ol' pinch") into a large heat proof glass measuring cup or ceramic pitcher, and pour in 2 cups boiling water. Cover and let steep for 20 minutes.

2. Remove the tea bags, taking care not to squeeze them because bruising the leaves and using these very concentrated drops of liquid will make the whole pitcher bitter.

3. Add the sugar to the still-warm tea, then pour this concentrate into a 2-quart pitcher and add 6 cups cold water. Let cool before refrigerating.

#62 How to Clean Your Kitchen
(Without Chemicals)

Learning the basics of cleaning and sanitizing in the kitchen keeps family and guests safe and healthy, and it keeps your kitchen free of dirt, odors, and food-borne contamination. Disease-causing bacteria hide out in more places than just cutting boards. Kitchen sponges, dishtowels, frequently touched surfaces such as the faucet or the inside of the sink, and even your own hands can harbor germs. Fortunately, you don't have to shell out for pricey, gimmicky, name-brand cleansers and gadgets, or depend on harsh chemicals, to keep your kitchen clean and safe. All you need is a little knowledge.

1 Clean wooden and plastic cutting boards, countertops, and the inside of the sink by scrubbing them with a paste made from equal parts baking soda, salt, and water. Rinse with hot water.

2 Rinse and wring kitchen sponges, and then microwave them on high for 2 minutes to kill bacteria. Zap barely damp dish towels on high for 1 minute.

3 To deodorize and sanitize cutting boards, rub with the cut side of half a lemon or wipe with undiluted lemon juice straight from the bottle.

4 Food particles cling to damp pipes in your drain, a perfect breeding ground for germs, not to mention clogs. Pour boiling water down your sink daily to keep pipes clean and odor-free.

5 For a natural abrasive cleanser, use a damp rag and a handful of kosher or rock salt to scrub anything from wooden cutting boards to cast-iron skillets to the tea kettle.

6 Spray undiluted white vinegar on stainless steel and chrome faucets, aluminum sinks, and on silver and copper items in the kitchen to clean and lightly disinfect, then polish with a soft, damp cloth.

7 Bleach's "green-ness" is hotly debated. Chlorine is natural and found in the human body, but overuse causes buildup in water tables, harming the earth. For home use, just a little bleach is needed to do the job. Use it in a ratio of 1 part bleach to 10 parts water to disinfect and kill germs. (Efficacy wanes with time and exposure to light.) If you prefer, substitute hydrogen peroxide, which also kills germs and removes stains.

Choosing and Using Your Cutting Board

Every type of board has pros and cons, so, if possible, keep several on hand and dedicate them to specific tasks to avoid cross-contamination. I recommend buying multiple sizes and thicknesses of wooden boards. As your cooking skills advance and you get a handle on your storage limitations, expand from there.

Thick plastic. Affordable, colorful, and dishwasher safe, thick plastic boards can double as trivets. Biggest pro: easy to bleach and dishwash. Biggest con: will nick and stain over time.

Flexible plastic. These are cheap and easy to store, clean, and sanitize. Biggest pro: bendable and rollable for easy food transfer. Biggest con: Sharp knives will eventually cut through them.

Corian. Tough like a countertop, these come in a variety of sizes and colors. Marks from use can be repaired. Biggest pro: The nonporous surface is virtually stainproof and resists bacterial growth. Biggest con: Heat will damage the surface.

Tempered glass. Stylish and complementary to kitchen décor, these durable boards are heavier than most but protect surfaces from extremely hot cookware. Biggest pros: the most resistant to bacteria; won't stain. Biggest con: The sound of the knife hitting the surface can be like nails on a chalkboard. And it's not very good for the sharpness of your knives, either.

Bamboo. Objects of beauty, these eco-friendly boards are water-resistant and durable. Harder than maple but lighter than oak, this material requires more care than some cutting boards. Before the first use, treat it with a food-grade oil. Biggest pro: won't shrink or swell like wooden boards, giving them a long lifespan. Biggest cons: cost and care. Bamboo tends to be more expensive, and you have to season it regularly.

Wood. Affordable hardwood boards, usually made from maple, are great for fruits and vegetables. Good ones can be sanded or replaned when the surface wears. I love the sound of a knife chopping on wood! Biggest pros: easy on knife edges; long-lasting; shown to be more sanitary than plastic. Biggest con: see "Bamboo."

When in doubt, throw it out. If your board's cracked, or too deeply nicked to sanitize or resurface properly, toss it. Yes, even if it was expensive! Safety first—if you can't afford another pricey one at toss time, buy some thin plastic ones and save up your pennies for a good one.

Bacteria Basics

Kitchens are notorious for hosting bacterial nasties and gruesome germs. Worst of all, these lurking monsters are invisible to the naked eye, which means vigilance is required.

Salmonella. Foods contaminated by animal feces transmit this bacteria, which can cause fever, intestinal cramping and diarrhea, nausea and vomiting, and chills. Symptoms appear within eight to seventy-two hours of contact. The most frequently reported bacterial infection according to the CDC, *Salmonella* poisoning often occurs when raw meat mingles with other foods through contaminated dishes, knives, countertops, and cutting surfaces.

Campylobacter jejuni. This bacteria travels in raw and undercooked meat and poultry, and infection targets the digestive tract, causing stomach pain, nausea, vomiting, and diarrhea. Unpasteurized milk often harbors it as do unpasteurized cheeses. The CDC estimates that 47 percent of raw commercial chicken breasts contain *Campylobacter*. When handling poultry at home, take meticulous care to sanitize surfaces (including the sink), and hands must be washed before touching other foods or serving utensils. Even a single drop of liquid from contaminated meat can cause infection.

Staphylococcus. The bacteria *Staphylococcus aureus*, found in animal products, produces a toxin when those foods are stored at the

(continued)

wrong temperature. When present in poultry and other meats, there is danger of cross-contamination of other foods such as in mayonnaise-based salads, poultry and egg dishes, and casseroles. Symptom, including nausea, vomiting, diarrhea, mild fever, and severe abdominal cramps, appear quickly, sometimes within six hours. Dehydration is a major danger.

E. coli. Many strains of *E. coli* (*Escherichia coli*) don't cause illness, but the most harmful can damage the small intestine, causing bloody diarrhea and death. Found in seafood, ground beef, unpasteurized milk, and raw vegetables, *E. coli* is easily transmitted human to human after improper hand-washing, and is perhaps the most difficult to ward against. Best practices include storing fish and meats at proper temperatures, thoroughly washing vegetables and fruits, and frequent handwashing.

What's in My Cleaning Products?

The obvious solution to all this potentially dangerous bacteria in the kitchen is to clean it. But be aware of the possible harm lurking in commercial cleaning products as well. Science has continued to uncover possible negative effects from the stuff we've long been squirting and spraying all over our cooking surfaces. Parabens and phenols, and bacteria-killers such as triclosan, even the strong fragrances that used to signal "clean," may be doing harm to our bodies long-term, and to our environment.

Increasingly, there are many widely available commercial cleaning products made with all-natural ingredients that are extremely effective. When our grandmothers used to scrub with baking soda and vinegar, turns out they may have known best! So even if you want to scrub your dirty floor with the heavy-duty cleaners, you might want to consider keeping industrial cleaning chemicals off your cooking surfaces, cutting boards, stovetop, counters, and pots.

⬠⬠

Environmentally Friendly All-Purpose Cleaner

Using a funnel, combine 1 teaspoon baking soda, ½ teaspoon dish soap, and 2 tablespoons distilled white vinegar in a 16-oz. spray bottle. Cap the bottle, shake gently, and let stand for 5 minutes. Fill the bottle about three-quarters of the way with warm water and shake again. For a nice scent, add 3 drops essential oil. For the kitchen, I like bergamot or eucalyptus.

SEWING

At one time, everyone but the very wealthy made their own clothes. With the advent of inexpensive machine-made clothing, sewing became a lost art for most people. Some sewing, such as hemming, repairing tears, and replacing buttons, can save you a lot of time and money if you do It yourself. Some of it is practical, such as making a pillow of an exact size. And some of it is not strictly necessary but easy and immensely satisfying: "See these curtains? I *made* them."

SEWING TOOL KIT

Pincushion or other holder

Measuring tape

Thread (multiple spools in different colors)

Seam gauge

Thimbles

Hand-sewing needles

Glass-head pins

Small sewing scissors

Color-ball pins

Flat-head pins

Buttons

Large sewing shears

Needle case

Fabric markers

Seam ripper

Sewing machine (optional)

#63 How to Thread a Needle

Many people may think *I can thread a needle*. They're probably right. But with some tasks, such as cutting an onion (see page 32), there may be a better way than the one you were taught. I don't have much advice about getting a rich man into heaven, but I can tell you how to reduce the pain of threading a needle.

Learning to Sew

You don't *have* to know how to sew in the same way that you should know how to cook at least the very basics. Sewing is not a daily task—the way eating is—and, yet, you *do* wear clothes every day and they *are* going to need some minor repairs. Being able to sew on a button is an incredibly valuable skill. There's something very satisfying, in our machine-made, store-bought world of clothing, about doing a peaceful, old-fashioned task like stitching up a tear with an invisible seam. And knowing how to hem your own pants is an economic skill, too—tailoring has become an extremely pricey proposition these days: perhaps because so few of us know how.

A sewing machine is not strictly necessary if all you want to do is make minor repairs. But very effective and efficient sewing machines have become seriously inexpensive and are widely available at big-box stores, so as you learn the joys of stitching fabric together, it makes sense to acquire one. It makes jobs such as stitching up a long torn seam, as in a bedsheet, into a breeze, and soon you may find that running up an easy set of curtains is well worth your time. Whether you ever make an item of clothing is up to you, but at least you'll be able to keep the clothing that you have in good shape with very little effort.

Here's the very core of what you need to know (and to have on hand) to start sewing.

Shopping for Thread

Don't be intimidated by the myriad brands and weights of thread available at fabric stores and in the notions departments of drugstores. They each have a different application, so it's good to have an assortment on hand if you plan to sew with various fabrics. Almost any project done by a beginner can be sewn with these five threads:

Polyester/cotton. Sometimes labeled "all-purpose," it's actually polyester thread wrapped in cotton. The best choice to have at home for hand or machine sewing, for use with cotton and cotton blends, polyester/cotton thread is also good for sewing on buttons because it combines flexibility with added strength.

100 percent polyester. A smart, basic choice for most hand or machine sewing, this thread is most suitable for synthetic fabrics or stretchy knits. If used on flat cotton, the stitches might look waxy and stand out.

100 percent cotton. Best for light- to medium-weight fabrics without much "give" or stretch to them. Cotton thread will not stretch, and the stitches can break if used on a stretchy knit fabric.

Fine cotton or silk. For use on sheer fabric and delicate goods such as light scarves or lingerie. For ultralight fabrics with lots of "give," choose silk.

Heavy-duty or T-40 weight. The best bets for upholstery fabric, pillows made of heavy fabric, thick woolen coats, and denim.

Shopping for Needles

It's a good idea to have a multipack of needles on hand. Most packaged kits come with everything a beginner needs for simple hand-sewing projects, from mending to buttons. Here are the five essential needles to start out with:

SHARPS

BALL POINT

QUILTING/BETWEENS

EMBROIDERY/CREWEL

CHENILLE

Sharps. The most common and useful type. They are of medium length, standard thickness, and of course, very sharp. Sharps are good for pretty much all cotton and synthetic fabrics.

Ball point. The second-most-common basic needle. Use with knits, as well as some laces and lingerie fabrics. The rounded point glides between the threads of the weave, and the narrow shaft makes it useful for fine work.

Quilting/betweens. Short needles with small, rounded eyes. The short length allows for faster, more accurate stitching. For detailed handiwork and appliqués but with heavier weight thread, quilting/betweens are also useful for heavy fabrics such as denim and canvas.

Embroidery/crewel. Same length and thickness as sharps, but with a longer eye to accommodate heavier threads.

Chenille. Very thick, very sharp, and with a long eye. Ideal for very thick thread, ribbon, or multiple strands of thread and for stitching through coarse fabrics.

1 Cut the thread with very sharp scissors, at an angle. A 45-degree angle is ideal for pushing thread through a small needle's eye, and a sharp cut reduces fuzz at the thread's end.

2 Hold the needle and thread over a white background. It'll make them easier to see. Keep an index card in your sewing kit, or pierce one with a hole punch, thread a loop of yarn through it, and pin it to your pincushion.

3 Stiffen the thread. A small tin of beeswax from a sewing or craft store is a great item to keep on hand. It's cheap, and it lasts forever. In a pinch, use saliva.

4 Buy a needle threader. This small gadget consists of a thin, flat disc of aluminum and a diamond-shaped, very thin wire. To use it, hold the disc and insert the wire through the eye of the needle. Poke the thread through the "giant" eye. As you draw the needle threader's wire backward through the eye, the thread follows.

5 Stop the shakes. If your hand isn't steady, use a pair of tweezers to hold the thread.

6 Make it a match. Your thread size and eye size should be compatible.

Don't even try to stuff thick embroidery thread through the tiny eye of a sharp.

7 Turn it around. Often, due to manufacturing, the eye of a needle will be larger on one side than the other.

8 Close one eye. This balances your close-up vision—human eyes are bifocal and threading needles is done at immediate range.

#64 How to Care for Your Needles

It's true that sewing needles aren't prohibitively costly, nor are they hard to come by. But why not use them to their best advantage, in the interest of economy and sustainability? With frequent use, the nonstick coatings wear off, the points dull, the eyes wear out, and the shafts weaken. Here's how to make 'em last.

1 Start with the best. Needles eventually wear out. Although inexpensive ones may be fine if you plan to sew on only the odd button here and there, if you plan to learn to sew, the good ones offer superior ease of use and longevity. Buy fewer, better-quality needles, like those that are platinum plated.

2 Use the right tool. Pulling a too-thick needle through fine fabric or jamming a soft tip through tough material will wear out your needles more quickly. If in doubt, test a needle on a patch of fabric that won't be seen, such as inside a hem seam: Thread it and run it through in a few loose stitches (that you can pull out) and make sure there aren't visible holes left behind.

3 Safe and dry. Store your needles in a good pincushion—emphasis on "good." Ideally, it should be covered with wool felt and stuffed with something like sawdust that will keep the needle dry and polish it each time it's inserted.

4 Out with the bad. A small nick or even a bit of debris on a needle may not be visible, but if you feel any sort of a pull in the fabric, or a faint catch as you try to push the needle through, start fresh. Otherwise, you may damage your fabric and you're less likely to get a smooth, flat seam.

#65 How to Sew on a Button

We've all had the experience of preparing for a date or a big meeting at work, or being late for a class only to find we've popped a button. I've resorted to stapling my blouse together or trying to hold the top of my jeans together with a paper clip. But now I play it smart. I don't go anywhere without my compact emergency sewing kit. With just three basic tools from your kit, you can sew on that button by following a few easy steps

The Basic Tools

Two needles. In your kit, you should have a sharp needle. This is your go-to and will work for almost any job. It's a thinnish, medium-length needle with a sharp point. For the second needle, choose a quilting needle (aka "between") for heavier fabrics such as denim or canvas. You'll need one of these needles to sew and the other to anchor the button. If you have only one needle, use a straightened paper clip, toothpick, or safety pin for the anchor.

Thread. Start with at least 12 inches of thread. I like to double my thread so it's stronger and easier to knot at the end—I suggest using 24

inches if you have enough to spare. You can match the color of either the garment or the button. If that's not possible, use black, white, or tan—whatever color is the most neutral.

A button. It's best to use the one that popped off. If that's not possible, check your garment for spare buttons. Sometimes extra buttons are sewn directly onto the inside placket of a shirt or into the waistband of pants.

Scissors (optional). If you can't lay your hands on a pair, use a nail clipper or saw the thread on the sharp edge of a table.

1 Thread the needle and make a knot. If you cut 24 inches of thread, double it over by threading the needle and hold the two ends together. Pull the needle until the thread is taut, leaving two equal lengths of thread on either side. Tie a knot at the end of the thread by making a circle, pushing the ends of the thread through, and pulling tight. If the knot seems so small that it will pull through the fabric, repeat this procedure, layering the knots until it's thick enough to catch the fabric.

If you have less than 24 inches of thread, don't double it over. Thread the needle and make sure that the "short end" is about 3 to 4 inches long. This end will remain unknotted. Holding the other end of the thread between your thumb and forefinger, loosely wrap the short end around your forefinger two or three times while keeping the thread in place with your thumb.

Slide your forefinger down toward the base of your thumb, twisting the threads together until the thread forms a loop and pushes off

the forefinger end. Grasp the loop between your thumb and forefinger at the point where the loop joins the rest of the thread. Pull the loop until a knot is formed. You'll be left with two lengths of thread: a short one with no knot and a long one with a knot at the end.

2 Find the target point. Insert your needle from the back side of the fabric to the front, where the button used to sit. Then insert the needle through the front, so that it comes out the back again. Using the same technique, make another stitch to create a small X where the button will be fastened. This X serves two purposes: It's the target you want to hit when sewing on the button, and it reinforces the spot, ensuring that future stress won't pull the button off again.

3 Position and anchor the button. Lay your button on the X and begin sewing it on. Insert the needle behind where the button sits and push it from the back to the front through one of the holes in the button. As you loop through one of the four holes (depending on the button), lay a needle, toothpick, or paper clip on top. This is your anchor: You'll loop the thread over it.

Pull the thread all the way through until the knot presses

against the back side of the fabric. Use your finger to keep the button in its place.

From the front side, insert the needle through the hole opposite the one you came up through. Push it through until the thread is taut. You'll now see a small line of thread across the button, connecting two of the four holes (or the two holes, if it's a two-hole button). Repeat this pattern three or four times for every set of two holes. The needle, toothpick, or paper clip you are using as an anchor will look like a silent movie damsel tied to a railroad track!

4 Create the shank. On the final pass of the needle, sew from back to front of the fabric, but don't push the needle through the button's hole. Pierce the fabric in the same position, turn the needle to the side, and pull it up next to the button, stretching the thread taut.

Next, wrap the length of thread behind the button, so that it encircles the threads you've already stitched. Do this five or six times,

effectively creating a tied bundle of thread.

When finished, pull the thread until it's taut, pierce the fabric behind the button, and pull it through to the back side. Now, you're ready to tie off the thread.

5 Secure the knot and free the needle. Create a knot on the back side of the fabric by inserting your needle to make a shallow dive into the fabric and, before pulling it taut, push it through the loop. Regardless of whether you tie the knot using your fingers or the needle, position it firmly against the back side of the fabric. Repeat this process three or four times.

Finally, pull out the anchor and voilà! Your button will likely be more secure than it was the first time it was sewn on.

#66 How to Make Your Own Sewing Kit

Pack this handy emergency sewing kit in your purse, backpack, or suitcase, and you'll never be caught unprepared—it contains just the basics, all in one place, for simple repairs. Here's what you'll need to include:

• A small, sturdy, puncture-proof container with a tight-fitting lid (think mint tin or lozenge box)

• A rectangle of medium-weight cardboard (cut from a cracker box, 3 by 4 inches)

• Safety pins (three different sizes)

• A needle threader

• Needles (sharps and ball points)

• All-purpose threads in basic colors:

• Several buttons of different sizes and weights

• A tiny pair of scissors (available in craft stores and the notions section of dry goods stores)

1 Using sharp scissors, cut very shallow slits up one of the long sides of the cardboard rectangle at regular intervals. Turn it around and do the same on the other long side, exactly across from each cut you've already made.

2 Wind black thread around the topmost part of the cardboard, inserting it into the slits to hold it in place and create a kind of a "skein." Don't pull too tight or the cardboard will buckle. After winding the thread around five or six times, tuck in the end so that you can easily find it again later.

3 Do the same with your other thread colors until the slots on the card are filled. It's useful to have white or off-white, black, navy, brown, green, and red.

4 Tuck the needles inside the thread, piercing the cardboard to hold them in place. You can also fasten your safety pins around a loop of thread so they're easy to find.

Some Helpful Glossary Terms

• *Pinking shears.* Scissors with a zigzag cutting edge that looks like a long row of little teeth

• *Tailor's chalk.* A thin flat piece of hard chalk or soapstone used by tailors and seamstresses for making temporary marks on cloth

• *Seam ripper.* A specialty notion with no moving parts that features a sharp, curved blade ending in a sharp point on one side and a small ball on the other edge that glides over fabric and helps protect it

• *Inseam.* The seam of a trouser leg that runs from the crotch down to the bottom of the hem, alongside the inner thigh and calf

• *Rayon.* Originally named artificial silk or wood silk, rayon is a transparent fiber made of processed cellulose. Cellulose fibers from wood or cotton are dissolved in alkali to make a solution called viscose, which is then extruded through a spinneret into an acid bath to reconvert the viscose into cellulose. Unlike nylon and polyester, rayon wicks water, so it's ideal for use as a clothing textile. ×

#67 How to Baste

Basting! It's not just for turkeys. Basting, also called tacking, means to sew easily removable stitches to temporarily hold fabric together. Why do double the work? Basting can help you save time in the long run and is often worth the extra step. It is possible to baste with a sewing machine set to big loose stitches, but hand-basting is more common. To hand-baste, you'll use a running stitch.

In Praise of Basting

- Basting stitches on seams let you test the fitting (side seams) or placement (darts) before final stitches.

- Basting can hold slippery fabric in place while you sew regular stitches.

- Basting allows you to hold together two layers of fabric in order to work them as one layer.

- Basting lets you hold trim or bric-a-brac in place until you firmly sew it on.

1 Use straight pins to pin together the layers or pieces the way you'd like them sewn.

2 Thread a needle and knot the end.

3 Do not baste exactly where you will sew the permanent stitches. If you sew over the basting stitches, it will be difficult to remove them.

4 Starting on the back side of the fabric, insert the needle through to the other side, through both layers of fabric, allowing the knot to stop the thread. Then push it back through in the opposite direction. Move on to repeat this process everywhere you intend to sew a final seam. This is called a running stitch.

You can choose the size of the stitches: long or short. (Long stitches take less time.)

5 Once you have basted the layers of fabric you want to attach, cut the thread at the needle and tie a simple knot to secure the stitching.

#68 How to Attach a Snap

When the fabric around a button seems worn and you want to secure it in a new way, consider a snap. The easiest way to install a snap doesn't involve sewing, but rather using one of two snap-specific tools that not everyone has handy: a cylinder piece for hammering or specialized pliers.

There are two sides to a snap: male and female. They both consist of two parts: the male, the stud and the ring prong, and the female, the socket and the ring prong. The stud "snaps" into the socket, which is the hollowed-out side; the prongs are what fasten both the stud and the socket to the fabric.

Tools and Hardware

If using a hammer tool, position it so that when struck by a hammer (which you'll also need), the prongs bend around the stud or socket. If using a plier tool, fit the head of the pliers around the stud or socket opposite the prongs and squeeze in order to bend the prongs.

If you don't want to invest in the hammer or plier tools, or if you don't want the metal rings to show, a sew-on snap is the best option.

This snap is best used in a place on a garment that won't be subjected to too much stress or strain. A snap is the best choice when one garment edge overlaps another, hiding the snap from view. What you see on the outside of the garment is smooth fabric with an edge.

Unlike the first snap defined in this section, the sew-on snap has two parts instead of four: the ball side (aka the stud side) and the socket side. Here's how to fasten a snap to your garments.

1 Determine and mark the placement of your snap.

2 Thread and knot a needle (follow Step 1 in How to Sew on a Button, page 124).

3 Lay the ball side of the snap on the inside hemmed edge of the layer of material that will overlap the other layer of material.

4 Holding the ball side of the snap in place, work from the back side of the material. Plunge the threaded needle through the fabric and one of the holes on the outer edge of the snap.

5 Sink the needle in at the outer rim of the snap. Keep the needle in between the outer layer of fabric and the layer to which the snap is being attached. This will hide the stitching from the right side.

6 Working with only one hole at a time, bring the needle up again along the outer edge of the snap next to the same hole your first stitch went through. Next, take the needle down again through the same hole. Repeat this process four or five times.

7 Repeat steps 4 through 6 for every hole in the ball side of the snap. Move from one hole to the next by slipping your needle through the two layers of material.

8 Secure the stitches by making tiny knots close to the first series of stitches.

9 Rub tailor's chalk along the ball of the snap and overlap the edges of the garment the way they will lay when the garment is finished.

10 Press down on the ball firmly so that a chalk mark is transferred to the underlying layer of material to mark where the stud or socket half of the snap will be sewn on.

11 Center the stud or socket half over the chalk mark and hold it in place.

12 Repeat steps 4 through 8, attaching the other side of the snap to the material.

#69 How to Fix a Rip in Your Jeans

Fixing a pair of blue jeans is the right project for a beginning mender. Let's just assume your jeans are more in the Levi or Lee class than the top-tier Joe's Jeans or 7 for All Mankind class. Unlike with a filmy nightgown, or silk shirt, repairs in jeans are fairly forgiving. Even if they're not perfect, they'll still be wearable. There are many types of tears: tri-corner tears, holes, frays, punctures, and rips. And these bad things happen to good fabrics. There's no "one size fits all" way to tackle these heartaches, but here's some advice to help you deal with common denim boo-boos:

Fusible Tricot Reinforcement

To repair a heavy fabric like jeans, an iron-on patch coupled with stitching may be your best bet. This works especially well with a three-corner (L-shaped) tear. Fusible tricot interfacing works best on 100 percent cotton fabrics like denim. You can purchase fusible tricot by the yard at sewing and craft stores, but beware! It must be preshrunk before you use it, or it will later buckle and bunch when you wash your jeans. To preshrink, simply soak the whole piece in warm water, then hang it to dry before using it. There is also tricot marked "preshrunk" available, so buy that if possible.

1 Once the tricot is dry, turn your jeans inside out, and cut a piece of tricot about twice as large as the tear or the hole so that there will be a solid square or rectangle over the ripped area. Preheat the iron to the highest setting.

2 Place a press cloth over the tricot, lightly spray it with water, and then hold the iron down firmly for about 15 seconds. Lift the iron, move it to the next area,

slightly overlapping where you have already fused the interfacing (like mowing a lawn), and repeat, until the whole sheet of tricot has been fused.

3 Next, turn the jeans right side out, keeping the press cloth in place, and repeat the process. Use a stamping motion with the iron, instead of a gliding motion, when applying the fusible tricot.

4 Let the whole project cool completely before taking the jeans off your ironing board. This will take only a few moments, but the freshly ironed synthetic material is very hot, so be careful.

5 Once the tricot is cool, thread a needle with dark thread. Working from the inside to the outside of the fabric, pull the thread until the knot is firmly in place on the inside of your jeans. Make evenly spaced stitches shaped like an X all around the perimeter of the tear. True, this won't be as dainty as a machine-sewn repair, but for work jeans, it will do the job and also make sure the torn section isn't vulnerable or weak.

Simple and Secure Hand Stitching

If you don't have access to an iron-on patch for reinforcement, hand sewing is a fine alternative. The doubled-over thread will hold up well, and hand stitching allows for freedom of movement as you work.

1 Take 24 inches of thread and double it by bringing the ends together. Push the ends through a quilting needle, so that you have a double string of thread for extra reinforcement.

2 Working from the inside of the jeans, push the needle through the fabric at one end of the tear. Using your finger, hold about an inch of the thread on the underside of the fabric. Go back through the fabric with the needle, making sure to pass it through the loop of thread you're holding secure on the inside of the jeans. This will secure the thread without a knot.

3 Holding the torn fabric in place, stitch along the edges of the tear by passing the needle up and down through the fabric, in a looping motion.

4 If you start to run out of thread, tie a knot on one of your "down" passes. To do this, pass the needle under a couple of stitches four or five times, then tie off the thread and cut it with scissors.

5 Thread the needle and repeat the process until you've stitched around the entire tear.

#70 How to Fix a Hole in Your Shirt

For finer fabrics, in places that show, you'll want to take extra care when mending a wardrobe mishap. Try this technique with a basic cotton or cotton-polyester blend shirt. Make sure your iron is ready to go on the appropriate setting for the fabric.

1 Start smart. With sharp fabric scissors, cut around the hole, making a neat square. Trim any loose threads or frayed edges. At each corner of the square hole, cut a ¼-inch notch at a 45-degree angle. Turn your garment inside out, then fold the narrow flaps formed by your cuts onto the material's inside, aka "wrong" side, and iron flat.

2 Match and mark. Find a matching piece of fabric. If the hole is small, you can sometimes use part of the shirttail. For broadcloth oxford shirts, it's sometimes possible to find a near match at the local thrift store. Barring all those, try your local fabric store. (Don't forget to bring the garment you want to match!) Mark and measure a square of the size you'll need from the matching fabric, and cut it a ½ inch bigger than the square hole you've cut in your shirt.

3 Line it up. Turn your shirt inside out and line up the patch on top of the square hole. Make sure the right side of the fabric is turned up and the grains are going in the same direction. Turn your shirt right side out and use straight pins to secure the patch. Baste all around the patch (see How to Baste, page 127). Remove the pins.

Over 2 billion T-shirts are sold every year, worldwide. A single T-shirt can require up to 700 gallons of water to produce (so learning to mend them is helpful to the environment)!

4 Sew it together. Turn your shirt inside out. Fold back the ½ inch of excess fabric so it's flush with the folded edge of the hole, folding the corners over each other. Insert the needle through the folded edge of the replacement fabric patch, just catching the very edge. Next, stitch up diagonally through the folded edge of the original shirt, securing the two fabrics together. Do this around the entire square. When you've sewn the whole square, remove the basting thread by snipping the knot off with scissors and gently pulling it out.

5 Add a finishing touch, or "create a clean edge." Use a catch-stitch to finish the edges of the patch inside the shirt. Catch-stitches hold fabrics against each other, as in hems or seam allowances. To make one, you need to "catch" a few threads from the underside of the top layer of fabric. Insert the needle, and then gently pick up a few threads from the very surface of the top fabric layer, without pushing the needle all the way through. It's a delicate procedure, and you have to kind of feel your way to it, so try a few sample stitches to get the hang of it. You may need to unstitch some initially. This style of stitching is referred to as "blind" stitching because it is invisible from the outside. It has some give, but it holds well. Using this technique will ensure that the patch stays in place.

6 Tack the patch. Cut off the tips of the patch's corners at 45-degree angles. Fold back each edge ¼ inch. Cross-stitch the edges to the shirt, picking up only one or two threads with each stitch. Inserting the needle from right to left, create a series of tiny Xs.

7 Press it and go. When you're finished with the sewing, iron the patch in place with the shirt inside out. Allow the area to cool, then iron the shirt from the front, starting with the patch.

#71 How to Hem Pants
(Measuring, Pinning, and the Invisible Hand Stitch)

Hemming a pair of pants is a great beginner project. Nice-looking results are easy to achieve, and the effort is rewarded in spades. Standard pant lengths for off-the-rack clothes simply do not flatter everyone. People's bodies vary: This man needs a large waist, so the pants are cut long. This woman has a long torso, but short legs. That kid grew six inches in a year, and their ankles are sticking out like a baby giraffe's. The correct pant length goes a long way toward cutting a fine figure.

Don't suffer pants that don't fit, and don't go broke over pricey trips to the tailor and dry cleaner. Follow these steps, and you'll be walking tall in no time.

Glossary of Hemming Accessories

Sewing pins. Used to temporarily hold fabric together prior to sewing and when attaching or cutting patterns. The shaft of the pin is typically made of brass, nickel, steel, or a combination of those metals. When used for machine sewing, you can quickly and easily remove them as you stitch. Sold in a variety of lengths and thicknesses, as well as with different types of pinheads:

- **Glass-head pins.** Straight pins topped with large, colored balls made of glass, making them easier to see and grasp, and allowing them to withstand heat from irons and dryers.

- **Color-ball pins.** Like glass heads, but less expensive, and topped with plastic heads. Not suitable for use with heat.

- **Flat-head pins.** The most common type of straight pin, they feature blunt-nubbed "heads" of the same metal as the pin shaft.

Seam gauge. A small ruler used in sewing. Generally 6 inches in length, it has a sliding marker, or flange, that is set to a specific measurement and is especially useful when measuring the same length repeatedly.

1 Wash it. Check the fabric care label on your pants. If your pants are made of cotton, rayon, or a blend of both, preshrink them by following the manufacturer's washing and drying directions. Iron the pants before you start to stretch and smooth the material. A warm wash also gets rid of any stiffener, which would make it more difficult to get an even hem.

2 Rip it. Using a seam ripper, take out the stitches of the original hem. If the fabric doesn't hang downward, iron it down.

3 Mark it. If possible, enlist a friend to help you with this. Try on the pants and stand on a chair. Have your friend fold the fabric at the bottom of the pants upward and inward, until the fold hits

about three quarters of the way down the back of your heel, and, using one straight pin at the back, mark the spot.

If you're on your own, do this in front of a full-length mirror. Be aware, though, that bending and standing will change the length, so you may have to try a few times to get it right.

4 Measure, fold, and press. Take off the pants you're hemming and turn them inside out. Measure the inseam, which is the seam that runs from the crotch down the inside of the leg, all the way to the bottom of the hem. Then measure the inseam on a pair of pants you already wear. Compare the two to make sure your measurements are correct.

Starting at the pin on one leg, use a tape measure to measure the length from the edge of the fabric to the bottom fold. Use that measurement to fold and pin the hem around the bottom of the leg with five or six straight pins. Repeat the process on the other leg. Iron the hems where you want them to be, making a crease. With the pants still inside

out, use your tape measure to measure 2 inches of fabric from the ironed hemline. Mark the pants with tailor's chalk, making a dotted line around the entire leg.

5 Cut. Take out the pins and cut the fabric on the dotted line (use pinking shears if you have them; the jagged scissor edge prevents fraying).

6 Pin the hem back into place using the five or six pins. Thread a sharp with the right thread for the pants. Don't double the thread over. Instead, pull about an inch of thread through the needle and knot the opposite end. With the pants inside out, sew a blind hem stitch (see How to Fix a Hole in Your Shirt, page 132) beginning at the side seam. Knot the thread on the inside of the pants when you've sewn the entire leg. Repeat for the other leg. When finished, iron the hems flat. Then iron the pants and hang them in the closet.

✕ ✕

Hemming Advice from My Mom

• If you like the way the original hem was sewn, examine it and take notes. There may be something about it you'd like to copy.

• Just like a carpenter does: Measure twice, cut once.

• If you have to work alone, tape a fabric marker to a chair leg and spin yourself against it, drawing a line.

• Compare your thread color to your pants both in natural sunlight and under harsh bathroom lights.

• Wear shoes with the same heel that you're likely to wear with your pants as you measure. Stand on a flat, hard surface.

• Measure both legs. All of us have one shorter and one longer leg, which may not be apparent to the naked eye. ✕

#72 How to Hem the No-Sew Way

usible fabric tape isn't the best permanent solution for hemming pants, but if you can iron, you can skip the sewing steps; the tape literally melts under the iron to stick the fabric together. It's great for times when you're traveling (many hotels have irons) or when the hem on your favorite pants falls and you're in a rush to get to a meeting or an appointment. Ready? Roll tape!

1 Measure your hem and iron the new hem in place as you would following the steps outlined in How to Hem Pants, Step 4, page 135.

2 Cut the tape to fit between the layers of the fabric. Make sure it doesn't stick out too far: Once you iron it, the tape melts onto the surrounding area.

3 Lay a damp press cloth over the area to be hemmed.

4 Press it with a hot iron to melt the fibers in the tape, taking care not to scorch your pants.

5 Remove the cloth and press the pants directly, melting the fibers of the tape.

6 Leave your pants on the ironing board until you are sure they are cool. Don't touch the newly fused part if you can help it. This is like letting glue dry between two sheets of paper.

⋈ ⋈ ⋈ ⋈ ⋈ ⋈ ⋈ ⋈ ⋈ ⋈ ⋈ ⋈

Fuse with Care

• It doesn't last forever. I don't tumble-dry garments with fusible fabric tape in them because the heat of the dryer can weaken or dislodge the tape.

• Use fusible fabric tape only on stiff, heavy fabrics because the tape itself becomes stiff and heavy after it's ironed into your garment.

• It's best for use on cottons and canvas. Fusible fabric tape doesn't stretch, so it will look odd if ironed onto flowy or stretchy garments. ⋈

#73 How to Thread a Sewing Machine

Threading a sewing machine is like riding a bike: easy once you've done it successfully once or twice. Sewing machines vary, of course, but the basic principle is the same. They create stitches by interlocking the upper thread (from a spool that winds through the needle) with the lower thread (that comes up through the bobbin).

1 Using the handwheel (or the "needle up" button), raise the needle to its highest position.

2 Raise the presser foot to disengage the tension discs. This will ensure that the needle doesn't "unthread" when you turn on the machine and begin stitching.

3 Place a spool of thread on the spool pin on the top of the machine. If your machine's pin is horizontal, add the cap to firmly secure the spool.

4 Take the thread between your thumb and forefinger and pull it across the top of the machine and through the first thread guide. The thread should unwind easily from the spool. If it doesn't, check the spool to find where the tension or snag is occurring.

5 Pull the thread to the front of the machine, down through the tension assembly, and around the next thread guide. Make sure the thread has passed between two tension discs as well as the hook that may be

attached to the left side of the tension dial.

6 Pull the thread up and through the hole or slot in the take-up lever.

7 Pull the thread back down through any remaining thread guides and put the tip of the thread through the needle eye. Some machines have built-in needle threaders that make quick work of threading the needle. To thread a machine needle manually, follow the groove in the needle shaft to determine from which direction (left

(continued)

to right or front to back) to thread the needle. Raise the presser foot so that you'll feel slight resistance when pulling the thread through the machine.

8 Lower the presser foot and gently pull the thread to check and ensure that the tension discs are engaged.

9 Insert a wound, full bobbin, taking care that its rotational direction is correct and that the bobbin tension spring is engaged. If applicable, close the throat plate.

10 Raise the presser foot and hold the upper thread (needle thread) while lowering and raising the needle one time to loop the upper thread around the lower thread (bobbin thread).

11 Gently pull the end of the upper thread to bring the lower thread up through the needle hole in the throat plate. Pull several inches of both the upper-thread and lower-thread ends under the presser foot together, toward the back of the machine.

Although he violated Elias Howe's patent (and later paid for it), American inventor Isaac Singer improved upon the design of the two-thread sewing machine and was responsible for popularizing it.

Quick Reference: The Parts of a Sewing Machine

1. **Spool pin.** Holds a spool of thread that feeds the upper thread
2. **Bobbin winder spindle.** Small pole to hold bobbin during the winding procedure
3. **Bobbin winder stop.** Stops the loading process once the bobbin is full
4. **Stitch-width dial.** Allows you to control the size of zigzag stitches
5. **Stitch-length dial.** Allows you to control the length of the stitch
6. **Handwheel.** Allows you to raise and lower the needle manually (useful for jams and for inserting or releasing projects from the machine)
7. **Pattern-selector dial.** Allows you to choose the stitch pattern by symbol
8. **Reverse-stitch lever (or button).** Allows you to run the fabric through the machine backward
9. **Power button or switch.** Controls on/off mechanism
10. **Bobbin-winder thread guide.** Directs the thread while the bobbin is being loaded
11. **Thread-tension dial.** Allows you to control tension on the upper thread.
12. **Thread take-up lever.** Moves up and down; it's where the upper thread is guided through
13. **Needle-clamp screw.** Locks sewing machine needle in place
14. **Presser foot.** Holds the fabric firmly in place and is controlled with a lever at the back of the machine
15. **Bobbin cover.** Holds the bobbin in place and keeps dust and debris off the thread
16. **Bobbin-cover release button.** Allows you to open the cover and gain access to the bobbin
17. **Feed dogs.** Pull fabric away from during the sewing process
18. **Needle.** Pushes and pulls thread through the fabric to create stitches
19. **Needle plate, or throat plate.** A metal plate located underneath the needle and presser foot; its openings allow the needle and feed dogs to make contact with the fabric

Troubleshooting Common Sewing Machine Problems

The good news is this: Many of your problems will be related to poor maintenance or neglect of your machine. Needless to say, the amount of maintenance needed depends on how much use your machine gets. As with any appliance, you should carefully read the owner's manual and follow recommendations for care and maintenance. If you don't have it, go online to download or order a copy, or check directly with a local dealer.

As usual, the best measure you can take to prevent your machine from malfunctioning is to keep it clean. Cover your machine when not in use. Dust, lint, and pet hair are enemies of a smooth-running sewing machine. Use compressed air to blast away dust particles, especially dust and lint from fabric as you sew (never blow because the moisture from breath can gum up the machine). Have a store of pipe cleaners, muslin squares, and sewing machine oil. Use the pipe cleaners for swabbing out crevices. Slide squares of clean muslin between tension discs (be sure to raise the presser foot). For more specific problems, try the following tips before spending money at the repair shop.

Breaking needles?

• Use the right size needle and thread for your fabric.

• Center the presser foot and make sure it's secure.

• Never pull the fabric through the machine. Let the machine feed it.

• Make sure your needle is securely fastened.

• Remove straight pins before sewing or position them so they don't run under the needle.

Noisy machine?

• Try cleaning and oiling, as oil may have dried and gummed up the machine.

• Check to see if thread is caught or is too tight in the bobbin case.

• Check the belt, and tighten or loosen as needed.

Seams puckering?

• Check to see if the tension is too tight.

• Check your stitches; if they are too long, the fabric can pinch and gather.

• Try a new or sharper needle.

• Make sure the upper thread size and bobbin thread size are the same weight and made of the same fiber.

• Avoid pressing down too hard on the foot while using lightweight fabric; a slower pace keeps light fabric from bunching.

Upper thread breaking?

• Make sure the tension isn't too tight.

• Check to see if your needle is dull or bent.

• Use the right size needle for the thread. Too small a needle will cause bunching as the thread slides through.

• Your thread could be old or of poor quality, causing knotting, stripping, and lint deposits in the machine.

Lower thread breaking?

• Make sure the tension isn't too tight.

• Use the right size needle for the thread. Too small a needle will cause bunching as the thread slides through.

• Check to see if the thread in the bobbin case is stuck or tangled.

• Take care not to pull the thread too tightly while winding the bobbin.

• Check for a possible sharp edge, or burr, on the throat plate that could be cutting the thread.

#74 How to Hem a Skirt

Although it's certainly possible to hem any skirt by hand, using a machine yields a more professional look—once you get the hang of it. And once you've mastered the techniques, hemming skirts on a machine takes very little time. You'll be richly rewarded if you take patience and care in measuring, pinning, and pressing the hems as you go. As with most sewing projects, the devil is in the details. Use these three basic techniques for hemming most A-line, dirndl, full, pencil, or tube skirts.

"Double Turn-Back" and "Topstitched" Hem

This is the most common hem. It simply involves turning the unfinished edge of the fabric under.

1 Using a seam gauge, divide the total hem allowance in half. For example, if working with a 1-inch hem, turn the garment inside out and iron the hem up a ½ inch on the wrong side. It's easiest to use glass-head pins to pin the fabric to the ironing board. Press the hem flat.

2 Turn the hem up another ½ inch, and then press the new fold flat. Some pros are able to skip this step,

but its worth the extra few moments of ironing to get a really smooth, flat hem.

3 Working from the outside of the fabric, so you can't see the raw edge, line up the fold against the left edge of the presser foot. You can feel the edge of the hem with your fingers even if you cannot see the "bump" through the fabric. Adjust the sewing machine needle to the left position, if your machine has a needle-right position. Topstitch the hem into place.

"Faced" Hem

Use this technique if you don't have much fabric to invest in the hem. It generally can be done with only a ¾-inch fabric loss. The bias tape used here will bend around curved edges, providing a polished, finished look.

1 Press the right side of the bias tape's fold open. Take care not to iron it completely flat. You need to be able to see the crease.

2 Lay the bias tape face-down on top of the right side of the fabric. Line up the raw edge of the tape with the raw edge of the fabric. Secure

(continued)

it with pins. Using your sewing machine, stitch in the crease.

3 Using a warm iron, press the seam flat.

4 Press the tape on the wrong side of the fabric and pin.

5 Using an edge stitch, machine-sew the tape in place, and then remove any pins.

"Blind" Hem

This technique makes a nearly invisible stitch. You can also use it on dressier fabrics where it's important not to see the stitching. Try to match the color and weight of the thread exactly with the fabric.

1 Install the blind-hem foot onto your machine.

2 Turn the skirt inside out and press 1 inch of fabric up on the wrong side.

3 Open the crease temporarily to fold ¼ inch of the raw edge into the hem and press. Then refold the crease from Step 2.

4 Set the machine to the blind-edge stitch. Nearly every modern machine has this setting, but if you're working on a really old machine, set it on the smallest stitch you can work with easily.

5 Use the handwheel to "walk" the machine. Do this until the needle swings to the far-left zigzag. Allow

---

The skirt is thought to be the second oldest form of clothing, preceded only by the loincloth. But—flashing forward many centuries—Christian Dior is credited with inventing the pencil skirt and the A-line skirt.

the needle to just barely catch the fold. Use the hand screw to adjust the bar on the foot so that it butts directly up against the fold. This will ensure even stitches.

6 The big zigzag of the stitch will catch just a thread of the fold, and the little zigzags will finish the

raw edge, guarding against future fraying.

7 Unfold the hem and use an iron to press it flat.

8 From the outside, you'll see a tiny stitch that looks like a dot about every ½ inch around the bottom of the skirt. If you see big stitches, it's an indication that you've stitched too much onto the fold. Carefully rip out the stitches with a seam ripper and begin again.

#75 How to Make a Pillow

Making and stuffing a pillow by hand is an excellent (and useful!) project for beginner DIY folk. That said, no maker should ever view themselves as too grand for the task. Homemade pillows are cheap and quick to make, and they instantly transform the decor of a room. Once you learn how, there'll be little need to purchase accent pillows ever again!

1 Figure out what size pillow you'd like to make. Add ½ to 1 inch for a seam allowance. If you aren't exactly sure of the size, I suggest

purchasing about a yard of fabric. If you'd like the front and the back to be different patterns, you may want to start with a ½ yard of each.

2 Cut the fabric to the desired dimensions.

3 Lay the fabric one piece on top of the other, right sides in.

(continued)

4 Sitting at your sewing machine, use a straight stitch to sew up three edges of the pillow.

5 When you get to side four, sew until you have about 5 inches unsewn, making, essentially, a hole in a pouch.

6 Turn the "bag" inside out by pulling it through the hole. Now the right side (or out-facing side) of the fabric will be showing.

7 Stuff polyfill or other filling, as desired, through the hole until the pillow is as plump as you'd like.

8 Tuck the unstitched fabric edges into the hole and pin them in place so the folded-over edge lines up with the outer seam. Pin the fabric edge to itself, but don't pin the hole closed.

9 Thread a sharp needle with a single knotted thread that best matches your pillow in color and weight.

10 You don't want a hand-sewn whipstitch or a machine stitch that will show on the outside of the pillow.

Use the following invisible stitch to keep the fabric closed and hidden beneath the folds of the fabric: Pierce the edge of the fabric on the inside of the pillow, so the knot remains unseen on the inside layer.

11 Take the needle and bring it through the seam crease right across from where the thread is coming out on the other side.

12 Keep the needle inside the fabric under the fold for about ¼ to ½ inch, and then poke it out a little.

13 Bring the point of the needle toward you and pick up some fabric (not too much) from the fold of the other side.

14 Pull the thread until it's taut, and then repeat the same action all across the opening.

15 Pierce the fabric across from where the thread is coming out, then travel under the fold and come out toward your body, grabbing a small amount of fabric from the other fold. Tie off the end by knotting inside the folds of the seam.

Pillow-Making FAQs

How much fabric do I need?

You'll need to use your math skills on this one because it's all about geometry. The amount of fabric depends on the width of the fabric and on the size of the pillow you desire. My advice? Stick with squares as you learn, then progress to rectangles. As you gain skill, you can branch out.

Every basic pillow has two sides. You need to add about an inch to each edge for the seams. Think of it this way: A 12-inch square pillow requires two 14-inch squares. One square in front, one in back, and extra fabric to sew the seams.

How do I buy it?

Fabric is sold by the yard (which is, as you know, 36 inches). In a fabric store, you'll see that most material is between 36 and 60 inches wide. The exception to this is upholstery fabrics, which are commonly 54 inches wide. A square of 54-inch fabric is 1½ yards long. That'll get you two 16-inch square pillows, plus a length of fabric left over.

How do I trim it?

Add fringed trim to pillows by pinning the trim between the two layers of fabric with the fringed portion facing the center of the pillow. You'll sew it inside out. When you turn the pillow right-side out, you'll have trim on the outside.

What fabric should I use?

The only rule is that you should use durable fabric for outdoor pillows. I suggest cotton canvas, duck cloth, vinyl, olefin, or use a shower curtain! (Hint: Make sure your fillings are 100 percent waterproof, too.) I like to make pillows out of blankets or bedspreads that have suffered a stain that I can cut out or sew around.

What fabric should I avoid?

Pillows can be a real art form for the inspired designer. But for everyday home use, consider avoiding silks or brocades that will show stains easily and that require dry-cleaning or special care.

Very different from their Western equivalent, pillows made in ancient China were often crafted from porcelain. The material was thought to have health benefits in this form—and may have been thought to inspire dreams.

#76 How to Make a Comfy No-Sew Fleece Pillow

All you need to make this cozy pillow is a pillow or pillow form, two pieces of fleece (or other no-fray fabric such as felt), a pair of scissors, ruler, and your own two hands.

1 Start with a square pillow to cover. Then select your fleece and wash it to remove any manufacturer's sizing.

2 Measure the pillow from seam to seam. Allow for the thickness of the pillow and the knotted closures by adding 8 inches to the width and length of your measurements. This is the size your fabric should be. Measure twice, cut once.

3 Lay the two squares of fleece on top of each other, right-sides together.

4 Place a ruler about 3 inches from the edge and cut into the fabric at 1-inch intervals. Cut out a 3-inch square from each corner.

5 You'll be left with 1-inch-wide, 3-inch-long fringe strips. Flip the pieces over, right-sides out, one on top of the other.

6 Tie double overhand knots using one fringe piece from each fleece layer.

7 Tie these knots around three sides, leaving one end open.

8 Insert your pillow into the open end.

9 Tie the fringes on the remaining side.

10 Check all the knots.

#77 How to Make a Super-Easy No-Sew Knot Pillow

No scissors? No ruler? No problem! All you need is a large square of fabric and a pillow or pillow form to make this very chic, knotted, decorator pillow. You need a piece of fabric three times as wide (plus a couple of more inches) and twice as long (plus a few more inches) as the pillow or pillow form.

1 Iron the fabric flat to stretch it out and to remove any wrinkles or bunches.

2 Lay out the fabric wrong-side up and center the pillow or pillow form in the middle.

3 Fold the top half of the fabric to the center dividing line of the pillow.

4 Fold the bottom half up so that it just extends past the edge of the first folded piece of fabric. It'll look like your pillow or pillow form is in a tube or like the beginnings of a wrapped piece of candy.

5 Take the squared-off corners of one end and fold them in one time each, as if you are wrapping a present, bringing the tube ends to triangle points. Repeat on the other side.

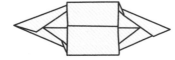

6 Fold the right triangle in across the top of the pillow. Then cover it with the other triangle end once you fold that across.

7 Tie the ends together in a square knot, by taking the fabric over-under, then under-over.

8 Tuck the ends securely behind the knot.

An old superstition suggests a key should be slipped into a child's pillowcase to ward off evil spirits.

#78 How to Make an Apron

Gathering fabric is exactly what it sounds like: "gathering" or bunching fabric together along one edge so that a ruffle effect is created. This technique is used in many sewing projects, such as puffed sleeves, can-can skirts, tote bags, and . . . aprons!

MATERIALS:

- 1⅓ yards of 45-inch-wide light cotton fabric
- Thread that closely matches the fabric in color and weight. Use 100 percent cotton thread.

Cutting the Fabric

1 Cut one piece of fabric 36 inches wide by 45 inches long to form the body of the apron.

2 Cut four pieces of fabric 3 inches wide by 45 inches long each to make the ties of the apron.

Making the Body

1 Turn the top edge of the body fabric down ¼ inch to the inside (you'll attach this edge to the ties). Using an iron, press this seam allowance. Turn again, and using your sewing machine, sew a running stitch close to the pressed edge.

2 Follow Step 1 for the hem, working from the bottom of the fabric, opposite the part you just sewed.

3 Follow Step 1 again for each side of the apron body. You now have, essentially, an edged rectangle.

Making the Apron Ties

1 Line up two of the four already-cut pieces, right sides together.

2 With the right sides still together, use the sewing machine to sew the 3-inch width, making a ⅜-inch seam.

3 Repeat Steps 1 and 2 with the other two pieces. You now have two 90-inch-long ties.

4 On each of the two apron ties, use a warm iron to press the long edges under ¼ inch to the inside.

5 Repeat Step 4 to press under the short ends of the apron ties.

6 Lay out the pieces, wrong-sides together. Pin them in place, and use the sewing machine to sew close to the edge for the entire perimeter length.

7 Pin and sew along the short ends of each of the apron ties. Use a small stitch and proceed slowly to keep the narrow ties as flat and smooth as possible, since long, narrow seams like this are inclined to pucker.

Sewing the Gather Stitch

1 Using the sewing machine, sew a gather stitch all along the top end of the fabric. (Choose the longest length possible on your stitch-length selector so the fabric gathers more quickly.) Place the presser foot about ⅛ inch or ¼ inch in from the edge of the fabric. Don't forward or backstitch at the beginning of the stitch (as you normally would). Keep a long tail of thread and sew a straight line parallel to the edge of your fabric. Grasp the thread with one hand and push the fabric over with the other hand. You'll see the fabric easily gather over the thread.

2 Continue gathering, pushing, and shifting the fabric until you have evenly spaced gathers and the top edge of the apron body measures about 20 inches.

Attaching the Apron Tie

1 Fold the gathered apron body in half to locate the center, and then mark it with a pin.

2 Fold the apron tie in half to locate its center, and mark it with a pin.

3 Lay the center of the tie over the pin in the center of the apron body.

4 Keep the tie at the very top edge of the body piece. Smooth the gathers at the inside of the apron body.

5 Double-check your measurement to ensure that you are maintaining the 20 inches at the top of the apron.

(continued)

6 Double-check to ensure that you will have the same apron tie length on both ends by checking the center of the tie.

7 Pin the tie in place and sew along the top edge.

8 Repeat Step 7 for the bottom of the tie.

9 Press.

In 16th and 17th century England, the color and pattern of your apron indicated your trade. Barbers wore a checked pattern, while butchers and porters wore green.

#79 How to Install a Zipper

Zippers are nothing short of miraculous when they function properly. When they jam or break in public, however, our love affair generally cools. But don't default to snaps, Velcro, or hook-and-eye closures simply because you're intimidated by zippers. It's not rocket science. It just takes a little practice. For your first-time zipper projects, try to choose a zipper with a slider on the smallish side. They're easier to deal with because they're less bulky. Also, do your best to match the length of the zipper with the length of the opening in your project.

Zippers are sewn into seams, for the most part. Rarely does a zipper run down the entire length of a garment's side. For most projects, like sewing a zipper into a pillow, you'll need to sew a regular seam before and after you sew in a zipper. Here's what to do.

Sew It Together

1 Take the two panels of fabric that will flank your zipper and finish the edges with a serger or a zigzag seam.

Then sew the two right-hand sides using a ⅝-inch seam allowance and a long stitch length (basting stitch). If you have a pattern or instructions with a different seam allowance, use that.

2 Turn out the wrong side of the sewn-together fabric and iron the new seams open flat.

Line It Up

1 Place the zipper so the teeth fall in the ditch of the seam you just made, with the right side of the zipper face-down. Now you'll need to figure out the exact placement.

2 You'll have a starting and stopping point for the zipper on the fabric. It could be the top edge of the fabric or ½ inch down. Wherever it is, place the end of the zipper where it needs to begin, with your zipper still face-down. Line up the center of the zipper teeth along the center of that open seam. Now it's time to pin the zipper in place.

Pin It

1 Pin the zipper into the seam face-down with the pins running parallel to the sides of the zipper.

2 Next, think about the way you will be sewing the zipper. You'll start on one side of the zipper, sew along it, then turn and sew the opposite direction. Position the heads of the pins so they face toward you as you sew; this makes them very easy to remove. In other words: The heads of the pins on the right side of the zipper will face one way while the heads of the pins on the left side will face the opposite.

Prepare to Sew

1 Turn the fabric over and mark it with a pin just above where the bottom of the zipper lays. This will show you where to stop sewing because you don't want to sew over the metal or thick plastic piece at the end of the zipper.

2 Attach a zipper foot to your sewing machine. Use thread that matches both the zipper and the fabric. Make sure the same thread is loaded for the upper and lower stitches. Many zipper feet have two locations where they can be attached to the machine to enable you to start stitching on either side of a zipper. In this case, attach the zipper foot on the left side.

Stitching It In

1 Stitch around all four sides of the zipper with a zigzag stitch, keeping the side of the zipper foot as close to the zipper as possible.

2 Stitch down the right side of the zipper, stopping just a few stitches past the end of the zipper with the needle in the down position.

(continued)

3 Rotate the zipper and fabric 90 degrees, then stitch just a few stitches beyond the edge of the zipper. Stop with the needle in the down position.

4 Rotate the zipper and fabric 90 degrees, then stitch up the left side of the zipper and a few stitches beyond the edge of the zipper. Stop with the needle in the down position.

5 Rotate the zipper and fabric 90 degrees. Stitch until you are about 2 inches from your starting point. Leave your needle down in the fabric to hold it in place.

Unpick, Unzip, Flip, Finish

1 With the needle still in the fabric, carefully begin to unpick the original center seam (the zipper is now underneath it, and you should be able to feel the closed teeth under the fabric) until just beyond the back of the zipper foot.

2 Unzip the zipper so that the pull is out of the way and just behind the zipper foot. Move the edge of the fabric a little to the right to give extra room for the zipper pull.

3 Continue sewing the additional 2 inches to the very end, and backstitch.

4 Flip the project over and unpick the entire center seam, exposing the zipper. Check to see that the zipper opens and closes correctly.

✕ ✕ ✕ ✕ ✕ ✕ ✕ ✕ ✕ ✕ ✕ ✕
The Parts of a Zipper

Chain. The continuous piece that is formed when both halves of a zipper are meshed together

Teeth. The individual elements that make up the chain

Slider. The device that moves up and down the chain to open and close the zipper

Pull tab. The part of the slider that you grasp to move it up or down

Tape. The fabric behind the zipper mechanism

Tape ends. The fabric that extends past the teeth at the top and bottom of the chain

Top stop. Two devices at the top end of the zipper that halt the slider from going off the chain

Bottom stop. A device attached to the bottom end of the zipper to halt further movement of that half of the zipper

Bridge stop. Similar to a bottom stop, this device is used at the top end of a zipper to prevent each half of the zipper from separating

Pin. A device used on a separating zipper that encourages the joining of the two zipper halves

Box. A device used on a separating zipper that helps correctly align the pin, so that the joining of the two zipper halves can begin ✕

#80 How to Fix a Broken Pull

For a super-quick, on-the-go repair, use a safety pin to replace a missing or broken zipper pull tab. To permanently replace it, try this.

1 Remove the pull tab from the slider.

2 Test to ensure that the slider can functionally slide up and down the chain (you might have to use a safety pin).

3 Using a magnifying glass, inspect the break in the pull tab.

4 Using a pair of pliers, bend the broken sections of the pull tab so there is ample space between them to allow the tab to fit back into the slider.

5 Using a metal file, file down any burred or sharp spots on the break point, taking care not to file off an excessive amount.

6 Insert the pull tab back into the slider, and then use the pliers to gently squeeze the broken sections back together. If possible, overlap the broken pieces slightly.

Unsticking a Zipper

If the teeth are sticking. Zip the zipper all the way to the top, if possible. Then, rub the teeth with a graphite pencil. Inch the zipper down a little at a time.

If the fabric is caught in the teeth. Use white vinegar or glass cleaner as a lubricant. These are not oil based and generally won't ruin fabric, but test an unseen or small patch before going all-in with this technique. Soak the fabric around the zipper with the white vinegar or glass cleaner. Really douse it. Don't be afraid because you are going to wash the garment as soon as you get the zipper free.

Very, very slowly (a millimeter at a time) pull the zipper in the direction you would to unzip the garment. Go a bump past the point at which you think it won't slide anymore, then relax your grip and rest for a second or two. Repeat. Each time the zipper should move a little tiny bit farther. If you see any fabric bunching, give it a hard tug while pulling opposite that bunch with the zipper.

#81 How to Fix a Separated Zipper

Of all the frustrating zipper mishaps, a set of teeth that refuse to stay closed is one of the most aggravating. Luckily—if you can locate needle-nose pliers and a needle and thread—there's an easy fix.

1 Using a small pair of needle-nose pliers, pry off the zipper's metal stop.

2 Move the slider all the way to the bottom of the zipper, going just below the bottom-most teeth.

3 Use your hands to realign the teeth so that they mesh.

4 Zip the zipper by sliding it to the top.

5 Thread a needle with embroidery or another very strong thread, and knot it off.

6 Starting with the thread on the back side of the zipper, make six stitches the size of the old stop across the bottom of the zipper where the old stop was.

7 Tie a knot on the underside of the fabric to secure the "stop."

✕ ✕

The History of the Zipper

Elias Howe, the inventor of the sewing machine, patented the "automatic, continuous, clothing closure" in 1851, but he never tried seriously to market or publicize the clever gadget. Forty-two years later, Whitcomb Judson marketed the "clasp locker," taking the same technology a bit further, and debuted it at the Chicago World's Fair. Thus, Judson is generally credited with inventing the device. B. F. Goodrich was the first to call it a "zipper," but it didn't enjoy popularity until 1937, when *Esquire* magazine touted it as the "newest tailoring idea for men." ✕

LAUNDRY AND CLOTHING

When you first start doing your own laundry, whether you're 12 or 22 or older, it can be a real shock to discover that just throwing things into the washing machine and then the dryer doesn't work! Clothes can look and feel much better if you know the tips and tricks to get them clean, keep them colorfast, and prevent shrinking or stretching. With a little skill and luck, you can cut down on dry-cleaning bills as well. Like dishes, laundry has to be done frequently. And it's too easy to end up with faded colors and graying whites if you don't exercise a little care. But despite the complex hieroglyphics of the modern laundry label, a little care and attention—and a few tricks up your sleeve—will keep your laundry fresh and bright.

LAUNDRY TOOL KIT

Chalk

Rubbing alcohol

Baking soda

Stain removal spray

Laundry detergent

Bleach

Glycerin

Ammonia

Distilled white vinegar

#82 How to Read a Laundry Label

" How should I best wash and care for my new top or dark-wash jeans?" you may ask. The obvious answer is, "Check the care label," right? Ummm, not necessarily. A dirty little secret about laundry care labels is that they don't always tell you how to best clean the clothes.

Why, you might ask, would the manufacturer bother to include them? Because they're compelled by law. The Federal Trade Commission (FTC) mandates that clothing companies meet federal agency regulatory requirements. Sadly, because sometimes laundry care labels are created with only the letter of the law in mind, they do not always communicate optimal instructions for care.

The mission then becomes how to interpret the secret code on these labels to know what you really can and cannot do to get your clothes clean. In some cases, clothing tags advise us to "dry clean only" or "machine wash, tumble dry." Making it still more confusing to average citizens, these phrases often have a different legal meaning versus practical meaning.

Practical Advice for Heeding Words on Common Laundry Care Labels

Some directions in the labels are more meaningful than others. You may have to ignore some of the more poorly written labels and use common sense. Still, it's always worth checking, and here's some translation to help you wade through:

- Check the label for important instructions like "wash separately" or "dry-clean only." These instructions are intended to lengthen the life of your clothes and prevent them from being ruined (see "When to Dry-Clean," page 174).

- Don't forget to look for drying instructions like "air-dry" or "tumble dry low." The way in which you dry your clothes is just as important as how they are washed, and placing delicate items in a hot dryer can ruin them. When in doubt, dry fragile items on a line or a drying rack.

- Interpret any laundry label symbols. (This can be daunting if you're not a visual person.) The system is intended to be a straightforward guide to give instructions on washing, bleaching, and drying. If you don't feel you understand what the symbols are trying to tell you, check other laundry care advice in this book such as How to Hand-Wash (page 173) or How to Care for a Sweater (page 166).

UNIVERSAL VISUAL SYMBOLS FOR LAUNDRY CARE

Recently, a new layer of complexity has been introduced to us from European standards and practices, in the form of labels featuring no words, only laundry symbols. These symbols can be confusing. Many clothing labels provide only pictograms and omit written instructions and important details for keeping our garments looking their best. Familiarize yourself with the chart, on pages 158–159, before you attempt to do your first load of laundry. I've included a common-sense translation of the symbols you'll most often find.

GUIDE TO UNIVERSAL HOME LAUNDRY SYMBOLS

CARE SYMBOL	DESCRIPTION OF SYMBOL	WHAT IT MEANS
	Washtub.	Indicates where you'll find washing instructions. Accompanying this symbol, you'll find additional directions.
	One dot in the washtub.	Machine wash in cold water.
	Two dots in the washtub.	Machine wash in warm water.
	Three dots in the washtub.	Machine wash in hot water.
	One line under the washtub.	Use the permanent press setting on the washing machine.
	Two lines under the washtub.	Use the delicate or gentle cycle on the washing machine.
	A crossed-out washtub.	Do not machine wash.
	A hand in the washtub.	Hand-wash only.
	Triangle.	With this symbol, you'll see full bleaching instructions. (Clothing made in Japan uses a lab flask.)
	Open triangle.	Without text, this symbol means to use bleach as needed.
	Two lines in a triangle.	Use nonchlorine bleach as needed.
	A crossed-out triangle.	Do not use bleach.
	Square.	With this symbol, you'll see drying instructions. (With a plain circle inside, it means machine dry.)
	A solid black circle within the square.	Tumble dry with no heat.
	A single dot within the square.	Tumble dry with low heat.
	Two dots within the square.	Tumble dry with medium heat.
	Three dots within the square.	Tumble dry with high heat.

CARE SYMBOL	DESCRIPTION OF SYMBOL	WHAT IT MEANS
	A single line underneath the square.	Use the permanent press setting on the dryer.
	Two lines underneath the square.	Use the gentle setting on the dryer.
	A crossed-out square.	Do not tumble dry.
	A horizontal curve inside the square.	Line dry.
	Three vertical lines inside the square.	Drip dry.
	One horizontal line inside the square.	Dry flat.
	Two diagonal lines inside the square.	Dry in shade.
	A crossed out twisted garment	Do not wring.
	Iron.	With this symbol, you'll find detailed ironing instructions.
	Single dot within the iron.	Iron with low heat.
	Two dots within the iron.	Iron with medium heat.
	Three dots within the iron.	Iron with high heat.
	An iron with crossed-out lines underneath.	Avoid steam while ironing.
	A crossed-out iron.	Do not iron.
	Circle.	With this symbol, you'll see specific dry cleaning instructions (meant only for professionals).
	A crossed-out circle.	Do not dry-clean.

#83 How to Sort a Heap of Dirty Clothes for Washing
(Including Fabric Types)

Doing laundry may seem like a mindless, simple chore, but in actuality, it requires high-level thinking. Basic knowledge of fabric types, a design eye to group clothes by color, a rudimentary understanding of the mechanics of the machine, and some smarts about the chemistry around bleach and detergent are necessary. The good news is that all of this can be learned.

As with any task, there is a starting line. With laundry, that line is the sorting of the pile. Here are the basics.

1 Dump your laundry onto an expanse of floor so you can see what you're working with.

2 Pick out any obvious non–machine washables that may have wound up in the hamper, including wool sweaters; delicate lingerie; fine silks; heavy woolen slacks, skirts, or jackets; and anything dry-clean only. Hand-wash or dry clean these items.

3 Do the first-round sort. Put all white items in one pile, and all colored items in a second pile.

4 Pull out any lint-shedding items, such as towels and terry-cloth robes, and put them in their own pile.

5 Sort by weight. Tumbling heavy denim or canvas items with light cotton nighties or undershorts will wear or possibly damage the light items. Plus, drying times for blankets are vastly different from those for socks.

6 Go through the colored piles, and pull out any noncolorfast items, including red garments, denim, and new black, navy, and deep purple items. (Always test brand-new garments for colorfastness before washing in loads. The exception to this is when washing like items: Wash new dark-wash jeans with jeans you want to keep dark, and new red items with other red items of the same fabric.)

7 Sort out heavily soiled items and wash them separately. For example, if someone in the family is a pastry chef with clothing coated in flour and food dye, his or her garments need to be removed from the general mix. Same goes for clothing caked with mud or saturated with automotive grease.

8 When it's time to machine wash, follow the instructions on the washing machines and dryers, the garments' care labels, and the laundry detergent packaging to ensure that you use the right water temperature, rinse temperature, and amount of detergent for each pile of laundry. Pay special attention to front-loading washers: You'll need to use high-efficiency (HE) detergent, and less of it.

#84 How to Remove Ketchup from a White Shirt

Murphy's law says if something can splash, plop, run, or spill, it will happen when you're wearing lucky khakis or your most beloved blouse. Fortunately, once you learn how to handle troublesome stains, you can keep your cherished clothes from winding up in the rag pile. Removing stains and keeping them from setting permanently takes a little know-how and a bit of elbow grease, but it's worth it to preserve your wardrobe and your budget.

All too common, and notoriously hard to remove: the ketchup stain. If you're like most diners in the Western world, you've overshot a plate of fries more often than you care to admit. Here's how to tackle the aftermath.

1 Remove the culprit. Scrape as much ketchup off the fabric as you can, as soon as you can. Use a spoon, butter knife, or credit card. Try not to rub it in further.

2 Force it into a back-pedal. Run cold water through the *back* of the stained fabric as soon as possible. This forces the stain out. (Don't run it through the front because you'll only set it in deeper.)

3 Get it in a lather. Rub a liquid detergent (or shaving cream, if you have it) into the stain, using a gentle, circular motion beginning at the outer edges of the stain and working inward.

4 Lather, rinse, repeat. Keep soaping and rinsing until the stain is fully gone. Hold the fabric up to a bright light. If you see the slightest hint of brown or pink, repeat the previous steps.

5 Use the big guns. The minute you can get some, apply a stain remover. Use a wipe, stick, gel, or spray. Allow it to saturate and do its job for at least a half hour.

6 Launder as usual. Wash the garment as you normally would. Check for the stain by holding the garment up to a bright light before tumble drying. Use caution here: If the stain isn't gone, the heat can set it permanently.

7 One last blast. If you still see a shadow of the stain, re-treat with stain remover, and let it sit overnight before laundering again.

8 Use bleach. If the garment is white or light colored (and you've tested it for colorfastness), use a mild bleaching agent. Try hydrogen peroxide, white vinegar, or lemon juice dabbed on with a damp sponge. Allow it to work for at least an hour, then relaunder.

╳ ╳ ╳ ╳ ╳ ╳ ╳ ╳ ╳ ╳ ╳ ╳

Before You Sort: Stain Screening

Ideally, you should treat stains at the moment of contact. If you spill red wine on your cotton shirt, it's a good idea to blot it with seltzer and a cloth napkin. Sometimes, that's not practical, so here are some tips.

• Deal with the stain when you undress. Don't toss the soiled garment in the hamper. If appropriate, presoak it in your washer with the right type of detergent or stain remover.

(continued)

- If you can't soak the item immediately, spray the stain with an on-the-spot stain remover.

- When you're sorting laundry, if you see a stain that's been left untreated, start the stain-removal process by soaking or treating the stain before washing it with a regular load (see below).

- If possible, do similar laundry with similar stains in the same load (i.e., grease stains with grease stains, grass stains with grass stains, and so on). ✕

Five More Common Stains (and How to Remove Them)

1. **Blood.** If the stain is new, soak the stained area in cold water with a splash of ammonia for a half hour. If the stain has set, dampen it with warm water, then pour on some unseasoned meat tenderizer, gently dabbing it into the stain. Cover with a lightly dampened, clean washcloth or dish towel and leave it overnight. The next day, rinse with warm water mixed with a few spoonfuls of ammonia, and launder as normal. Do not tumble dry until you check the stain. If the stain persists, carefully apply bleach (test for colorfastness!) or dry-cleaning solvent from the inside of the garment, and allow it to soak for an hour. Wash again as usual.

2. **Coffee.** Soak immediately in lukewarm water. Gently dab the stain with laundry detergent or a vinegar-and-water solution. Launder the garment in the hottest water recommended for the fabric, check to see if the stain is gone, and repeat as needed. Avoid bar soap, which can set the stain permanently.

3. **Ring-around-the-collar.** Rub white chalk over the stain. It will lift out some of the oils in the collar, then you can launder as normal. (It won't remove the stain completely, like bleach does, but it will improve the look.) If the stain persists, launder again, using a cup of distilled white vinegar in the rinse water. If that doesn't work, launder again adding a cup of baking soda in the main wash. If the stain remains, and the shirt is white or colorfast, use diluted bleach dabbed on with a sponge, then launder as normal.

4. **Ballpoint pen.** For ballpoint pen ink stains on your dress-shirt pockets, rinse the stain with glycerin, not water, at your earliest opportunity. Let the fabric soak for at least 10 minutes, up to an hour, then apply detergent mixed with water and add two or three drops of ammonia. Let the ammonia soak in for an hour, blotting occasionally. Rinse thoroughly. If the stain remains, dab on a solution of bleach and water, but only if the garment is white or colorfast.

5. **Crayon.** Scrape off the excess wax with a spoon, butter knife, or credit card. Lay the stained area face down on a white paper towel and cover the garment with another paper towel. Smooth a warm iron over the top paper towel. The heat will melt the greasy wax, which will be absorbed by the paper. Repeat the process, using fresh paper towels until no more stain transfers to the paper towel.

✕ ✕ ✕ ✕ ✕ ✕ ✕ ✕ ✕ ✕ ✕ ✕ ✕ ✕ ✕ ✕ ✕ ✕

Testing for Colorfastness

A garment that isn't colorfast may bleed its dye in the wash and stain other clothing. Luckily, it's easy to test colorfastness before washing. Simply soak the fabric in soapy (room temperature) water, and, after a half-hour or so, take it out and check for dye in the water. Set your garment on paper towels to dry. If no dye bleeds into the water or onto the towels, your garment is colorfast. ✕

A Glossary of Common Household Stain Removers, A to Z (er, W)

Ammonia. Helps fade perspiration stains from light-colored and white shirts (see "How to Remove Pit Stains from a White Shirt," page 177).

Baking soda. Removes odors and helps remove stains from chrome and stainless steel.

Bleach. Probably not your first line of defense, but bleach works well on faint, lingering stains (especially food or dirt marks) on white cotton.

Cream of tartar. Excellent on rust stains and food stains; mix it with lemon juice to make a paste.

Denture-cleaning tablets. Great for food stains on tablecloths; stretch the fabric over a bowl, dissolve one tablet in ½ cup water, and pour directly on stain or spot.

Dishwasher detergent (liquid). Use this for any stain that you might normally bleach (heed fabric-care labels regarding bleaching).

Dishwashing liquid. Great spot-treater; use undiluted on tough stains like chocolate.

Glycerin. Effective on sticky stains such as tree sap, gum, and tar; also useful for juice and condiment stains (such as those from ketchup and mustard).

Hydrogen peroxide. Very effective on blood stains and stains on bathroom tile and grout; excellent for bleaching out stains on white clothes (mix 1 cup hydrogen peroxide with 1 tablespoon ammonia for a great liquid stain-fighter).

Laundry detergent. Seems obvious, right? When you cannot launder clothing right away, spot-treat with some detergent rubbed directly onto the spot.

Lemon juice. Use this to bleach spots out of white cotton and linen; use as a pre-laundry stain treatment for diaper, baby formula, grass, and tomato sauce stains.

Meat tenderizer (unseasoned *only*). Mix with very cold water to treat protein-based stains such as blood, milk, broth, or egg yolk stains.

Mineral spirits. An intense treatment for very stubborn greases like asphalt, tar, and motor oil; do not use on fragile or delicate materials; wash clothing thoroughly after treatment and air-dry.

Rubbing alcohol. Great for grass stains, shoe polish stains, and plant-based food stains.

Salt. Combine salt and lemon juice to tackle mildew stains; sprinkle salt on red wine or grape juice stains to prohibit setting until fabric can be laundered.

Seltzer. Safe for any fabric or surface that can be treated with water; inhibits stains from setting and brings staining agents to the surface of fabrics.

Shampoo. Use this for dirt and mud stains, cosmetic stains, and ring-around-the-collar.

Shaving cream. Shaving cream is basically aerated soap; use it to immediately spot-treat stains by applying it to fabric, then rubbing the area with a wet washcloth.

Sunlight. Not only will sunlight naturally bleach and fade stains, but it is germicidal; laying cottons and other fabrics out in direct sunlight can fade scorch marks, blood stains, mildew stains, and diaper stains; if you have the space, consider dragging mattresses out on hot, dry, sunny days to whiten and refresh them.

WD-40 lubricant. A great spot-treater for oil-based stains such as lipstick, salad dressing, meaty sauce, or motor oil.

White vinegar. Use undiluted as a spot-treater on suede items; on other fabrics, it's great for beer or berry stains.

#85 How to Wash a Load of Clothes

L earning how to do your own laundry will save you a boatload of money in drop-off fees and dry-cleaning bills. As with cooking, if you are a beginner, this task can seem daunting. My advice: Roll up your sleeves and learn. It's a basic life skill, like cleaning a toilet or shopping for groceries. Mom won't be willing to do it forever, and even if she is, sooner or later every grown-up should take charge of their own underwear!

How Big Is a Load of Laundry?

"But the lid stayed shut!" isn't a good reason to stuff your entire pile of dirties into a washing machine. Industry professionals judge load size by weight. The definition of "a load" of laundry depends on the capacity or size of the machine at hand.

Small-capacity top loaders may hold only 5 to 6 pounds of dirty clothing. Medium-capacity top loaders can usually handle 7 to 8 pounds. Large-capacity top loaders can clean about 12 to 15 pounds per load.

Front-loading washing machines can hold as much as 18 pounds of clothing. To find out how much your loads weigh, first weigh yourself, then weigh yourself holding a load of laundry in a lightweight, collapsible hamper. Subtract your weight from the weight of you the laundry. Some average weights of common laundry items:

- Twin-size quilt: 3 to 5 pounds
- Complete child's outfit: 2 to 4 pounds
- Complete adult's outfit: 3 to 5 pounds
- Traditional square laundry basket (filled): 18 to 25 pounds
- Standing rectangular hamper (filled): 21 to 28 pounds
- Down or synthetic comforter: 2 to 7 pounds

1 Sort and separate into piles. Divide by weight, level of dirtiness, type of fabric, and color. Categories can include whites, delicates, towels, noncolorfast garments, jeans, and blankets (see How to Sort a Heap of Dirty Clothes for Washing, page 160).

2 Pick a pile and prepare. Scan items for stains and spot-treat them. Empty pockets of coins, papers, and folding money. (Look twice for pens. Ink will ruin the laundry forever.) Turn colorfast items and garments with heavy hardware (like metal buttons) inside out.

3 Add the detergents. Carefully follow instructions on both the machine and the product packaging for adding detergent to the machine. For example, if you're using a high-efficiency washer and your local water is soft, you should use the bare minimum of detergent recommended. Use more for standard washers with hard water. Add liquid softener and bleach to the appropriate dispensers, if needed. Dilute bleach with water, using a separate plastic container, and taking extreme care not to splash it on surfaces or the clothes you're wearing. Never pour laundry chemicals directly onto dirty garments.

4 Select the appropriate water temperature. Colors require cold water. Whites, under most circumstances, can be washed in warm water.

When bleaching cotton whites, like sheets, use hot. To kill mites, lice, or bedbugs on bed linens (especially pillowcases), use the hottest water available.

5 Honor the care labels. Follow the recommendations and set the temperature on the machine.

6 Add the clothing to the machine. Don't overstuff it or the clothes won't get clean.

7 When the cycle is complete, prepare to dry. After the garments are washed, shake out individual items so they'll dry more quickly, with fewer wrinkles.

8 Before drying, clean and empty the lint trap. Do this every time. Dryer lint is responsible for a great number of house fires. Make this a mindless habit and a step you never skip.

9 Dry like clothes together. Dry heavy towels with other heavy towels. Dry jeans with jeans. Otherwise, your heavy items won't dry and your delicate items will wear out faster.

10 Get 'em while they're hot. Don't let warm clothing languish in the dryer: Remove it as soon as possible once the cycle is done. Not doing so will leave you with a pile of wrinkled clothes.

11 Fold and hang. The same applies here. The sooner you neatly fold or hang your garments, the fewer creases you'll face when you dress.

#86 How to Wash a Down Comforter

Recommendations say to wash your down comforter every two years. Good-quality comforters are expensive, and they can last a lifetime when well cared for. Follow these tips before tossing yours in the washer.

1 Don't use your top-loading machine. With a capacity of around 12 to 15 pounds, it usually can't handle a queen- or king-size comforter. Often, the agitator will be in the way. For better results, use a high-efficiency front loader with no agitator. Take it to a laundromat if necessary.

2 Treat it gently. Use cold water and set the machine to the gentle or delicate cycle. Down feathers are fragile, so use a mild soap without enzymes, such as Ivory Snow or Woolite. Do not use fabric softener in the water, as it will cause feathers to clump and not dry properly, leading to unpleasant odor.

3 Spinning and dampness. When the wash cycle is over, check the comforter for wetness. Generally, running it through one or two more spin cycles is a good idea. If it still feels soaking wet, wrap it in beach towels and wring it out to remove excess water. Once it's damp but not soaking wet, it is ready to be dried.

4 Dry and dry again. Use a large dryer for comforters: the bigger, the better. Dry on low heat to avoid damaging the feathers. It will take longer, but it will preserve your investment. Once the comforter is halfway dry, throw a clean tennis ball in the dryer to fluff the down.

#87 How to Care for a Sweater

Mating socks and tossing underwear in a drawer are great beginner skills to master along the road to learning proper maintenance of your own wardrobe. Caring for a sweater is a more sophisticated undertaking. Here are my favorite tips and tricks.

1 Sweaters should be folded. Don't hang sweaters on hangers or hooks because the fibers will become misshapen, stretched out, and eventually damaged permanently.

2 Sweaters should be groomed regularly. Use a clean baby hairbrush to remove lint, hair, and dandruff. To get rid of pills, purchase a small shaver or handheld depilling machine. Or, you can pick them off by hand, one at a time.

3 Sweaters require timely repairs. When zippers break, buttons are lost or broken, or holes appear, make the fixes right away. Unchecked holes will only get bigger.

4 Sweaters last longer when dry-cleaned or hand-washed. This is especially true of sweaters made from animal fibers.

5 Sweaters require careful off-season storage. Stow your sweaters in dust-proof bags layered with sachets of lavender, cedar chips, or dried bay leaves to keep them smelling nice. Make sure all sweaters are freshly washed and completely dry before storing to keep unseen stains from becoming permanent. These tips will also help to deprive hungry moths of meals.

#88 How to Save a Shrunken Sweater

If you pull a suddenly shrunken sweater out of the wash, don't panic. You may have to chalk it up to a laundry learning experience, but don't give up hope immediately. With emergency care, there's a chance of saving it.

1 First, when you spot the horrifyingly transformed garment after the wash cycle, never put it in the dryer. That will seal the deal. Instead, gently squeeze it in a thick towel to absorb moisture.

2 Next, fill your sink with cold water, and add 1 to 2 tablespoons of baby shampoo and ½ to 1 tablespoon of gentle conditioner. Gently swish the sweater in the water to thoroughly saturate all fibers. Soak for an hour, then remove it without rinsing.

3 Using a piece of cork board and stainless-steel push pins, gently begin stretching the sweater back into its original shape and size and pinning it into place. Check on it every few hours to reshape as needed.

#89 How to Dry Sweaters on a Drying Rack

Few people seem to have the patience anymore to care for sweaters, but if you take the time to wash and dry them properly, you will be richly rewarded. By following these basic tenets of sweater care, you'll extend the life of your favorite cotton or woolly wonder exponentially.

1 Acquire a drying rack. The ideal racks for drying and reshaping sweaters are stackable, made of plastic mesh, and have the surface area of a card table. They are inexpensive, fold and store easily, and can be found at any housewares store. Airflow is optimal, so allow space for sweaters to be stretched out to their full length and width.

2 Avoid racks with bars. Racks with bars are great for underwear and socks, cotton items to be ironed later, and synthetics like nylon and polyester. When you lay sweaters across the bars, however, lumps and bumps will form.

3 Always lay flat. First, water and wood don't mix. You run the risk of ruining nice hangers by dampening them. The rule of thumb: *Never* hang a wet sweater on *any* kind of hanger. The weight of the wet fibers will stretch the garment as it dries, leaving the shoulders stretched out. Not only will the sweater look odd on your body, but you will permanently damage the fibers.

⨯ ⨯

Rejuvenate Sweater Cuffs, Necklines, or Waistbands

Don't send your hard-worn, favorite sweater to the charity shop without giving this refresher a try.

1. Attack only one problem at a time. Choose cuffs, neckline, or waistband.

2. Pour boiling water into a large, heatproof bowl set on a secure surface (a heatproof kitchen counter covered with a damp dish towel to anchor the bowl will do).

3. Dip into boiling water to dampen the cuffs (or neckline or waistband) of your cotton, alpaca, cashmere, wool, or angora sweater. Use your fingers to pinch together the fibers and to reshape as desired.

4. Use a blow dryer on the cuffs (or neckline or waistband) as you shape them. ⨯

#90 How to Reshape a Wet Sweater

1 After washing, gently remove excess water by squeezing the sweater in an absorbent towel and laying it out flat on a new, dry towel (or two, if needed, to accommodate your sweater with both arms extended), spread out on a waterproof surface, such as a plastic-topped card table or net drying rack.

2 With very gentle stretching and manipulation, arrange the sweater into its original shape. Gently push the ribbing together at the neckband, wristbands, and waistband. Fasten all zippers or buttons. If there is a tab collar, fold it into place. Dry a

(continued)

removable belt separately and spread out an attached belt to its full length.

3 Allow the sweater to dry for a full day and night.

4 Switch out the old towels for new, dry ones. Flip your sweater over and arrange it into shape, and allow it to dry for another 24 hours.

5 If the sweater is still damp, replace the towels and shape it again.

6 Once your sweater is bone dry, without a hint of dampness, fold and store it.

#91 How to Fold a Fitted Sheet
(and Storage Tips for Other Items)

Folding fitted sheets neatly, with their rounded, elasticized corners, is hardly intuitive. Don't despair and resign yourself to living with lumpy, balled-up bed sheets in your linen closet. The method for taming them involves tucking the corners into each other to achieve a crisp, flat rectangle. This technique is written for a right-handed person. Lefties: Simply do it in reverse.

1 For sheets with the fewest possible wrinkles, fold them straight from the dryer. Grab a warm, fitted sheet and shake it out.

2 Stand holding the sheet by the two adjacent corners of one of the shorter edges. (The bulk of the sheet will be lying against your body as you fold.) With the sheet inside out, insert one hand into each of these two corner "pockets."

3 Bring your right hand across to your left and fold the corner in your right hand over the one in your left, enveloping it.

4 Next, reach down and over and pick up the corner hanging in front (this is the third corner). Bring that corner up and fold it over the

two corners you're holding in your left hand. The visible corner will be inside out.

5 Bring up the fourth corner and fold it over the others. It should not be inside out. You want the correct side to be visible. This corner will envelop the three others.

6 Next, lay the folded sheet on a clean, flat surface and straighten it out.

7 Fold in the two edges so the elastic is hidden.

8 Now, fold the sheet into a rectangle.

9 Fold the sheet into as many rectangles as you require until it's the size you prefer.

The average person spends one third of their life in bed. After a lifespan of 75 years, that amounts to 25 years, or 9,125 days, of sleep.

How to Safely Store Off-Season Garments

We all know the drill: In the spring, pack up your sweaters, coats, and ski wear and bring out the shorts, bathing suits, and Hawaiian shirts. In the winter, reverse. To preserve your clothing for years to come, it's imperative to store off-season garments with care to avoid damage from insects, mildew, and mold.

Here are a few basic rules about storing any type of clothing:

- Wash and thoroughly dry all fabric items before storing.

- Never store clothes or blankets in plastic bags or airtight containers.

- Wicker hampers or wooden and rattan trunks are best for storing garments and linens because they breathe.

Safe Storage of Some Common Fabric Types

Leather and suede. Store in a dry closet. When possible, cover the garments with clean, white cotton sheets. For soft leathers, store garments flat and wrap them in white tissue or sheets.

Rayon. Store flat, wrapped in white tissue paper or sheets, or hang garments, and cover with sheets.

Linen. Roll the items, don't fold, and cover with sheets.

Silks and knits. Store flat, wrapped in tissue paper or sheets.

Fur. Professional cold storage is the way to go for expensive or valuable garments. If you must store at home, be sure to store in a cool, dark place, and cover with sheets.

Wool. Lay flat and cover with sheets. Store in a cool, dark place.

#92 How to Iron a Shirt

My mother saw the advent of synthetic fabrics as freedom from tyranny. Give her a nice drip-dry blouse and some wrinkle-free bed sheets, and she's one happy camper.

I, on the other hand, relish the feel (and smell!) of a crisp, white dress shirt or Egyptian cotton linens. I don't mind putting in the work now and then because the payoff in luxury can be worth it. Sometimes, I actually like to iron. Repetitive and relaxing, it puts me in a zenlike state enhanced by the heat of the steam and the aroma of the starch.

Most people hate ironing because they simply don't know how. The good news is you can learn quickly and say good-bye to scorching skirts and ironing wrinkles into pillowcases.

1 Preheat your iron. Warm the iron using the manufacturer's listed settings. The highest temps are usually for linen and cotton. Start with the collar. Lay the shirt on your ironing board, front facing downward. Spray the collar with water, and with starch, if desired. Next, iron the underside, moving the iron from one point to the other with a pressing motion. Smooth wrinkles to the bottom of the collar as they appear. When finished, flip the shirt and repeat on the top side.

2 The cuffs. Start by unbuttoning the cuff. Now, iron the inside of the cuff, moving all wrinkles to the edges. Repeat on the outside. Next, carefully iron around the buttons, even on the back side, where the button is sewn on. Ironing over buttons leaves a mark.

3 Shirt front. Start around the buttons, carefully working the iron point around the buttons on the placket. Move back up to the top of the shoulder and work your way down the front of the shirt, pressing the iron in long, smooth strokes. Repeat on the other side. It's worth spending a bit more time on the front placket and areas near the collar to make them perfect, especially if you're not planning on wearing a jacket over the shirt.

4 Shirt back. Lay the shirt flat on the ironing board, front facing downward. It works best to position one of the sleeve heads into the square edge of the board. That presents half of the back of the shirt smoothly. After completing the first half, you can neatly slide the shirt over to iron the remaining half. Start at the top by ironing the yoke (back shoulder area), then slowly slide the iron down to the bottom of the shirt with a pressing motion.

If your shirt features a center box pleat, iron around it. After the back of the shirt is wrinkle-free, reposition it lengthwise on the board, and take a few seconds to iron the pleat back in so it looks crisp.

5 Sleeves. I prefer to iron sleeves last. This is the trickiest part of ironing a shirt. The issue here is that you're ironing a double layer of fabric. If one of the layers is bunched, you'll be ironing wrinkles into your shirt. Take the time needed to make sure your fabric is fully flat and aligned before applying heat. Using your fingertips, pick up one sleeve by the seam and lay the whole sleeve (along with the better part of the shirt)

flat on the ironing board. If there are visible creases on the top of the sleeve, left over from previous ironing, match them again. This ensures that you'll have a single crease line. Start ironing at the shoulder and armpit area, where the sleeve is sewn onto the shirt, then smooth down with a pressing motion toward the cuff. Next, turn the sleeve over and repeat the motion.

Finally, repeat the process with the other sleeve.

6 Spot check, and hang. When you're finished with a shirt, do a quick check of the key areas. If you see wrinkles, touch up the shirt, and then hang it on a hanger immediately. Make sure the shirt has plenty of space: Hanging hot shirts too close together causes them to form new wrinkles that will set as they cool.

Completed in 1902, the Flatiron Building in New York City is so named because of its unusual triangular shape that resembles an early clothing iron.

Why Iron a Dress Shirt?

No-iron and wrinkle-resistant shirts are widely available at reasonable prices. So, why on earth would anyone iron a dress shirt? There are many reasons.

Because you hate no-iron shirts. Many people don't like the feel or smell of no-iron shirts. Manufacturers treat them with a formaldehyde resin bath, which makes the cellulose strands bond to one another at the molecular level. Those chemicals emit an odor when these

shirts are new, and the smell can last through several washings. Generally, no-iron shirts are stiff and a bit scratchy instead of being soft and slick. Unlike pure, untreated cotton, these processed fabrics don't breathe well. If you like the feel of cotton, you have to iron because wrinkly cotton shirts are a sartorial no-no.

Details matter. Wearing wrinkled clothes sends a signal that you lack discipline and attention. Even in a casual work environment, wrinkles convey sloppiness.

(continued)

Customized shirt care. You know your own clothes best. Wine stain on the placket? Unlike some dry cleaners, you'll work to get it out before you apply heat. Prefer stiff collars and cuffs? You'll starch.

Cotton shirts at the ready. Those who use dry cleaners inevitably find themselves stuck without a favorite (or any!) pressed shirt when they need one. Do it at home and take back control.

Your shirts will last longer. Hand-washing combined with hang-drying help prevent wear on the fabric as well as shrinkage. Dry cleaners can stretch and abuse shirts, as evidenced by the small tears and missing and broken buttons on the ones I've received back. Wash and press your own shirts, and you can concentrate on the stained portions and heavily soiled areas, like collars and cuffs, and ease off on the less-abused areas.

It's kind of fun. Seriously, though—it's easier than you think, and when you do it right, the rhythm can lull you into a calm state. Plus, there's a true sense of pride and accomplishment that comes from turning a large wrinkled pile of shirts into a small, orderly stack.

Getting Started: Tools of the Trade

1. A well-built iron. Irons have come a long way since your great-grandmother had to heat two cast-iron triangles on the woodstove, alternating them to always use the hot one. You don't have to spend a large amount to get a high-quality one, but here are some things to look for:

• A smooth, solid soleplate. This is the flat metal plate that heats up and is pressed onto fabric. Look for aluminum-coated cast iron, solid steel, or titanium-coated metal. Poor-quality irons can heat unevenly or have burrs and nicks, leading to damage.

• High heat. Some natural fabrics, such as cotton and linen, require high heat to loosen and reform the shape of the fibers. A very hot iron helps slash ironing time in half, so that you're not passing the hot iron over the same spots repeatedly, stretching and wearing the fibers. The heat from the soleplate helps the steam heat up and maintain a high temperature.

• A steaming device. Hot moisture attacks the toughest wrinkles, smoothing them with minimal work by helping distribute heat throughout fibers.

2. A good ironing board. Make sure it has a large surface area, is easy to fold without pinching fingers, and is adjustable to a height that is comfortable for your back. Invest in a good pad and cover, and replace these as they wear or become soiled.

3. A spray bottle. Fill this with water, and water only, and dedicate it to your ironing. I advise purchasing a new bottle. When using a spray bottle that previously contained a cleaning product, residues can transfer to garments. Have it at the ready for spot-spraying or in cases when you disable the steam feature.

4. Spray starch. Use starch in moderation, if you like crisp-to-stiff shirts. Overdoing it can stifle cotton's breathability and encourage wrinkling. Spray lightly, too, because

excessive application can cause visible flaking of the starch. If you don't like aerosol cans, make your own by dissolving 1 tablespoon of cornstarch in 2 cups of hot water, and spraying it from a pump bottle.

#93 How to Hand-Wash

In my great-grandmother's day, Monday was Wash Day. Back then, laundry was washed by hand with lye soap, and you were lucky if you had a crank roller to wring out heavy items like sheets and quilts.

Today's hand-washing isn't the backbreaking chore it once was. Generally, we reserve it for pricey and delicate items, to save money on dry cleaning, or occasionally, when we find ourselves short of skivvies, we do it to avoid wearing a bathing suit under our clothes. Before you (or your delicates!) take the plunge, here's the least of what you need to know.

1 Start with a clean sink or bathtub. Scrub off scum, then make sure all cleanser has been washed down the drain. Bleaches and dyes from cleaning products could discolor or weaken your garments.

2 Keep your cool. Wash in lukewarm water, cooler than bathwater. Never use hot water—colors could bleed, and fibers could shrink.

3 Mild, not wild. Choose detergent formulated especially for delicates. It's not harsh enough to fade colors, and it dissolves in cool to warm water.

4 Keep it light. Save hand-washing for smaller, lightweight items. Lingerie, silk shirts, scarves, and dress socks are all good candidates. Don't use this method for towels and jeans—for one thing, you'll use gallons of water for a clean rinse, and for another, they require days to line dry.

5 Assess the risk. If a laundry item is marked "dry-clean only," you could ruin it forever by saturating it with water or the wrong soap.

6 Hand-washing does not equal the delicate cycle. Agitation causes stress on a garment. Even front-loading machines toss and tumble. For sturdier items, such as synthetic nightgowns or top-quality men's undershirts, washing on delicate with similar colors and fabrics shouldn't cause harm. If you have doubts, wash them in the sink.

7 Rinse, then repeat. This step takes time and effort. You'll need to fully drain the sink or bathtub, and then refill it with water twice—if not several—times. Add ¼ cup distilled white vinegar to a sinkful of rinse water or 1 cup to a bathtub of rinse water to help dissolve detergent residue. TIP: You'll need to rinse at least twice after that to wash away the vinegar so you don't smell like a dyed Easter egg.

8 Squeeze, don't wring. After the final rinse, use your hands to push and squeeze out the water without twisting your garment. Twisting stretches and pulls fibers, leaving you with saggy clothes. Then lay the garment out on a drying rack or a clean towel (if using a towel, you'll have to switch out damp for dry one or two times).

When to Dry-Clean

"Do I really have to schlep to the dry cleaner and shell out the big bucks to clean this garment?" you may ask yourself. Maybe not. Many garments labeled "dry-clean only" can be safely washed on the gentle cycle or by hand (see How to Hand-Wash, page 173). Use these steps to help you decide.

Decipher and interpret the care label. Manufacturers are required to list only one way to clean a garment. If the label says "dry-clean only," it's smartest to obey it. If it says "dry-clean," that means that is the recommended method, but not necessarily the only method.

Examine and think about the fabric. Unless the label says something different, dry-clean silk, acetate, suede, leather, velvet, wool, and taffeta. Cotton, rayon, linen, microfiber, cashmere, polyester, acrylic, and nylon can generally be washed at home on the delicate cycle, or by hand. First check for colorfastness: Moisten a cotton ball with mild detergent and a little water and dab it on a hidden seam or hem to see if any dye comes off. Wash noncolorfast items with like colors always.

Consider and test the detailing. Some care instructions are for the fabric only—not the embellishments or hardware, which may have been attached at another factory. This is why some labels come with caveats, such as "exclusive of decorative trim." Before attempting to wash items featuring beads, sequins, fringe, or tassels, make sure they are sewn on (not glued) and colorfast.

Dry-Cleaning Myths Debunked

Dry cleaners may seem like magicians, but once you know the inside scoop, you'll feel more empowered when making the decision "to dry-clean, or not to dry-clean."

Dry-cleaning is not dry. Water isn't used, but a toxic cocktail of other wet chemicals is. The most common liquid used is perchlorethylene, and even so-called "green" dry cleaners use liquid carbon dioxide and silicone fluids.

Men's shirts aren't necessarily dry-cleaned. The placard outside the cleaners may say, "Men's shirts: $2.50," but that doesn't mean they're being dry-cleaned. They're laundered in a big machine with detergent, starched if requested, then pressed and dried on a shirt form.

You'll never get reimbursed for ruined clothes. Not fully, anyway. Legally, the dry cleaner can cite depreciation. In some cases, you'll get the full value if the garment is less than four months old. If your garment is older than two years, expect no more than 20 percent of its original value.

Say good-bye to lost clothes. Once gone, they're likely gone forever. In many cases, your garments will be sent home in a bundle with another customer who won't bother to return them. Wash irreplaceable items at home or pay top dollar at a reputable white-glove or French cleaner.

Some stains are permanent. Dry cleaners have tricks, but they aren't magic. The key is to rush stained garments in as soon as possible. Natural fabrics like silk, cotton, and wool absorb and retain stains over time.

Only half of complaints are resolved. According to the Better Business Bureau, in 2009, only half of consumer complaints to dry cleaners were even addressed. It's a good reason to take more control of your clothing's care.

#94 How to Hand-Wash Curtains

You may want to consider taking very expensive drapes with heavy liners to a dry cleaner. Same goes with antique drapes or curtains with intricate pleating or folds. But for many styles—if the drapes and the liners are both made of washable fabrics like cottons or sturdy synthetics—hand-washing is a perfectly good (and economical) choice. Here's how to do it right.

1 Before you wash, vacuum. Most vacuum cleaners have hoses and brush attachments for cleaning curtains and drapes. Suck out the dust before washing.

2 Remove any ornaments or trim. If they're tacked on, carefully remove them with a seam ripper and tack them back on after washing the curtains.

3 Using a sturdy ladder or step stool, remove the curtains from their rods.

4 Remove all hardware, such as pins and hooks, and store in a zip-top bag or shoebox.

5 Hand-wash the drapes in lukewarm water with mild detergent. Sheers and light panels will fit, one at a time, in the sink. Larger panels may require the bathtub.

6 After several rinses, squeeze (don't wring) the panels. If your dryer has a no-heat setting, you can tumble the panels one at a time. Do not use heat. Otherwise, dry panels on a clothesline or stretch them across drying racks.

7 Press panels with a cool iron, using a press cloth to avoid scorching or leaving a "sheen" on the fabric.

8 Reattach any hardware you removed, and hang the panels while still the slightest bit damp: The weight of the fabric will help pull out the wrinkles and allow the drapes to dry as they are meant to hang.

They that wash on Monday
Have all the week to dry;
They that wash on Tuesday
Are not so much awry;
They that wash on Wednesday
Are not so much to blame;
They that wash on Thursday,
Wash for very shame;
They that wash on Friday,
Must only wash in need;
And they that wash on Saturday,
Are lazy folks indeed.
--from *A Book of Nursery Rhymes*
   by Charles Welsh

#95 How to Whiten a Dingy T-Shirt

Bright white clothing screams "clean." Even if it's not seen and admired by the public, a fresh, new shirt, pair of socks, or set of underclothes can make a person feel more confident, adding a little spring to the step. And don't forget the warning handed down by my Mom and mothers like her about clean underwear! Making sure your whites are sparkling falls under the category of "plan for every inevitability." The good news is that you don't have to constantly toss and rebuy basics to maintain your bright whites. With a little know-how, you can keep them shimmering long past their expected expiration date. Here are some tips for keeping your whites bright.

1 Sorting. Keep whites separate. Sort whites from colored clothes. Dye molecules will bleed into the water and subtly tint your whites.

2 Treating stains. Attack spills and smudges immediately. Use a solid stain stick or spot-treating liquid and carefully follow package directions because all fabrics and all stains are unique.

3 Loading the washer. Pack the washing machine loosely, allowing enough room for the dirt to lift out and float away rather than be redeposited.

4 Bleaching. Don't always reach for the chlorine bleach. Overusing it on pure cotton fabrics can increase yellowing. An oxygen-based bleach will generally do the job and is safer in most cases. Use chlorine bleach every fourth wash and follow package directions carefully.

5 Recalibrating hard water. Because minerals deposit on whites, leaving them looking dingy, if your local water is hard, invest in a water-softening device or add softener to each load.

6 Line drying. When possible, allow whites to dry in the sun. Ultraviolet rays, although undesirable for humans, help whiten already white fabric.

How to Remove Pit Stains from a White Shirt

It's hard to exude confidence when you're sporting half-moon rings in the underarm region. These unsightly patches can be caused by the aluminum chloride used in many deodorants or from minerals in your perspiration. Try these tips to keep your white shirts brilliant, from collar to hem.

- Wash the shirt with every wear, even if it looks and smells clean. Chemicals from products, and your own body, can get to work over time. In other words, while your shirt languishes in the hamper, the stain will grow.

- For newish stains, turn the shirt inside out, rinse the pits, then allow the shirt to soak in cold water.

- If soaking doesn't remove a new stain, use a solution of 2 tablespoons ammonia to 1 cup water. Pour the solution onto the stain and let it rest for an hour. Then wash the garment on the hottest setting the care label recommends. Then allow the shirt to air-dry because the heat of the dryer will set the stain. Repeat if necessary.

- If ammonia doesn't remove a new stain, try chlorine bleach (use only color-safe bleach on light pastel colors). Use a solution of 1 tablespoon bleach to 1 cup water. Pour the solution onto the stain and let it rest for an hour. Wash the garment on the hottest setting the care label recommends. Allow it to air-dry and repeat if necessary.

- For older stains, pour distilled white vinegar onto the stain and let it rest for an hour. Wash the garment on the hottest setting the care label recommends. Allow the shirt to air-dry because the heat of the dryer will set the stain. Repeat if necessary.

Little Laundry Facts

- To keep black clothes black, use an antifade detergent. This keeps the chlorine in the water from fading the dye. When washing, turn the garment inside out and hang or lay it flat to dry.

- To reduce odors, add ½ cup baking soda to 1 gallon water and presoak the garments for at least three hours. Then, as you machine wash them, add ½ cup distilled white vinegar to the rinse cycle.

- To disinfect your washing machine, pour in ½ cup mouthwash and run it through a regular cycle using hot water.

- To dry clothes in a hurry, twirl the load on the spin cycle in the washer an extra time. Then, when putting them in the dryer, throw in a dry towel or two. Finally, as with a pot of rice, don't open the dryer door to keep checking if they're done.

#96 How to Fold a T-Shirt the Retail-Store Way

1 With the shirt face down in front of you, fold the sleeves, one at a time, in to the center. If the sleeves are too long (as they will be on an adult shirt, but not necessarily on a child's shirt), fold each sleeve down toward the bottom hem after they've been folded in to the center.

2 Fold the bottom half up toward the shoulders, making a rectangle.

3 Stack shirts in large rectangles or, if you prefer, bring the bottom fold up to the shoulders once more to make a smaller base rectangle. Once you start folding T-shirts in this simple clean line, it's hard to go back to anything more elaborate.

DOMESTIC ARTS

General housecleaning has to be done at some time or another, or eventually the dust bunnies gather into a herd and start peeping out at you from under the beds and furniture. It's true that these days people seem less inclined to spend a lot of time mopping and polishing than perhaps they once did. As with most things, domestic work is inclined to fill the space allotted to it, so once you start looking, you'll always find more dirt that needs cleaning. How scrupulous you want to be is entirely up to you, but here's how to do the basics and delve into the nooks and crannies.

DOMESTIC ARTS TOOL KIT

All-purpose surface cleaner

Baking soda

Broom and dust pan

Sponges

Paper towels and soft cotton rags

Window cleaner

Vinegar

Vacuum

Mop and bucket

#97 How to Hand-Wash a Dish

E ven those who have a dishwasher will occasionally have to wash dishes by hand: after a big Thanksgiving meal, when your dishwasher breaks down, when you run out of dishwasher detergent, or while on vacation or visiting loved ones.

No one I know enjoys hand-washing dishes, but do it we must for hygienic and aesthetic reasons. Take heart; when done properly, this chore can be accomplished efficiently and effectively with a minimum of dishpan hands and floor puddles. Here's what to remember.

Roll up your sleeves. This is always a good idea, unless, of course, you're already wearing short sleeves.

Tie on an apron. This is optional, but I prefer to wear one because it allows me to work faster without fear of soaking my clothes.

Don rubber gloves. As with an apron, this is optional, but for those with dry skin or other skin conditions, it's a good idea.

Set up a dish tub. If you don't have one, go out and buy a proper plastic dish tub because this inexpensive tool will save you not only time but also water and energy (and therefore, money). If you don't have a dish tub now, use your largest plastic bowl. Set up a drying rack. Again, if you don't have one, buy one. They're easy to find and cheap. I suggest a metal one with a metal run-off tray; they resist mildew better than rubber or vinyl-covered ones.

Scrape first. Thoroughly scrape plates and dishes into the trash or compost bin before you start.

Have hand lotion at the ready. I keep a large bottle on my windowsill. (It also encourages good health practices during cooking. Family members are more likely to scrub up when soothing lotion is available.)

1 Soak pots and pans. If dirties include pots, pans, or casserole dishes crusted with baked-on food, fill them individually with hot water, then set them out of the way on the counter to soak about 15 minutes. If you have encrusted spatulas, ladles, or other small items, drop these in the larger vessels to soak. For heatproof pots and casseroles lined with baked-on food, fill with water and set on a low burner to simmer off the matter.

2 Fill the tub with water. Use the hottest water possible without burning yourself (rubber gloves help with this) and add one or two squeezes of dishwashing liquid. The hotter the water, the more likely glass and silverware will dry without marks or streaks. Don't fill the tub all the way to the top because dirty dishes will displace water, causing overflow.

3 Wash in the right order. Begin with the crystal, then glasses, plates, and dessert dishes. Move on to flatware, then servingware, then serving dishes. Empty the soaking water from pots and pans, and wash them last. Throughout the process, empty your tub and refresh the water as needed. To wash, immerse the dishes in the soapy water, then scrub off grease, sauce, and food with a kitchen brush, sponge, or steel wool pad. (Steel wool is abrasive—don't use it on delicate items made of crystal, porcelain, china, or stainless steel.)

(continued)

4 Rinse the dishes. As you finish scrubbing each item, rinse it off under the running tap in groups of six or seven items at a time. Use lukewarm water. Begin with the outsides of glasses, and the backs of plates and bowls. Rinse the eating surfaces last. Alternatively, you can fill the sink with lukewarm water and immerse the items, refreshing the rinse water as needed.

5 Check the dishes. After you rinse each item, double-check for residue. Any remaining sauce or food will be fairly obvious, but it's a good practice to remove your gloves and check with your fingers to ensure that all grease has been removed. Rewash stubborn soil from unclean pieces. If dairy products or starchy residues (such as flour, cornstarch, or gravy) remain, wash again using cold water because hot water forms a chemical reaction that causes gumminess. For heavily soiled pots, pour in kosher salt and scrub with paper towels before repeating the washing process.

6 Dry the dishes. Once you're sure each dish is clean, let it rest on your rack (or dish towels) to air-dry. Stack bowls and glasses upside down so water drains instead of pooling. If you are ready to put dishes away immediately, you can hand dry them with a dish towel, one item at a time. Don't use bath towels or hand towels because they'll leave lint behind. If you can, recruit a friend or family member to help you dry items and to get them neatly put away.

╳ ╳

Super Secrets for Doing the Dishes

There are secrets to making any chore seem less daunting. Here are five to keep in mind when you're the one in charge of setting the rules around the kitchen sink.

• Wash dishes immediately after meals. Never let dishes pile up or sit in a sink overnight. It isn't going to get any easier or any more fun. Trust me. Just do it!

• Have every household member stick to one cup or glass. Rinse it between uses and set it aside. Washing twenty cups and glasses a day is time-consuming and wastes resources.

• Use good-quality dish soap. For cutting grease, it really is worth the extra pennies to buy Dawn.

• Don't throw sharp knives into soapy water. Soak them in their own bowl or dishpan, or wash them by hand under the tap and put them away immediately. Better safe than sorry.

• Don't stack heavy casseroles or pots on top of fragile glasses or dishware. This seems obvious, but it's tempting to take the risk when you're surrounded by dirty dishes after a big party. Work slowly and steadily, and make good choices. Remember the old riddle: How do you eat an elephant? One bite at a time! ╳

In a 2015 study, Swedish researchers determined that children were 40 percent less likely to develop allergies if their families hand-washed their dishes.

#98 How to Load a Dishwasher

I lived many blissful years of married life without a dishwasher, without feeling slighted. Once our family grew to include our two sons, I decided it was time for this labor-saving device. Not counting the days my babies were born, I'd say that the arrival of my dishwasher was one of the happiest days of my life! Of course, that's an exaggeration, but I won't lie—I do love it.

From the get-go, however, my husband hovered over me as I stacked the dishes, telling me what to put where. I'd walk away, and he'd restack the whole load! I decided to get the real skinny on how it should be done. And I'm happy to share.

1 Provided your dishwasher was made in the last ten years, you don't need to rinse the dishes first. In most cases, scraping should be enough. Water temperatures are higher, spray power is stronger, and rack design and sprayer placement are now very effective.

2 Load it up. Generally the rule is heavy on bottom and light on top. But there are many nuances to the game of dishwasher Tetris. See "How to Load a Dishwasher David's Way," page 184.

3 Select a detergent and rinse agent. Use tabs or all-in-one packs. They contain premeasured detergent and add a rinse agent for you so you don't need to remember to fill the reservoir. If you choose not to use a premeasured pack, there's no difference between liquid and powder. You will, however, need to use a rinse agent. This will get food debris off dishes effectively and reduce spotting on glasses.

4 If you have a disposal, run it and make sure it's clear before starting the dishwasher. Dishwashers usually share a drain pipe with the sink, so you don't want anything blocking in there.

5 Make sure spinning arms are not blocked and that no small items have fallen into the drain area. Close the door and select a cycle based on what you're washing and the manufacturer's instructions.

Scrape, but don't pre-wash! Your dishes need to be dirty in order for the detergent to clean them properly. (Enzymes in the detergent are made to cling to food particles.) Plus, pre-washing can waste up to 6,000 extra gallons of water per year.

How to Load a Dishwasher David's Way (aka "The Right Way")

• Scrape first. Use a brush or spatula for stubborn bits.

• Put pots, pans, and heavy-duty casseroles on the bottom rack, open side down.

• Insert plates in the slots in the bottom rack, facing center. If they lean, lean them inward. Make sure there are spaces in between so sprayers can do their job.

• Glasses, crockery, and delicate items go on the top rack—don't position them with the prongs inside the items. Instead, use the prongs to hold them in place like fences. When possible, stack bowls on an incline.

• Yes, even wineglasses, all but the super-thin type, can be dishwashed. Either lower the top rack to make space for the stems or make sure they don't butt up against other dishes. Even crystal can go in, if your dishwasher features a crystal mode or a temperature setting under 149° F.

• Plastic items like storage bowls with lids go on top. Heating elements on the bottom might melt them.

• Don't overpack the cutlery basket. Knife points and fork tines should go heads down for safety. Make sure spoon surfaces are separated so water can flow between them. (Mix different types in the same compartments so they don't nest.) Lay very long pieces in the upper basket, as they can impede the spray arm. Put small teaspoons in the special spoon basket if your model has one.

• Lay long serving utensils, like tongs and spatulas, in the upper basket. Make sure spoons and ladles face down so they don't collect water.

• Put cutting boards or baking trays in the outermost slots of the bottom rack.

✕ ✕

Betcha Didn't Know . . .

You can put silver flatware in the dishwasher! But there are a few rules to follow if you do:

• Rinse the pieces under the tap before loading them. This removes potentially damaging substances like lemon, vinegar, and salt, which could mar surfaces if the items are left sitting.

• Never put stainless steel with sterling or silverplate in the dishwasher. The two metals react with each other, and you'll do permanent damage to both.

• Hand-wash and dry new sterling and silverplate at least three times before putting them through your dishwasher.

• When putting real silver in the dishwasher, use half the normal amount of detergent and make sure it contains no citrus or lemon additives. Don't worry—unless heavily soiled, your dishes will still come out clean.

• Pay special attention to knives. If your knives were made prior to World War II, then hand-wash them. Knives consist of two elements, the hollow, silver handle and the blade. High heat can melt the resin commonly used in antique knives that seals these components together.

• Skip the heated dry cycle when washing silver in the dishwasher. Take out the pieces and dry them by hand. ✕

#99 How to Mop a Floor

"**D**on't come in here, I just mopped!" is something I heard my mother shouting from inside the kitchen when I was a kid. Even then, I treated that warning seriously, as did my siblings. We steered clear until drying time was over because a wet floor felt unpleasant under the feet. Mopping is well worth it, though: Nothing signals "clean kitchen" like a gleaming floor. Now that I'm in charge of my own kitchen, I'm the shouter. But I look forward to a time when my boys will do some floor cleaning of their own. Here's what moppers need to know.

- **Sweep floors daily.** This protects floors from abrasions caused by feet walking across particles of debris. It also reduces your need to mop.

- **Some flooring, such as polyurethane-coated wood, can't handle harsh detergent**s. When in doubt, consult the professional who installed it or the home-improvement store where you purchased it.

- **Old-fashioned hardwood floors shouldn't be mopped with water.** Instead, sweep with a broom and clean with a dust mop. Spot-clean stubborn areas with commercial hardwood cleaner or distilled white vinegar dissolved in a little bit of water, then wring out the mop or sponge until it's almost dry. If the floor is damp after cleaning, dry it with a soft towel.

- **When your sponge mop begins to crumble, chuck the head and buy a new one.** For rag or string mops, rinse and wring repeatedly, or throw in the washing machine.

- **Start with a clean bucket.** Refilling one that's less than sparkling sets you up to spread germs.

1 Before you start, give the floor its daily brush or sweep.

2 Check for marks and stains. If you find any, clean them up using the guide provided in "How to Tackle Stubborn Spills and Stains on Floors," page 186.

3 Fill your bucket with hot water and mix in the quantity of floor cleaner specified on the cleaner's label.

4 Wring the mop so that it's not dripping, but barely damp. Wear rubber gloves and squeeze it out with your hands or buy a commercial bucket that includes a sturdy wringer.

5 Work the room starting from a corner, working backward rather than forward so you are not stepping on your cleanly mopped floor.

6 Empty and refill your bucket with water and cleaner mixture as soon as the water starts to become dirty.

7 If the room you're mopping is a high-traffic room, dry the floor on your hands and knees with an old towel rather than waiting for it to air-dry.

How to Tackle Stubborn Spills and Stains on Floors

Before you mop, survey the area for any of these common stains. Or, better, stay ahead of the game and attack these issues as they arise.

Blood. Wipe up any excess with paper towels. Then clean with a sponge dampened with very cold water. If the stain persists, sponge it with a solution of half ammonia and half very-cold water, making sure to blot excess water away with a clean towel.

Crayon or wax. Put a clean rag over the spot and iron with a warm iron. Next, rub the affected area with mineral spirits applied to a soft cloth. If dye from the candle or crayon persists, put on a pea-size dab of white toothpaste and rub gently with a soft, dry cloth.

Ink. If pooled, carefully dab up with a soft cloth (don't use paper towels because they may stick, making the mess worse). Then rub with a cloth dampened with warm water and Dawn dishwashing detergent.

Oil. Soak up the majority with lots of paper towels. Then saturate a soft cloth with dry cleaning fluid (you can buy this at a hardware store) and lay the cloth over the spill for 10 minutes. Next, wipe with a cloth barely dampened with distilled white vinegar and a squirt of Dawn dishwashing liquid. Dry the area with a clean cloth.

Scuff marks. First, try to erase them with a gum eraser. If stains persist, dab on a small amount of liquid floor wax and rub gently with a fine-gauge sandpaper. Sprinkle on a small amount of baking soda and rub with a sponge, dampened with hot water. Dry excess dampness with a clean cloth.

Shoe polish. Using a square of superfine steel wool, rub the area gently. Work very slowly because you are essentially sanding off the top layer. Then wipe with a cloth barely dampened with distilled white vinegar and dry with a clean cloth.

Tar. Fill a zip-top bag with ice cubes and lay it on the patch of tar. Then, using a plastic knife or spatula, scrape off the tar. If a fine layer remains, follow the directions for removing oil by using dry cleaning fluid.

Urine. Soak up the majority of the puddle with paper towels as soon as possible.

Wine. Rub the stain with a sponge barely dampened with warm water and Dawn dishwashing detergent. Then rub with a cloth dampened with denatured alcohol. Repeat the process as necessary, alternating between the two cleaners.

Sweep First, Mop Later

Guess what happens when you try to mop an unswept floor? You make mud! Even if you think you know how to sweep, using the proper technique makes the job easier.

Get a good broom. Invest money in a good one, and when it starts to wear, replace it. For floors with lots of dirt or hunks of debris, consider a broom with a broad end, to cover more surface with fewer strokes. For lightly dirty floors, a dust mop will do the trick.

Clear your space. Sounds obvious, but lots of people try to "sweep around it." Trust me, the few minutes you spend decluttering pays off. You can finish the job in broad strokes instead of working around obstacles.

Close off the area to pedestrians. This includes pets.

Start in the far corner and sweep toward the middle of the room, using overlapping strokes. Pull the broom against the floor (and toward your body) to either the right or left, then lift it back to that edge in the opposite direction.

Be sure the broom reaches into the angle of each corner. It's important to be able to access all of the nooks and crannies where dirt accumulates.

Working around the room, collect debris in small piles. Leave them!

When finished, use a dustpan and brush to collect the piles. When you see a "line" of dirt left, turn the dustpan to the opposite angle and sweep it in the pan. If the lines aren't vanishing, wipe them up with a damp paper towel.

#100 How to Vacuum

Vacuuming. Informal surveys tell me that some people love it and some people loathe it. The lovers talk about the soothing hum that drowns out the noise of the day and the relaxation that comes with the repetitive motion. The haters say it's boring and takes too much time. Love it or hate it, we all have to do it.

1 Vacuuming should be your last chore. Dust, clean mirrors, wipe down surfaces, and take down curtains and drapes *before* you vacuum. Any dust rustled up by other tasks will fall to the floor. You don't want to vacuum twice.

2 Clear the way. This sounds obvious, but I have stood and watched my sister vacuum around items ranging from a cardigan sweater to a pile of blocks. Pick up the clutter and your job will go faster.

3 Use a detective's eye. Now that you've cleared shoes and books, think smaller. Use your hands to pick up thumbtacks, balls of hair, gum wrappers, or pebbles. It's easy, and it will extend the life of your vacuum.

4 Surround the area. If you plan to vacuum a rug sitting on a wooden or linoleum floor, sweep those areas with a broom before starting the vacuum.

5 Scope out the outlets. The less cord you have to let out, the less chance you'll have of knocking something

over. Change outlets as you move from area to area.

6 Start your engine. Begin by the door and work your way across the room, going back and forth, overlapping each strip by a few inches. Don't push backward and forward, using short, tiny movements; this takes longer and requires more energy. Long, smooth strokes will achieve results.

7 Cutting corners. If you have wall-to-wall carpet, you need to focus on the corners only every third or fourth vacuuming. You may need to use the wand or nozzle attachment for hard-to-reach parts. If your floor is a hard surface or wood, you may need to do this each time because of dust bunnies. Warning: Vacuums can

(continued)

scratch wood floors. Check and wipe down the vacuum's wheels before you begin to get rid of grit. Switch off the beater bar and work parallel to the planks.

8 Slow down at the fringes. Vacuum rug fringes by moving the vacuum from the rug to the ends of the fringes (not the other direction), or the fringes may get sucked up and jam the vacuum's moving parts.

9 Act fast. If you hear a loud or unusual noise, or if your self-propelling vacuum stops moving, shut it off immediately. When this happens, it's likely something is caught in your brush bar. Running the motor when there's a blockage is likely to burn it out.

Vacuum FAQs

How do I vacuum blinds?
Use the brush attachment. A plain nozzle will scratch or chip them. Close the blinds so that they're flat. Vacuum across the slats, not up and down. Then reverse the slats and vacuum the other way.

How do I vacuum curtains?
Use the lowest suction setting and the upholstery attachment. Begin vacuuming at the top of the curtain and work your way down in overlapping "strips."

How do I vacuum furniture?
For upholstered pieces, use the upholstery attachment. Use the crevice tool attachment for corners, edges, and between cushions. Use the brush attachment for vinyl or leather furniture. To do cabinets or bookshelves, use either the dust brush or crevice tool attachment. I don't recommend vacuuming fine wood furniture because it's not worth the risk of scratching it. Do these pieces by hand with a dust cloth and a mild wood soap, if necessary. In general, however, avoid wetting or dampening wooden furniture. A wipe with a microfiber cloth may be all that's required to remove dust.

Can I vacuum drawers?
Yes! Especially cutlery drawers, where crumbs tend to collect. Remove the contents and use the wand or crevice tool attachment.

Can I vacuum dust mites from my pillows?
You can vacuum pillows with the soft brush attachment. Or you can place a pillow inside a thick plastic bag, and while holding the bag closed around the nozzle, suction all the air from the pillow. Afterward, refluff the pillow.

Can I use my vacuum as an air freshener?
To remove airborne dust, allergens, and odors from a room, remove the hose and leave the vacuum on for 15 minutes with the doors shut. This is a great practice after a big spring cleaning or if you've had a smoker in the house. Caution: Don't leave the vacuum on for extended periods, as you risk burning out the motor or starting a fire.

How about the walls?
Yes. Vacuuming is a great idea, especially before a thorough washing or painting. Use a brush attachment.

What's Wrong with My Vacuum?

Here are the top four most likely diagnoses:

1. Broken or loose belt, or broken brush roll. The cleaning head of an upright or canister vacuum cleaner is equipped with a spinning brush roll that fluffs and moves the carpet fibers. The belt is connected to the vacuum's drive shaft and to the brush, thus spinning it. The movement of the carpet fibers loosens dirt and dust so the suction can capture it and move it to the dirt collector.

A damaged brush roll can't agitate the carpet, and a broken or loosened belt will not spin the brush roll. At this point, the only action left is suction, making the vacuum far less effective.

2. A clog in the bag or filter. The bag collects dirt and dust sucked through the vacuum's hose. The bag also functions as a filter that the air passes through. When the bag is overfull, suction decreases. Bagless vacuums rely on filters to force air from the vacuum. Blocked, wet, and clogged bags and filters impede exhausted airflow, thus decreasing suction power.

3. Clogged hose. Upright vacuums rely on the hose to suck air from the cleaning head into the dirt collector. Clogged hoses have less air to pull dirt and dust from carpet fibers, upholstery, and other surfaces. Canister vacuum cleaners are particularly tricky because the hoses are often longer. It goes without saying: Air cannot flow through a clogged hose.

4. Electrical failure. The electric motor powers the fans used to provide airflow and to power the driveshaft that spins the brush roll. If electrical problems occur in the motor itself, you'll need a new motor or electrical trouble-shooting and repair performed by a qualified technician.

#101 How to Make a Bed

"What's the point of making my bed?" my teenage brother used to reason with my mother. "I'm just going to sleep in it again tonight." This argument did not fly with my father, whose military training included learning to make hospital corners and to pull a sheet taut enough to bounce a quarter.

I, for one, cannot stand to slide into an unmade bed. To my mind, a crisply made bed is a welcoming combination of style and comfort. Cozy comforters and bed linens, properly layered, result in a safe and dreamy refuge. In short, there's a lot more to making a bed than simply slapping on some sheets and blankets.

1 Start with your bare mattress. Buy the best one you can afford. You'll be spending a lot of time on it. Make sure it's clean and fresh. I advise vacuuming it regularly, turning it (if it's not a pillow top), and occasionally laying it out in bright, direct sunlight if possible (see How to "Spring Clean," page 197).

2 Layer on a mattress cover or mattress pad. For one, it will prevent you from ever coming in direct contact with the cold, slippery mattress if your sheets come untucked. It also adds a layer of padding and wicking for comfort. Finally, it extends the life of your mattress by adding a line of defense against spills or stains.

3 Next up are the sheets. Because sheets directly touch your skin, you want to make sure they're soft and comforting; I prefer cotton ones, with a high thread count. These are the most expensive option and require the most labor to care for (special washing and ironing), but I think they're worth it. Alternatively, you can seek out some budget-level

(continued)

poly-cotton blends that still feature breathability. Start by stretching the fitted sheet across the mattress, pulling the elastic hem all the way over the bottom edge of the mattress. Tuck in the sides and corners as tightly as possible.

4 Lay the flat sheet on top with the top edge meeting the end of the mattress, and tuck the sides and bottoms under. I suggest making hospital corners (see "Perfect Hospital Corners," opposite).

5 Layer on a cozy blanket for color, texture, and warmth. You can tuck this in just like you did with the sheet, or leave it hanging evenly over the sides.

6 The crowning glory is the comforter, duvet, or bedspread. The top layer is your visual statement, so let it reflect your personality. This layer should tie the look of the linens together and complement other visual elements in the room. I suggest switching top covers seasonally. Having three or four of different weights and thicknesses also allows you to rotate them for washing.

7 Pillows come next. Choose feather or down for warmth and softness, or firmer synthetics for support.

Replace pillows when you notice obvious signs of fraying or wear, and do it pre-emptively every year to discourage proliferation of allergy-causing mites. In addition to comfort and neck support, pillows can be decorative. Consider shams to tie your bed's look together, and square European-style pillows are great for adding a decorative touch that anchors the bedding to the headboard. Round bolster pillows make a grand statement and also serve as back support for reading in bed. Have fun with small, decorative throw pillows and use them as statement pieces.

#102 How to Start a Bedroom Routine

For me, the bedroom is a refuge from the noise and chaos of the outside world. In order to relax my mind and body, I need my surroundings to be as free from chaos as possible. For that reason, I tidy daily. Doing a little bit each day keeps the chore from feeling insurmountable.

1 Make the bed. (Obviously!)

2 Open the shades and the window(s). Regardless of the season, I leave a window open for a short portion of the day. The fresh air makes the room smell good, and it promotes health.

3 Fold and hang all clothes (and put away jewelry, belts, and shoes). Dirty clothes go in the hamper.

4 Straighten the bedside table. Put away accessories, and arrange books or magazines.

5 Go over surfaces with a microfiber cloth or a feather duster (this will make deep cleaning less frequent).

6 Spot-vacuum the floor, if necessary, using a handheld model (the full vacuuming is done with the rest of the house).

✕ ✕

Perfect Hospital Corners

A neatly made bed is like a gorgeously gift-wrapped box. For a fresh and finished feel, you'll want to learn the art of folding orderly hospital corners. Here's how:

1. Start by putting on the bottom sheet. Tightly secure the first corner, then move to the one diagonal to it. Pull firmly and secure. Repeat, pulling and tucking until you have a flat, taut surface.

2. Spread your top sheet (the flat sheet) over the bottom sheet, centering it. Make sure to pull it from the corners, then the sides, until it rests flat.

3. Tuck the bottom edge of the sheet (by your feet) firmly under the bottom of the mattress, letting the sides hang down.

4. On one hanging side, grasp the edge of the sheet about 12 to 18 inches from the foot of the bed. Pull it straight up to form a triangle. Then just lay it there. Tuck the end that drapes tightly underneath the mattress.

5. Still leaving the triangle, tuck in the long part that hangs down on the sides.

6. Now, pick up the triangle and pull it straight down with a firm force, making a diagonal line.

7. Finally, tuck the triangle tightly under the mattress.

✕

While top sheets have long been admired as a hygienic and attractive barrier between sleepers and their blankets, the use of flat sheets is on the decline. An estimated 40 percent of Americans have chosen to go top(sheet)less.

#103 How to Hang Curtains

So you've decided to dress your window! Congratulations. But get mentally prepared. That first decision just set off a chain of other decisions to consider: What style will you choose? How much coverage is ideal? What measurements are most important?

Curtains and drapes do a lot for a home. They ensure privacy, they keep out furniture-fading sunlight, they put the finishing touch on room décor, they make a room appear larger, and, depending on the season, they can block out or hold in heat and coolness. Here are some hints to help you navigate this unfamiliar terrain.

1 Decide on the style of the window dressing. Some choices include floor-length formal drapes, informal tab-top curtains, or whimsical café-style curtains.

2 Figure out where you'll hang the rod. You might choose the customary 4 inches above the top of the window frame. Depending on whether the curtains have tucks, flat tops, tabs, or ruffles, you may choose to hang them higher or lower. For a tall, deep window, you could consider hanging the rod inside the window frame.

3 Determine the level of coverage. A good rule of thumb is to extend the top of the curtain 4 inches above the top of the window frame, 2 inches to the sides of the window frame, and 2 inches below the bottom of the window frame. Choose dimensions based on how much privacy you require, how much light you want to block out, and whether you want the window to appear larger than it actually is for aesthetic reasons.

4 Now you can measure! Use a tape measure to measure from the curtain rod to the desired bottom point and from side to side. Double the side-to-side measurement so that you'll have enough fabric for full, gathered

curtains. Now, measure the window. Take three sets of measurements: Measure the inside of the window frame, the frame itself, and the extra space outside of the window frame. You may get to the store and decide to switch from one type of window dressing to another. Having all relevant measurements will save you a trip.

5 Procure your supplies. Make sure the person helping you at the fabric or home-improvement store understands the difference between the projected dimensions of the curtains and the actual dimensions of the window. Have the actual dimensions of the frame on hand, too.

Make windows look larger by hanging curtains above the top of the frame and letting them hang to the floor.

X X X X X X X X X X X X X X X X X X X X X X X X X X X X X X X X X X X X X X X X X X X X X

No-Sew Curtains

If you like the homespun look of plain linen, and hate to sew, have I got the curtain solution for you!

If you don't already know, drop cloths are available at hardware and home improvement stores, and they come hemmed on all four sides.

The very first thing you'll want to do is iron the fabric, so that it's crisp, flat, and stretched out. Then re-measure regardless of what the package says.

Drop cloths are commonly 6 feet by 9 feet. It's quite possible to make those dimensions

work, especially for floor-length curtains with a bit of romantic, pooling fabric at the floor level. If you need to adjust the length, you can hem them quickly with iron-on hem tape (see How to Hem the No-Sew Way, page 136).

To affix your curtains to the rod, open the sides of the top hem and slide the rod through or purchase snap-on grommets or clip-on rings from any craft or fabric store.

To embellish, I suggest iron-on bric-a-brac that you can find at the same craft or fabric store! X

THE ROD

As I mentioned earlier, the most common mount for a curtain rod is 4 inches higher than the top of the window frame, allowing the curtains to hang 2 inches below the bottom of the window frame. To give the illusion of a taller window, hang the rod 8 inches above the frame. For a very dramatic effect, you could opt to hang it all the way up to the molding by the ceiling. To give the illusion of width, extend the rod farther than the common 2 inches beyond each side, anywhere up to 6 inches. Unless your goal is to make a strong statement and buck convention, having a rod no wider than a third of the window-width makes for nice proportions.

THE WIDTH

Most people like the look of curtains hanging in folds. You want to be generous with the amount of fabric, so the panels should be at least one and a half times the width of the window (or of the rod, if your goal is to give the illusion of a wider window). For a flatter, more modern look, measure your fabric at the width of the window, plus 1 inch on either side. For a luxurious, baroque look, measure the fabric at three times the window width.

THE LENGTH

For floor-length drapes, measure from the top of the rod all the way to the floor, then subtract to allow for the hanging hardware. When purchasing premeasured drapes and curtains, bear in mind that the length given is from the top of the pocket into which the rod is inserted to the hemmed, bottom edge. When in doubt, round up. Hemming curtains is easier than lengthening them.

The Care and Maintenance of Your Drapes and Curtains

In addition to the occasional machine washing or trips to the dry cleaner (see How to Hand-Wash Curtains, page 175), your drapes and curtains will last longer and look fresher if you follow these tips:

Keep 'em dry. Close the window when it's raining and don't subject curtains and drapes to direct steam, such as from a radiator or humidifier. Water stains can become permanent, as can mildew stains.

(continued)

Buddy up with blinds. Even inexpensive plastic mini-blinds can help protect your curtains. In direct sunlight or under conditions of extreme heat, draw the blinds. This will keep fabric fibers in curtains and drapes from breaking down, and dyes from fading.

Rotate! If several of the windows in your room have the same dimensions and have identical curtains, swap them out. Conditions are different from window to window. Or keep several sets of curtains available in your linen closet for any given window. Rotating will not only make your favorites last longer, but it's also a great way to refresh the room's look from season to season.

Shake 'em down. Between vacuuming and washing, beat and shake your curtains (while they're still on the rod) to loosen dust and debris, and to rid them of minute mites. Do this with the windows open or with your vacuum set to "suction" with no hose attached (see How to Vacuum, page 187).

#104 How to Remove Gum from a Rug

No matter how vigilant, tidy, or house-proud you might be, there will come a time when a stealthy piece of chewing gum will find a patch on your carpet or rug and take up residence. My advice is to take a deep breath and keep these tricks up your sleeve, not only for the gum, but also for some of the more stubborn staining culprits.

1 Fill a zip-top freezer bag with ice. Lay it on the patch of gum and let it rest there at least 15 minutes.

2 Using your fingers and fingernails, pick as much of the freezing cold gum out of the carpet fibers as possible.

3 Repeat. Freeze the gum again and use your hands to remove more gum. Smaller pieces should chip off as you pick through the fibers.

4 Pour a generous amount of olive oil onto the corner of an absorbent rag or old dish towel. Dab it onto the gum patch, scrubbing as you do. Keep adding oil, but only by dabbing. Resist the temptation to pour oil directly onto the spot.

5 Using a serrated-edged knife, scrape at the spot to loosen gum particles. Alternate this with scrubbing with your lightly oiled cloth. Repeat until all of the gum is gone.

6 You might be thinking, *Now I have an oil stain instead of a gum stain!* You would be right. Cover the spot with baking soda and press it into the carpet fibers. Allow it to soak up the oil for at least 15 minutes.

7 After the resting period, use your hand to rub in even more baking soda. Vacuum up the oily baking soda.

8 Finally, clean the area by dabbing it with a sponge soaked in a solution of warm water and a few drops of Dawn dishwashing liquid. Rinse and repeat as necessary until all the soap and oil are removed.

9 Dab dry with a clean towel, then allow the area to air-dry fully.

#105 How to Erase an Ink Spill from Carpet

Rubbing Alcohol Method

1 Immediately dab at the liquid with paper towels, absorbing as much as you can without pressing.

2 Saturate a rag with rubbing alcohol and dab at the spot. Replace your rag and resaturate with alcohol as needed. You don't want to dab ink back onto the carpet.

3 Repeat until the ink has been fully removed.

Lubricant Method

1 Immediately dab at the liquid with paper towels, absorbing as much as you can without pressing.

2 Grab a can of spray-on lubricant, such as WD-40. Test a small patch of carpet near an edge or under a piece of furniture. Spray it on, sponge with a solution of warm water and Dawn dishwashing detergent, and then rinse with another damp sponge. If the stain is still there after drying, proceed to Step 3.

3 Spray the lubricant on the stain, covering it but without forming a pool. Let sit for 15 minutes.

4 Using a sponge saturated with warm water and Dawn, dab at the spot. Change sponges and add more water as needed.

5 Once the ink is gone, rinse the area with clear, warm water, press a dry towel into the carpet to absorb dampness, and allow it to air-dry.

╳ ╳

Liquid Spill? Don't Rub or Scrub!

For a liquid spill, the first line of defense is soak and dab. When possible, place a layer of paper towels on top and allow physics to do the work. You want liquid to transfer to the place of least concentration (the clean towels) from the place of most concentration (the spill site). Pressure can force the staining agent deep into the rug's fibers. ╳

#106 How to Remove Pet Stains from Carpet

(or, What to Do When You Love Spot, but Not "Spots")

They don't mean to make a mess! Really! Frustrating as pet stains and odors in your carpet may be, most people who love animals consider the cleanup to be a small price to pay in exchange for the cuteness and companionship. Here are three green ways to tackle the accidents.

1 Seltzer water. The bubbling action in the seltzer is what makes it an effective stain fighter. Before pouring on a small amount of fizzy water, blot and dab urine stains with paper towels. Once the liquid has stopped fizzing, blot the spot again and repeat as necessary. For a fresh stain, this may be all the treatment you need. For old or set-in stains, consider this a pretreatment. Allow the carpet to dry, then treat with the baking soda method (Step 3).

2 Distilled white vinegar. Vinegar's acidity helps neutralize odors, making it a great option for dealing with fresh pet urine. Lightly dab and blot with clean paper towels.

Remember: Don't rub or scrub! Using a solution of equal parts cold water and distilled white vinegar, sponge the soiled area. Wring and repeat several times. When you're satisfied that the urine has been removed, blot the carpet with a thick, dry towel and allow it to fully air-dry.

3 Baking soda. For old or dried urine spots, baking soda is the answer. Pour a generous pile on the spot and rub it in lightly with your (gloved) fingertips. Let it sit overnight, then vacuum it up. Caution: Pets may be tempted to play with or eat the pile. Overturn a large plastic bowl or a laundry basket over the area and weight it down with thick books.

#107 The Poop on Poop

Handling another creature's waste is not at the top of anyone's wish list. Once you become a pet owner (or a parent!), however, duty trumps squeamishness.

1 Get your tools. You will need rubber gloves, a dustpan, a scrub brush, and a paint scraper or spatula.

2 Put on rubber gloves. (For the chemical and the ick factor!)

3 Use the scraper to scoop the bulk of the feces into the dustpan.

4 Dab up any excess waste with damp paper towels, taking care not to grind it into carpet fibers.

5 Spray the stain with a prewash laundry stain remover. It must be a product that's labeled "oxi-action," "oxygen power," or "oxygenated." Scrub it in with the scrub brush.

6 Dab the area with a damp sponge saturated with a solution of dishwashing liquid and cold water.

7 Spray again with laundry prewash. Alternate with dish soap solution as necessary.

8 Do this until there is no visible stain. When finished, blot the area with a clean, dry towel and allow it to air-dry.

9 Once dry, if an odor persists, treat the area with distilled white vinegar or baking soda.

10 Soak whatever tools you used in a sink filled with a gallon of hot water, with 1 cup of bleach poured in. Take great care not to splash the solution on anything: Bleach discolors clothing, hair, and some countertops and flooring. Not to mention— it's really bad for your skin.

Pets can provide many health benefits, ranging from reduced blood pressure to elevated seratonin and dopamine. Some studies have shown that dog owners are less likely to experience depression than those without pets.

#108 How to "Spring Clean"

In the days before modern conveniences, the first warm weather made it possible to do a sweeping housecleaning. After a long, hard winter, it must have felt great to throw open the windows and let the dust blow out, to wash walls down with water that didn't freeze, and to toss out your sour mattress ticking.

These days, most of us clean throughout the year, but there's no denying that the brighter sun and the longer days still invigorate us, filling us with the desire for a fresh start. Here are some suggestions for ways to kick off the warmest part of the year with renewed and refreshed surroundings.

Kitchen

• **Freezer.** Empty it completely and toss anything with freezer burn (grayish brown and dried-out). Dissolve 3 tablespoons baking soda in a quart of hot water. Using a soft, mesh sponge, wipe down the inside.

(continued)

• **Refrigerator.** Repeat the freezer-cleaning process detailed above, but toss anything growing a culture.

• **Stove and oven.** Remove control knobs, burners, and spill catchers, and soak them in a sink of hot water, Dawn dishwashing detergent, and 1 tablespoon baking soda. Run the oven cleaning cycle or do it manually. Clean the stove top with nonabrasive scouring liquid.

• **Countertop appliances.** Thoroughly clean the toaster oven, blender, coffeemaker, and food processor. Run removable parts through the dishwasher or soak them in a sink of hot water and dish soap.

• **Behind the scenes.** Enlist help to pull out the stove and refrigerator. Vacuum, then mop around them. Vacuum out the refrigerator coils.

• **Sink.** Soak the drain cover in a bowl of hot water and dish soap. Pour a box of baking soda into the drain and let it sit for an hour. Then pour in distilled white vinegar to loosen any clogs, followed by a whole kettle of boiling water down the drain to flush out grease and debris.

Living Room

• **Declutter.** Put away items where they belong (shoes to closets, school books to bedroom shelves, quilts to linen closets). Enlist the help of everyone in the household to make this a regular task, weekly, or, even better, daily.

• **Shelves.** Dust knick-knacks and bookshelves. Remove each item, dust the shelves themselves, and then carefully dust each item before replacing.

• **Rugs and carpets.** Shampoo or steam-clean the rugs and wall-to-wall carpet. Vacuuming and spot-cleaning are for maintenance. The big clean must be done regularly. Have antique or precious rugs professionally cleaned.

• **Curtains and drapes.** Throw curtains in the laundry if their care labels indicate that it's safe. Send expensive drapes to the dry cleaner.

• **Lamps.** Dust the bases and wipe off any greasy areas with a solution of hot water and distilled white vinegar, making sure to dry thoroughly with a clean towel. Dust or vacuum the shades.

• **TVs, tablets, and computer monitors.** Clean screens by wiping them down with a microfiber cloth lightly dampened with distilled water. Dust the plastic parts, then wipe down with a vinegar-and-water solution as needed, avoiding electronic components. Use compressed air to dust in crevices.

Bathroom

• **Medicine cabinet.** Toss expired medications and deteriorating cosmetics. Take inventory. Wipe down the interiors, then clean the mirrors.

• **Fans and vents.** Take them apart with a screwdriver and soak individual pieces in a solution of hot water and Dawn dishwashing detergent.

- **Shower curtain.** Replace the interior liner and machine wash the shower curtain.

- **Towels and washcloths.** Make rags of the ones with frays or stains, or donate them to an animal shelter, where they'll be used for bedding.

- **Floor.** Scrub the floor with a brush. A flick with a wet mop is fine for maintenance, but you'll need some elbow grease to really get the scum out of cracks and crevices.

- **Drain.** Pour baking soda into the drain and let it sit for an hour. Then pour in distilled white vinegar, followed by a whole kettle of boiling water, to flush out debris.

- **Showerhead.** De-scum the showerhead. If you can easily remove the head, soak it in a sink filled with a solution of half distilled white vinegar and half boiling water. Once the water has fully cooled, scrub it with a stiff brush. If you can't remove the showerhead, fill a heavy-duty zip-top freezer bag with vinegar and warm water and tie it to the pipe with kitchen twine or a rubber band. Let it hang there overnight. Remove the bag and scrub the showerhead with a stiff brush, taking care not to scratch the finish.

Bedroom

- **Mattress.** Strip the mattress of bedding and lay it in the sun on a clean blanket in the backyard (if you have one!). Mark which side was last facing up; if your mattress is not a pillow top, flip it.

- **Pillows.** Machine wash them, if possible. Most down- and fiber-filled pillows can go through the wash (check the label). Don't overstuff the machine; run one or two pillows through per cycle, using gentle detergent. Make sure all pillows are completely dry to avoid mildew.

- **Dressers and armoires.** Remove all items from the interior. Vacuum and dust inside cabinets and drawers.

- **Bed linens.** Wash pillow shams, the mattress pad, the bed skirt, and the duvet cover. Check labels; send anything not machine washable to the dry cleaner.

- **Windows.** Use a bucket filled with warm water and a drop of dish soap, and a soft, microfiber cloth. Be sure to do the sills and frames. Finish by washing the panes with a nonstreaking glass cleaner.

- **Blinds and curtains.** Vacuum blinds using your vacuum's wand attachment and machine wash curtains or send them to the dry cleaner.

Closets

- **Take inventory and declutter.** Go through each item in your closet. Decide if you are going to keep, donate, or trash the contents, one piece at a time. For items you are keeping stored away, make a list of the contents and whereabouts.

- **Seasonal clothing.** Rotate seasonal clothing and store what's not needed.

- **Boxes and trunks.** Label the contents on all sides, as well as on the top.

- **Regroup.** Organize your clothes by color, type, or use.

(continued)

• **Shelves.** Remove all items and clean as needed, vacuum and dust the shelves, then reshelve the items.

• **Floor.** Vacuum and mop the floor.

Around the House

• **Metal fixtures.** Clean and polish all brass and metal fixtures, including outdoor doorknobs, the door knocker, pot and pan racks, and finials.

• **Wood.** Using proper wood soap and wax, clean fine woods, including banisters, finials, and art pieces.

• **Wall hangings.** Remove mirrors, wall art, and photos from the wall. Dust around them, clean the frames, and then clean the glass.

• **Air-conditioning filters.** If you don't have disposable filters, gently pull out each filter and rinse it with warm water in the bathtub. For spot-cleaning, use a small brush and some dish soap diluted in hot water. Allow them to dry, then pop them back into place.

• **Light switches.** Fill a bucket with a gallon of hot water, a drop of dishwashing detergent, and ½ cup white vinegar. Wipe down every switch and switch plate in the house.

• **Doorknobs.** Fill a bucket with hot water and household cleaner, following the instructions on the bottle. Wipe down every doorknob inside the house.

LIFE SKILLS

There's more to running a home than cooking and cleaning, laundry, and (occasionally) sewing. You may have to write things such as checks and thank-you notes, invite friends or family over for food, set a table, and perhaps even get dressed for a fancy event. Some life skills are simply acquired over time by seeing things happen in the homes of others, but here's a general overview of some of the basics and also a crash course on a few of the little grace notes for the finishing touches of pleasant living.

#109 How to Make a Household Budget

If the word *budget* makes you want to take to your bed and turn off your phone, you're not alone. "I don't want to be told what I can and cannot do with my money," you might say. But the fact of the matter is that a budget is your key to feeling calm and happy in relation to your money. If you take a deep breath and read on, you'll see that a budget isn't Big Brother or a straitjacket. It's a tool designed to help you live your life with as little stress, fear, and worry as possible. Here are some guidelines to keep in mind:

Know you're in control. Repeat: I am the boss of me. If the idea of taking your head out of the sand and creating a budget makes you uncomfortable or scared, remind yourself that you are the final word. You don't *have* to carry through with adhering to it, but information is power. Once you know what there is to know, you are free to ignore the whole idea.

Keep it simple. My husband loves the idea of Excel spreadsheets and Quicken. Gadgets and apps excite him. I'm the opposite. I still enjoy my Rolodex and my pen and notebook. If you love using apps, great! Use the tools. If not, don't put the obstacle of learning the program or software in your way. Use an old-fashioned sheet of paper.

Identify a goal or dream. Decide what would make you happy. Paying off a student loan? Buying a car? A down payment on a house? Having zero credit card debt? Keeping the prize in mind will help you stick to your budget.

Commit to a trial period. For me, the idea of doing something—or anything—forever is overwhelming. It makes me not want to start. As with exercising, eating healthfully, or keeping a clean house, I hold myself accountable for only short periods. Then, if I like what I'm doing, I re-up. Sometimes, a new practice becomes a lifelong habit.

1 Write down your total monthly income. For freelancers and project workers, this may be trickier, and you may have to estimate. Look at your monthly income over the last six months to gauge best- and worst-case scenarios for the future.

2 Separate your spending into fixed, variable, and discretionary categories.

In one column identify essential fixed expenses, such as rent and mortgage payments, car insurance, medical insurance, cable bills, and student loan payments. These payments will be the exact same amount each billing cycle.

In another, list your monthly essential but variable expenses, such as utilities, phone bills, groceries, gasoline expenditures, credit card

payments, clothing costs, car maintenance, household repair, medication, and medical bills. Try to round off numbers to the nearest $10 if possible, or $50 if more breadth is needed. Base your estimations on past bills, if you have them.

In a third column, list reasonable amounts for nonessential expenses. These include gifts for birthdays and holidays, eating out, entertainment, hobbies, personal care, and travel. Check old credit card statements by the month to ground yourself in actual numbers of dollars spent.

3 Attack debt first. The bottom line is that your money isn't your money if you're in debt. If you're reeling from the weight of credit card bills or other debt, a budget can help you see how to dig your way out. Overbudget so that you are always paying more than the minimum on credit cards. If you have extra money from another category at the end of the month, make extra payments to reduce debt. If you have a serious debt problem, you may need the help of a credit counseling agency. Beware, though: Some purport to be helpful and instead prey on the indebted. Confirm their authenticity through the National Foundation for Credit Counseling or the Association of Independent Consumer Credit Counseling Agencies.

4 Build in a buffer. What was the amount of your highest-ever utility bill? Write that number into your monthly budget. Also budget amounts for emergencies and, if you have enough, for "mad money" to be spent without any questions asked or eyebrows raised. With that covered, you're likely to feel more comfortable investing a designated amount monthly. This investment could simply mean putting $10 into a savings account. Do not, however, invest large amounts of money if you are in debt. Look for places to cut without pain. This is personal. For one person, giving up their favorite subscription box might feel like a cruel breakup. They might, however, be fine with eating out less. Another may not be able to fathom buying store brand foods but would be happy to give up premium TV channels. The idea here is to decrease spending without feeling deprived.

5 Follow the plan as closely as possible for several months and analyze the outcome. Although "forever" is too long, you will need to give the plan a chance to play out. After a reasonable amount of time, reassess. Are you paying down debt or at least not incurring new debt? Are you paying bills on time without robbing Peter to pay Paul? Have you banked or saved any money? Has it been painful, tolerable, or exhilarating?

✕ ✕

Budgeting Tips and Tricks

Sticking to a budget reduces stress and helps personal relationships. Financial issues can cause families and couples to fight, but being in control and knowing the facts about money and spending can bring peace.

• For each expense, label an envelope in a cardboard box (or use hanging files or a foldover binder). Put the cash for each category in its proper place. There's nothing like a hands-on illustration to bring the cold, hard facts home.

• Pay cash for everything for at least one month. This gives you the real-world sense that your money isn't just an idea.

• Instead of endlessly scrolling or binge-watching TV every night, look for coupons in circulars, newspapers, or shopping apps. There are TV shows and online communities dedicated to this money-saving practice. Many people get a thrill out of the "game" of couponing. ✕

#110 How to Set the Table for a Fancy Formal Dinner

Special occasions, such as engagement announcements, anniversary and birthday dinners, and holiday feasts call for something fancier than the traditional place setting. Although today's customs allow for more individual creativity than in the past, there are some basic rules. Once you learn them, you can observe them or bend them as you like.

The Basic Layout

The place setting wasn't devised as a puzzle or a test. It's based on logic and grew out of rhyme and reason. Utensils to be used first are laid on the outside. Diners work their way inward as courses are served and cleared.

The main dinner plate is right in front of the diner. Glasses and stemware are placed above the dinner plate and to the right because the majority of diners are right-handed and glasses are reached for repeatedly. Bread plates are placed above the dinner plate and to the left. The setup makes it easy to eat without much movement, which could lead to spills and breaks.

Setting the Table

Here is the traditional formula for a basic "cover" or place setting, in order of setup. Remember, you aren't just setting the table, you're setting the tone for the event.

1 *Charger and dinner plate (or "service plate").* First, put down the charger plate. A charger is a plate larger than the dinner plate and is used to dress up the table. Ideas about when to clear the charger vary. Sometimes, chargers are removed as guests are seated. It is becoming more common for charger plates to remain on the table during the service of soups and first courses, to act as a base on which food-bearing plates and bowls will sit. If the design of the chargers complements the design of the dinner plates, they may remain on the table throughout the courses of the meal. Charger plates are, however, always removed before serving dessert. If your dishware is already formal or pleasing, and you choose not to use chargers, lay out the dinner plate only.

2 *Soup bowl.* Center it on top of the charger and/or dinner plate.

3 *Bread plate.* Place this above and to the left of the charger or dinner plate. Lay the bread knife on it, facing the blade tip away from the charger. It should be horizontal, lining up with the edge of the table.

4 *Coffee cup.* Place this, on its saucer, slightly below and to the left of the bread plate.

5 *Forks and napkin.* To the left of the dinner plate, working from the edge of the plate outward, lay the dinner fork, the fish fork, and then the salad fork (or rearrange to match the order of your courses). Next to the salad fork, lay the rectangular napkin. NOTE: All flatware should align with the bottom of the plate.

6 *Spoons and knives.* To the right of the dinner plate, working from the edge of the plate outward, lay the dinner knife, fish knife, and salad knife (blades facing the plate), and the teaspoon. If you have a soup course, put a soup spoon on the far right. If your courses move in a different order, rearrange so the last knife used is on the inside.

7 *Glasses and stemware.* Above the spoons and knives, to the right of the plate, set the water glass on the inside (closest to the bread plate) and two wineglasses beside it, grouping the two together. Just above the wineglasses, set a Champagne glass.

8 *Dessert spoon and fork.* Place these horizontally above the dinner plate, with the spoon on top with its handle facing to the right; the fork sits below with its handle facing left.

When electricity was first invented, not all households could afford it. Even if you could, it was considered polite to avoid boasting. To make guests feel comfortable, hosts kept candles with charred wicks on the tables so that no one could be singled out as having more affluence.

A Word on Tablecloths

Like a bedspread, the tablecloth is the icing on the cake. It unifies the table settings and the décor of the room. On a practical level, the tablecloth can protect the table itself and dampen the noise at crowded or lively parties. Here are some points to consider as you choose tablecloths for various occasions:

• **Overhang.** For a formal dinner, a deep and dramatic overhang is the order of the day. A drop of 10 to 15 inches will allow it to rest in guests' laps. For a relaxed, casual dinner, a drop of 10 inches is appropriate.

• **Silence cloth.** The silence cloth is used underneath the decorative tablecloth to give it a fluffy, drapey, luxurious effect. Silence cloths are commercially available in materials such as felt, foam-backed vinyl, wool, and quilted cotton, but you can easily make them yourself because they simply require cutting and measuring—no hemming.

• **The basic tablecloth.** If you buy only one, get it in a solid color that matches or complements your dinnerware and accent pieces. Remember, the more precious the fabric, the more care you'll have to take with spills and splashes. Some very nice tablecloths are sold in poly-cotton blends and are machine washable. For Grandma's heirloom lace or linen, however, you're looking at a trip to the dry cleaner after each event.

At the Center of It All

Nothing indicates the mood of a festive meal more than the centerpiece. If there's a horn of plenty on the table, you know it's Thanksgiving. With centerpieces, you are limited only by your imagination—and the height of your guests. Don't stack anything on the table that might prevent easy eye contact during conversation.

Although you can buy lovely centerpieces at home goods stores, here are some fun DIY alternatives:

• **Floating the idea.** Use fruit in a glass bowl or large vase. Try using lemons for a cheerful spring luncheon or create a tableau of plums, blueberries, and red grapes floating in water for a romantic deep-winter's dinner.

• **Falling for flowers and leaves.** Spread apart the leaves of small purple and green cabbages, and plunge stems of flowers into the centers. Or invert various sizes of bowls, drape them with ivy, fall leaves, or bunches of grapes, and place pomegranates or squash on top.

• **Stack it.** Use a flat platter or plate with a rim, and pile it high with pinecones, palm fronds, or anything that suits the theme.

Tips for a Successful Dinner

Hosting can be stressful, but with a few advanced considerations your dinner can be a memorable—and enjoyable—evening. Here are a few tips (keeping in mind of course that, as with all matters of etiquette, your guests' comfort trumps any rule).

• If you're having more than twelve guests, cater, staff, or provide buffet service.

• Have one or two spares of everything on standby in the kitchen, in case something gets broken or dropped.

• Don't crowd your guests. If you need space, don't set out the coffee cup or dessert flatware until the other dishes have been cleared. If it's very crowded, consider seating guests at two tables.

• Formal tables are beautiful and indicate that an occasion is special and should be treated with honor.

#111 How to Answer a Wedding Invitation

Responding promptly to a wedding invitation shows the sender your gratitude for being included. It also shows that you understand customs and are willing to participate in them, therefore ensuring future inclusion and connection. Most of all, though, it really helps the person planning (and paying for) the wedding estimate how many chairs will be needed and what the grand total of the bill might be. Here's a to-do list.

1 If there's a response card, fill it out and send it back as soon as possible. Most are preprinted, and you need to check boxes and fill it out. If you see "M_____ will attend _____ will not attend," it means to finish the courtesy title and write in your name. For instance, a single man, might write something like "r. Smith" on the line, a married couple might finish it with "r. and Dr. Smith."

2 Some invitations include entrée selections. If yours does, and you're responding in the affirmative, check the box or boxes for your desired entrée.

3 If your invitation doesn't include a response card, you are often expected to hand-write a response (although nowadays a website where you can RSVP may be provided). Use the plainest, nicest cardstock you can find. If the invitation is formal, respond in kind. You are elevating the event and giving it the gravitas it deserves. Say something like, "Ms. Flattered Guest accepts with pleasure your wedding invitation for Sunday, the tenth of June, at four o'clock in the afternoon."

⌕ ⌕ ⌕ ⌕ ⌕ ⌕ ⌕ ⌕ ⌕ ⌕ ⌕ ⌕

The Plus One

If you are single, unless the invitation specifies "Mr. Happy-to-Attend and Guest," you are **not** invited to bring anyone. Plates at weddings are costly. Don't put the couple in an awkward position by increasing numbers. Also, children are not invited with parents unless their names appear on the envelope. Many couples want weddings to be adults-only affairs. ⌕

Although rumor has it that a wedding guest has an entire year to send a gift, it's considerate to send one before the wedding or shortly (no more than three months) thereafter.

#112 How to Pack a Suitcase

Packing a suitcase is an art. Flight attendants, globetrotters, and frequent business travelers can attest. Have you ever suffered the embarrassment of being invited to a fancy restaurant when you've packed only hiking boots and sandals? Or the discomfort of shivering in a tank top, envious of those around you who thought to pack fleeces (even though it rarely snows in Florida in March)?

With ever-increasing baggage fees, and constantly shrinking carry-on space, knowing how to pack your bags efficiently can also save you money when you fly. Whether traveling by train, bus, or car, packing the right items can take the stress (and high cost!) out of travel. Minimizing the number of bags you carry helps make the journey as sweet as the destination.

Most important, you'll be secure in the knowledge that you have what you need when you unpack. It's easy when you plan ahead by following these tips.

Before You Travel

Prepare like an athlete. See your doctor before you travel to discuss any health complaints or to get refills on medications or prescriptions for anything new you might need. For the week leading up to your departure, maintain your health and fitness: Eat well, sleep well, and de-stress. Travel requires stamina. There's luggage to haul, time zones to negotiate, and you'll want to be at your calmest in case of irritations like flight delays or lost bags.

Be a good citizen. For foreign travel, don't assume you know what paperwork or vaccinations (and proof thereof) you'll need. Check individual countries' websites or contact the US State Department. Then make an appointment with your primary care doctor to make sure you're up to date on any required vaccines.

Avoid a postage pile-up. Have a friend pick up your mail or fill out a card (or online form) to have it stopped temporarily while you're away.

Pay your bills. This sounds obvious, but you never know when travel delays could put you behind, racking up costly late fees or harming your credit. If you don't want to pay in advance, call providers and lenders, and arrange for delayed due dates.

Alert the bank. If you're traveling abroad, tell the banks that issue your credit and debit cards. To protect you from fraud, they might shut down your account after recognizing a sudden spate of atypical activity like purchasing several sets of skis in Switzerland, or frequenting a beer garden in Germany. Also, check with your bank to make sure that your credit card will be accepted where you are going. And remember that currency conversion fees may apply to foreign purchases; you may want or need to use particular credit cards to avoid such unnecessary fees. Be aware that you'll likely get the best conversion rates simply by taking cash from a local bank machine with your normal debit card.

Let the loved ones know. Give your itinerary and contact information to loved ones. They may need to reach you in case of an emergency (or to let you know you won the lottery!).

Planning and Prep

Make a list. And then, check it twice. You can probably wait to decide if you'll take the yellow shirt or the blue, but some items are nonnegotiable. Avoid that sickening feeling of remembering something crucial just as the plane is taxiing down the runway. Eyeglasses, contact lenses, passports and visas, medicines, host gifts, and work-related documents top the list of forgotten items.

- **Don't wait until the last minute!** If you're furiously throwing things into bags at midnight before your 5:00 a.m. flight, you may wind up in Paris with a camp lantern. Instead, start packing a week in advance. Leave your suitcase open in a corner of the room, and stash items you have multiples of, like socks, underwear, and dental floss. (Keep your packing list and a pen nearby.)

- **Check the weather.** Even if we can't fully predict conditions, in this age of advanced technology, you'll be able to gauge likely temperatures. Why drag a winter coat if Amsterdam will be enjoying a warm spring?

- **Survival of the fittest.** Plan so you'll always have food and water at hand. It's true that you can't carry more than 3 fluid ounces of liquid through airport security, but you can carry an empty water bottle to refill on the other side. Bring a granola bar, nuts, or other small snack that will keep to help maintain your blood sugar levels.

- **Wear it; don't carry it.** Yes, you'll have to take off heavy shoes and jackets going through airport security, but it's a huge space-saver payoff. Once aboard a plane or train, you can stash your heavy coat overhead or under the seat.

- **Color coordinate.** Pack clothes that match. Bring coats and jackets in neutral colors, and have every top match every bottom. Save pizzazz for accessories.

Get Packing: The Hand Luggage

- **Keep essentials close.** Carry medicines, a light wrap or jacket, travel documents, make-up, a pair each of clean socks and underwear, credit cards, and money in a large purse or backpack (along with your snacks and water). And don't let it out of your sight!

- **When asleep, loop the strap around your feet.** Once you're off the plane, never hand it to a porter or valet. Think of it this way: If all your luggage were lost but this piece, could you get through a week in a strange place?

- **Save your screen.** Tuck laptops and tablets into your hand luggage, when possible. You'll have to present these at security, so try not to have to dig deep.

Get Packing: The Big Bag

- **Roll 'em! Roll everything.** It's the most efficient way to use space and the best packing method for avoiding wrinkles. You can even roll a suit by actually turning the jacket inside out, folding it in half lengthwise, then folding it in half, top to bottom, and rolling. For pants, lay them out as you would hang them up. Fold dress shirts the way they're boxed at the dry cleaner; place the shirts on the top part of the pants, then fold the pants over the shirts. Another way to keep shirts wrinkle-free is to fold them into thirds from outside to inside, with the sleeves folded in. Next, fold the shirt into roughly 3- to 5-inch sections, working upward, until the collar is on top. Once you've rolled everything, set it aside.

- **The shoes fit.** Line sides of the case with shoes, putting each one in a shoe bag or gallon-size zip-top bag. Stuff rolled-up socks, scarves, neckties, and underwear inside them. If your shoes are smelly, try following the instructions in "Banish Odors and Keep Shoes Smelling Fresh," page 216.

- **Go heavy duty.** Line the bottom with jeans, canvas coats, and other heavy rolls. This will help if the suitcase won't close and compressing is needed.

(continued)

- **Layer it on.** Continue layering on and filling in cracks with medium-heavy items, such as jackets.

- **Lighten up.** Move on to lighter items, such as knits, shirts, lingerie, and pajamas.

- **Keep it dry.** Pack any nonessential toiletries in side pockets, making sure they're sealed in zip-top bags in case of leaks.

- **Cut the cord.** Don't take a hairdryer unless you know your host or hotel doesn't have one to lend. If you need one, invest in a small travel version and tuck it, along with any other appliances such as shavers or curling irons, into cracks between clothes rolls.

- **Sheathe your jewelry.** Never travel with expensive jewelry. There's too much value in such small items, and the threat of loss or theft is too real. For the jewelry you do pack, place each item in a separate zip-top bag, lay out a pillowcase, and space the bags out within the pillowcase. Roll the pillowcase and pack it in your pajama and lingerie layer.

#113 How to Tie a Scarf

U nisex, utilitarian, and fashionable, the right scarf, tied with aplomb, marks the wearer as the kind of thoughtful dresser who goes the extra mile to look perfect and polished. These styles are ridiculously easy to execute; most are complete in three steps or less.

The Classic Once-Around

This is a classic way to tie a warm winter scarf for a commute to work or an evening out. This style is casual, and with a wool scarf, will help you hold in precious body heat during cold winter days. Drape the scarf around your neck, letting one end drop lower than the other. Take the long end, wind it loosely around your neck, and let it drape over your chest.

The Parisian Knot

This is likely the most popular knot for all genders. It's an all-purpose knot for any scarf and looks great when used for a silk or cashmere blend that accents a smart outfit or for a thin wool scarf. Take a scarf in both hands and fold it lengthwise. Drape it around your neck, then insert both ends through the loop and pull them through.

The Asymmetrical

A timeless look, perfect for adding an accent to a neat, traditional suit, double-breasted coat, or suit jacket. Open the scarf fully and wrap it around your shoulders like a shawl. Now, pull the right side down, so that it's longer than the left side by a third. Toss the right side over your left shoulder and allow the left side to hang down.

The Bohemian

Best with lightweight cotton or open-weave scarves. This method makes a statement. Try using it to complement an unzipped, short leather jacket or close-cut, trendy blazer. It can pair with any cardigan, jacket, or coat, or it can be worn with blouses and dresses to amp up the style. Drape the scarf around the back of your neck and allow both ends to hang down in the front, one equally as long as the other. Cross the ends over themselves, and tie them together to create one parallel knot. Repeat this three to five times, until you have a braided necktie effect.

THE ESSENTIALS: Items Every Wardrobe Needs

Forget the trends. Invest in the top-of-your-budget versions of these staples, and you'll never spend the hours before a big date, interview, or any other occasion thinking, *I don't have a thing to wear.*

TIP: If you have the option, get your clothes tailored! Many adjustments pay for themselves because you will get much more wear out of something that fits well. Clothing made to fit your body builds confidence and instantly creates a more polished look.

UNISEX

1. Gray suit. Equally at home in the conference room or cocktail lounge.

2. Navy jacket. Easy to throw on over jeans, or the matching trousers it came with when you purchased it as a "four-season suit." It's as indispensable as underwear.

3. A crisp white shirt. Dress it up or dress it down. Look for high-quality cotton and a highly tailored look. Try on lots of styles, find the one that fits you best, and invest in two or three.

4. French blue dress shirt. Doubles for work and play. Tuck it in and top it with a tie for the office, or untuck it with black jeans and boots for hanging out.

5. Leather (or high-quality pleather) jacket. Rugged but sophisticated, it transforms you from casual to polished.

6. Elegant black/brown belt. Choose a 1-inch width with a simple buckle and it'll complement any pants or trousers.

7. Neutral chinos. Buy flat-front, slim-legged, 100 percent cotton. Try on as many pairs as it takes to find your perfect fit.

8. Perfect jeans. You may have to try on a hundred pairs to find the style that flatters you best, but when you find your denim soul mate, you'll be glad you did. Buy them in a dark wash, so they dress up more easily.

9. Leather, waxed cotton, or other sturdy duffel bag. This bag will take you anywhere and match anything you wear. Don't get caught on a business trip with your logoed nylon gym bag.

FEMININE STAPLES

1. Black pencil skirt. Flatters every figure and looks neat and polished with any top, from a cashmere shell to a silk bow-front blouse to a cotton scoop-neck tee.

2. Little black dress. The LBD is a foolproof way to look pulled-together, and it goes from daytime, paired with ballet flats or low pumps, to evening, paired with strappy sandals or peek-toe high heels.

3. Tailored pantsuit. Buy the best one you can afford, in a neutral color and an all-season fabric. Spend the money to have it tailored. Mix and match accessories, and you could wear this every day.

4. Slim black pants. Pull them on, and your look is instantly sleek and polished. These can be dressed down for everyday wear, but they'll never stoop to sloppy.

(continued)

5. Classic-cut, colorful blazer. Choose the most basic of cuts, and you'll be able to throw this blazer over every skirt and pair of pants or jeans you own. Buy it in a bright color like red, purple, or royal blue.

6. A good leather tote bag. Doubles as a briefcase or computer bag during working hours and a shopping bag or weekender hand luggage during leisure hours.

7. A cashmere cardigan. Tuck it into your bag to protect you from winter drafts or summer air conditioning.

8. The right bra. It's really worthwhile to be fitted by a professional. The right bra perks you up, refines your figure, and makes all of your clothes look great.

#114 How to Tie a Tie

If you've never tied a necktie, you may gape in wonder as you watch an experienced businessman whip the ends of his about, without even a glance in the mirror. The art of tying a tie lies simply in practice. Here are instructions for tying the three most popular styles with ease.

The Four-in-Hand Knot

This asymmetrical method of tying is slightly youthful, jaunty, and casual. Some call it "the schoolboy." Very easy to execute, and a great choice for button-down shirts. This style works best with heavier-weight fabrics and wider cuts.

1　Drape the necktie around your neck. The wide end should drop down about a foot below the narrow end of the tie.

2　Now, cross the wide part of the tie over the narrow end.

3　Turn the wide end back underneath the narrow end.

4　Continue by bringing the wide end back over in front of the narrow end once again.

5　Pull the wide end up and through the loop around your neck.

6 Hold the front of the knot loosely with your index finger and bring the wide end down and through the front loop.

7 Remove your finger and tighten the knot carefully to the collar by holding the narrow end and sliding the knot up.

The Half-Windsor Knot

This is the junior version of the Windsor knot. This triangular and symmetrical shape is best used with dress shirts and light- to medium-weight fabrics. For shirts with standard collars, it's a safe and traditional choice.

1 Drape the necktie around your neck. The wide end should drop down about a foot below the narrow end. Cross the wide part of the tie over the narrow end.

2 Bring the wide end of the tie around and to the back of the narrow end.

3 Push the wide end up and pull it down through the hole between your collar and tie.

4 Bring the wide end around the front, over the narrow end, from right to left.

5 Bring the wide end up and back through the loop again.

6 Pull the wide end down through the knot in front.

(continued)

Famous for their perfect dimple, Windsor knots came about in the early 20th century when the fashionable Duke of Windsor (briefly King Edward VIII) inspired their creation.

7 Tighten the knot and center it with both hands.

The Windsor Knot

A bold, thick, and symmetrical knot, this style has long been associated with confidence and power. This knot pairs best with a wide-spread collar and is appropriate for important events like job interviews and work presentations, as well as formal events like business dinners and awards ceremonies.

1 Drape the necktie around your neck. The wide end should drop down about a foot below the narrow end. Cross the wide part of the tie over the narrow end.

2 Bring the wide end of the tie up through the hole between your collar and the tie, then, pull it down toward the front.

3 Pull the wide end to the back of the narrow end, and then to the right.

4 Take the wide end back through the loop one more time. You will have a triangle now, where the necktie's knot will ultimately be.

5 Wrap the wide end around the triangle by pulling that end from right to left.

2 Bring the wide end up through the hole between your collar and the tie, then, pull it down toward the front.

6 Bring the wide end up through the loop a third time.

7 Pull the wide end through the knot in the front.

8 Tighten the knot and center it with both hands.

#115 How to Tie a Necktie on Someone Else

Are you a fan of classic film tropes and all things sophisticated and nostalgic? This may be the skill for you. Helping someone with their necktie will surely elevate you to the status of classy co-star!

Or maybe you want to help out a haberdashery-loving gal who dreams of dressing up like Annie Hall but is clumsy with knots.

Or maybe, like me, you've needed merely to quickly dress two little boys for a wedding. Either way, it's a nice skill to have.

If you can tie a tie for someone else, you'll be the hero of the day. Which is the go-to knot to use for doing a tie-wearer a favor, you ask? Why, the half-windsor, of course. Once tied on yourself, it can be loosened and slipped over your head, then transferred to the grateful recipient.

Begin with the tie around your neck, following the instructions for the half-Windsor knot on page 213, and omit Step 7. Then simply place the loop of the necktie around the neck of the man, woman, or child who will be wearing the necktie and push the knot up to the neck.

But if you'd like to tie the tie directly on the other person, try this.

1 Flip up the shirt collar and drape the necktie around the neck of the recipient, with the wide end on your right. Allow the wide end to drop down about a foot below the narrow end.

3 Swing the wide end to the right, passing it under the narrow end.

5 After this, push it up through the neck hole. Now, tuck it through the knot and let it hang down.

2 Cross the wide end over the narrow end and bring it up through the neck loop and down the front.

4 Cross the wide end back over the narrow end to the left.

6 Tighten the tie and fold the shirt collar down, and voilà: He (or she) will be dressed to the nines!

#116 How to Polish a Pair of Shoes

There's an old saying that goes "If you're wearing good shoes, and carrying a good bag, the rest of the outfit doesn't matter." Good-quality shoes, kept meticulously neat, speak volumes about the wearer. Actor Conrad Cantzen felt so strongly about the impression shoes make that in 1945 he bequeathed his estate to The Actors Fund with the stipulation that it be used to help actors buy shoes so they did not appear "down at the heels" when auditioning for jobs. In short, good-looking shoes can vastly improve your life!

Here are some ways to keep your shoes sweet smelling (or at least *not* smelling), spick-and-span, and in good repair.

1 Cover an area of the floor with sheets of newspaper or an old towel.

2 Check your shoes for spatterings of dirt or debris. If they're filthy, wipe them down with a damp rag and let dry.

3 Take a horsehair shoe polish brush and rub it into your wax shoe polish. Scrub your shoes vigorously. Use plenty of polish so that you leave a film on the outside of the shoe.

4 Let them absorb the polish for a few minutes, then wipe down the outside of the shoes with a soft, lint-free cloth. Use a circular motion and rub hard to buff them to a high gloss.

✕✕

Banish Odors and Keep Shoes Smelling Fresh

- *Use a powder.* After taking off your shoes nightly, sprinkle a thin layer of baking soda inside. In the morning, take them outdoors and clap the soles together. The odor will be carried off with the powder.

- *Make room in the freezer.* Put each shoe in its own gallon-size zip-top freezer bag, and put them in the freezer overnight to kill odor-causing fungus and bacteria.

- *Raid the laundry room.* Before bed, crumple up dryer sheets and insert them into shoes. ✕

In the 1800s, the first commercially available shoe polish—or shine—was made from sugar, vinegar, black dye, and water. Shortly thereafter, tallow (an animal by-product) was introduced as an ingredient to prevent the polish from rubbing off on clothes, but it wasn't until 1904, when the Kiwi brand introduced a vastly improved formula, that commercial shine began to resemble the modern shoe polish available today.

When Good Shoes Go Bad: Shoe Repair and Maintenance Tips

SELF-SUFFICIENCY: WHEN TO DO IT AT HOME

Channel your inner cobbler, and your shoes will last longer and perform better.

Heels wearing out? This seems obvious, but I'm going to say it: Alternate the pairs of shoes you wear to preserve the ones you love most.

Slick bottoms? Rub the bottom with sandpaper or a wire brush to add traction. Still slick? Spray the bottoms with hairspray and let it dry completely before wearing.

Waterproof it. Rub a new pair of leather shoes or boots with mink oil. This neutral-colored oil softens the leather and makes it water resistant. Allow it to dry fully, then treat shoes with spray-on water repellent at the seams and all over the insides.

Soles or heels coming off? Glue them on at home with glue specifically designed for shoes (ask for it at a hardware store). Before you start, rub the surfaces to be glued with sandpaper to improve the bond. This works especially well on sneakers.

Scuffed-up suede? The best tool to erase surface marks is a dry cleaning bar, usually sold with a stiff-bristle brush. The bar is like a pencil eraser; use it to remove marks from suede. Then use the brush to bring the nap back up. Finish with a deep-cleaning suede spray.

Mark on nonpatent leather shoes or boots? Try rubbing the stain off with a gum eraser. If that fails, invest in a small bottle of shoe polish that matches the shoe color precisely and paint over the scuff.

Crack or nick in leather? Find a Sharpie marker in the same color as the shoe, and simply draw over the affected area, and then let it dry.

SHOE STORE SUPPORT: WHEN TO PAY FOR IT

An investment in a trip to the shoe repair store for repairs and maintenance can save you money in the long run. Buy the highest-quality shoes you can afford and keep them in good repair. Here's what to pay for:

New shoes too tight? Have them stretched. Some places can even stretch specific parts of the shoe, such as the heels or the "bunion" area. It's an inexpensive service that can make a big difference.

Uncomfortable standing all day in your new shoes? Invest in gel insoles. Slide them inside your shoes to absorb shock between your feet and the sidewalk. It's worth the investment because they'll relieve and prevent pain.

Want to make them last? Have your shoemaker put on rubber heels and toe taps. It's a great way to keep the bottoms from wearing out. Replace the taps as they wear down or fall off.

Slippery soles? Have your shoemaker install sole protectors. They'll add life to a quality pair of shoes and provide traction to help you avoid slips on the ice or slick flooring.

#117 How to Write a Thank-You Note

Polite behavior and good manners in a person are universally appreciated. Why? Because they indicate regard and respect for fellow human beings. Behaving in this way also marks you as a person who not only knows the right way to act, but also cares enough to follow through. My favorite thing about proper etiquette is that participation is open to everyone. One needn't be born into a blue-blood family, or have piles of money in the bank, in order to have lovely behavior. And it's that behavior that marks someone as a quality person, not connections or wealth.

Thank-You FAQs

How long do I have to send a thank-you note?
For a regular gift, try to write the note and mail it within two to three days, so it arrives within the week. Notes for wedding gifts should be sent out two weeks after the wedding date.

Can I type a thank-you note?
No. Even if your handwriting is terrible, write it by hand.

Is there a rule about stationery?
Not really, but have something on hand like postcards of a local landmark or museum art piece, a box of unisex "Thank You" cards, or a pack of neutral-colored stationery. The need to shop for supplies will delay the thank-you! The classic choice is a card with your initials at the top.

1 Write a greeting. It need not be more complicated than "Dear Uncle Frank."

2 Name the gift. Never just say: "Thank you for the gift." The giver will wonder if you mixed it up with other gifts and lost the tag. For an added bonus, compliment the gift, as in: "Thank you so much for the beautifully hand-knit wool scarf." However, there are exceptions.

- **Money.** Here's an instance where you do not name the gift. Instead, say, "I'm truly grateful for your generous gift."

- **Intangibles.** If your friend let you borrow her beach house, or if someone did you a favor, define the gift in a flattering way. Don't say, "Thanks for the couch and the grub," but do say, "Thank you for your gracious hospitality." It's okay to be simple.

3 Tell how you use the gift. If you love a new bathrobe, say, "I've barely taken off my robe since I opened the box." Don't lie, though. Say something that's true, even if you hate the gift. "The practical umbrella hat is such a pretty shade of purple!"

Regarding money, it's okay to mention how it will be used. "Your generous gift will help when I buy my new bike," is fine, but don't write, "Your fifty bucks will get me two butter knives and a serving spoon off my registry."

4 Talk about the past and the future. This is a time to underscore your connection to the giver. "It was so nice to see you at my graduation party, and I look forward to sharing Thanksgiving with you." If you see the giver often, try "I know we'll talk at work, but I wanted to take a moment to express my

gratitude." If it's someone you rarely see, use a phrase like, "I'm thinking of you, and wishing you all the best."

5 Wrap up. Say thanks again with a short, simple phrase. "Thank you again for the present," and then the

sign-off. If "Love," or "Yours Truly," work, say that. If not, simply sign your name.

#118 How to Stock a First-Aid Kit

How many times have you had a bump, scrape, or burn only to find that your medicine cabinet lacks basic first-aid supplies? There's no better time than the present to put together complete kits and stash them where they'll be needed most. And if you do it the DIY way, buying in bulk for several kits at a time, you'll save some green, too.

Where Do I Need First-Aid Kits?

- In every bathroom of your home
- In your car
- In the workshop or garage
- In your disaster evacuation backpack
- In the home office
- In your hiking and camping equipment
- In a child's stroller or diaper bag

What Should a First-Aid Kit Contain?

The basics, as recommended by the American Red Cross:

- 2 absorbent compress dressings (5 by 9 inches)
- 25 adhesive bandages (assorted sizes)
- 1 adhesive cloth tape (10 yards by 1 inch)
- 5 antibiotic ointment packets (approximately 1 gram each)
- 5 antiseptic wipe packets
- 2 packets of aspirin (81 mg each)
- 1 blanket (thermal space blanket)
- 1 breathing barrier (with one-way valve)
- 1 instant cold compress
- 2 pairs of nonlatex gloves (size: large)
- 2 hydrocortisone ointment packets (approximately 1 gram each)
- Scissors
- 1 roller bandage (3 inches wide)
- 1 roller bandage (4 inches wide)
- 5 sterile gauze pads (3 by 3 inches)
- 5 sterile gauze pads (4 by 4 inches)
- Oral thermometer (nonmercury/nonglass)
- 2 triangular bandages
- Tweezers
- First-aid instruction booklet

(continued)

The concept of the first-aid kit has been around for quite some time—aviator Charles Lindbergh carried one across the Atlantic on his first successful ocean crossing in 1927.

Clearly, first-aid kits should be tailored to their specific uses. If you live in an urban area, you probably don't need a snake-bite kit in your bathroom. You might, however, need one if you live in or near the woods or to stock your hiking backpack.

What Specifics Should I Have for a Children's First-Aid Kit?

- Eyedrops
- Anti-itch lotion
- Baby wipes
- A list of emergency phone numbers (doctor, hospital, Poison Control)
- Rectal thermometer
- Mouthpiece for administering CPR (available from your local Red Cross)
- Children's ibuprofen and acetaminophen (but never aspirin, which can cause fatal Reye's syndrome in young children—check with your doctor, even before giving baby aspirin)
- A tooth preservation kit
- Activated charcoal powder (to use only when advised by Poison Control)

How Can I Personalize My First-Aid Kit?

- Be sure to include your prescription or over-the-counter medications when you're traveling. Make sure to check expiration dates every so often and replace as needed.

- If you wear eyeglasses or contact lenses, have extra lenses as well as extra cleaning and storage solutions in first-aid kits in your car or camping gear.

- If you are allergic to nuts, bee stings, shellfish, or any other potentially anaphylaxis-inducing substance, have an EpiPen in every kit.

- If you have sensitive skin, consider packing emollients for dry skin or cornstarch-based body powder (avoid talc, as it's harmful when breathed into the lungs).

✕ ✕ ✕ ✕ ✕ ✕ ✕ ✕ ✕ ✕ ✕ ✕ ✕ ✕ ✕ ✕ ✕ ✕

What about Syrup of Ipecac?

Once a standard in every home first-aid kit, syrup of ipecac does not necessarily help a person who has swallowed poison. Parents are now advised not to use it. Instead, in the case of a suspected poisoning, call Poison Control at 800-222-1222 or call 911. ✕

✕ ✕

Twenty Safety Tips for Every Home

1. Keep car keys and cell phone on your nightstand. If you hear suspicious noises in the night, press the panic button to set off the car alarm. Given the commotion, an intruder is likely to flee the scene. Landlines can be cut; having a cell phone near at

night secures the opportunity to call 911 if necessary.

2. Keep shrubbery trimmed. Heavy, dark shrubbery growing tall close to a house can give someone a place to hide when you're coming home at night.

3. Enlist a neighbor to check for leaflets. When you're away from home for an extended period of time, even if you stop the mail and the newspaper, marketers could still leave fliers, brochures, or pamphlets stuck in the door crack or lying on the porch. Don't broadcast that household members are away. (This includes on social media; be mindful of what you post publicly about your travel plans.)

4. Install smoke detectors. Smoke detectors should be on every floor and carbon monoxide detectors near bedrooms. Test them regularly and replace the batteries every daylight savings time change.

5. Secure tall bookshelves to the wall. This is especially important in households with young children. Climbing on them can cause them to topple over and injure someone.

6. Cover all unused outlets. Plastic outlet covers are cheap and readily available. Even if no kids or pets live in your home, you never know when you might have visitors.

7. Don't pile firewood along the outside of your house. Intruders can climb aboard, gaining access to windows. It can also fuel house fires. Instead, pile it next to a fence or shed, at least 20 feet away from the dwelling.

8. Put up a security-system decal. Even if you don't really have a system in place, this could discourage inexperienced burglars.

9. Take care with extension cords. Never place them under rugs or heavy furniture. Wear and fraying could lead to fires.

10. Create a plan in case of fire. Practice a fire escape plan with your family. Identify two exits for every room and assign jobs for rescuing small children or pets.

11. Avoid burns in the shower and bath. Set your water heater below 120 degrees Fahrenheit to avoid potential burns (and to save energy).

12. Invest in fire extinguishers. Place all-purpose fire extinguishers in key locations in your home: the kitchen, bedrooms, and the basement. Check expiration dates regularly.

13. Skid-proof your tub or shower. Use rubber mats, adhesive decals, or strips to help prevent falls.

14. Store heavy items properly. They should be organized in cabinets at waist level or below.

15. Don't overload outlets. Be certain that you have no more than one high-wattage appliance plugged in to any given power point.

16. Spring for a chimney sweep. If you burn wood in a fireplace, be sure to have the flues and chimneys professionally cleaned and swept annually.

17. Be strict and unfailing about firearms. If there are guns in the house, make sure they are locked up, unloaded, and stored separately from ammunition.

18. Fence in the pool. All pools by law require a four-sided fence and a child-proof gate. If you have a temporary pool—even a small wading pool—empty it when it's not being supervised.

19. Make sure your house number is visible. Visitors should be able to read the number from the street. This will lead emergency workers directly to your door when needed.

20. Paint the bottom steps of the stairs white. This will help reduce tripping and falls.

INDEX

CONVERSION TABLES

INCHES TO CENTIMETERS

½ = 1.3	5 = 12.7	9½ = 24.1	18 = 45.7
1 = 2.5	5½ = 14.0	10 = 25.4	19 = 48.3
1½ = 3.8	6 = 15.2	11 = 27.9	20 = 50.8
2 = 5.1	6½ = 16.5	12 = 30.5	21 = 53.3
2½ = 6.4	7 = 17.8	13 = 33.0	22 = 55.9
3 = 7.6	7½ = 19.1	14 = 35.6	23 = 58.4
3½ = 8.9	8 = 20.3	15 = 38.1	24 = 61.0
4 = 10.2	8½ = 21.6	16 = 40.6	
4½ = 11.4	9 = 22.9	17 = 43.2	

FEET TO METERS

1 = .304
1½ = .456
2 = .608
2½ = .760
3 = .912
3½ = 1.064
4 = 1.216
4½ = 1.368
5 = 1.520

Use these formulas for precise conversions:

inches × 2.54 = centimeters   feet × .304 = meters

APPROXIMATE EQUIVALENTS

1 stick butter = 8 tbs = 4 oz = ½ cup = 115 g
1 cup all-purpose, pre-sifted flour = 4.7 oz
1 cup granulated sugar = 8 oz = 220 g
1 cup (firmly packed) brown sugar =
  6 oz = 220 g to 230 g
1 cup confectioners' sugar = 4½ oz = 115 g
1 cup honey or syrup = 12 oz
1 cup grated cheese = 4 oz

1 cup dried beans = 6 oz
1 large egg = about 2 oz or about 3 tbs
1 egg yolk = about 1 tbs
1 egg white = about 2 tbs

Please note that all conversions are approximate but close enough to be useful when converting from one system to another.

OVEN TEMPERATURES

°F	GAS MARK	°C	°F	GAS MARK	°C	°F	GAS MARK	°C
250	½	120	350	4	180	450	8	230
275	1	140	375	5	190	475	9	240
300	2	150	400	6	200	500	10	260
325	3	160	425	7	220			

Note: Reduce the temperature by 20°C (36°F) for fan-assisted ovens.

LIQUID CONVERSIONS

US	IMPERIAL	METRIC
2 tbs	1 fl oz	30 ml
3 tbs	1½ fl oz	45 ml
¼ cup	2 fl oz	60 ml
⅓ cup	2½ fl oz	75 ml
⅓ cup + 1 tbs	3 fl oz	90 ml
⅓ cup + 2 tbs	3½ fl oz	100 ml
½ cup	4 fl oz	125 ml
⅔ cup	5 fl oz	150 ml
¾ cup	6 fl oz	175 ml
¾ cup + 2 tbs	7 fl oz	200 ml
1 cup	8 fl oz	250 ml
1 cup + 2 tbs	9 fl oz	275 ml
1¼ cups	10 fl oz	300 ml
1⅓ cups	11 fl oz	325 ml
1½ cups	12 fl oz	350 ml
1⅔ cups	13 fl oz	375 ml
1¾ cups	14 fl oz	400 ml
1¾ cups + 2 tbs	15 fl oz	450 ml
2 cups (1 pint)	16 fl oz	500 ml
2½ cups	20 fl oz (1 pint)	600 ml
3¾ cups	1½ pints	900 ml
4 cups	1¾ pints	1 liter

WEIGHT CONVERSIONS

US/UK	METRIC	US/UK	METRIC
½ oz	15 g	7 oz	200 g
1 oz	30 g	8 oz	250 g
1½ oz	45 g	9 oz	275 g
2 oz	60 g	10 oz	300 g
2½ oz	75 g	11 oz	325 g
3 oz	90 g	12 oz	350 g
3½ oz	100 g	13 oz	375 g
4 oz	125 g	14 oz	400 g
5 oz	150 g	15 oz	450 g
6 oz	175 g	1 lb	500 g